The Mindful College Applicant

The Mindful College Applicant

Cultivating Emotional Intelligence for the Admissions Process

Belinda H. Y. Chiu

ROWMAN & LITTLEFIELD
Lanham • Boulder • New York • London

Published by Rowman & Littlefield
An imprint of The Rowman & Littlefield Publishing Group, Inc.
4501 Forbes Boulevard, Suite 200, Lanham, Maryland 20706
www.rowman.com

86-90 Paul Street, London EC2A 4NE, United Kingdom

British Library Cataloguing in Publication Information Available

Library of Congress Cataloging-in-Publication Data Available

ISBN: 978-1-5381-1983-9 (cloth : alk. paper)
ISBN: 978-1-5381-7590-3 (pbk. : alk. paper)
ISBN: 978-1-5381-1984-6 (electronic)

∞™ The paper used in this publication meets the minimum requirements of American National Standard for Information Sciences—Permanence of Paper for Printed Library Materials, ANSI/NISO Z39.48-1992.

Contents

Introduction

You're Going to Make It

If you are anxious about what happens after high school, you're not alone.

I have been part of the frenzy that robs many of you of sleep, leading to early-onset burnout and stymieing the cultivation of compassion. Yet I have also been part of the legions who seek healthier pathways to "success."

COLLEGE ADMISSIONS

In this book, I am going to focus on selective institutions of higher education that accept less than 25 percent of their applicants. This is not to say that these institutions are any better or worse than any other, but rather, it is this narrow band of institutions that has helped to drive the level of "crazy" to new highs. The not-so-great news is: Yes, it's a super-competitive process and statistics suggest that, no, the majority of you won't get in. The good news is: You're going to be OK. The key is to recognize your greater purpose and to be more intentional about choosing the *right* school for you, *and* to prepare yourself to thrive there so you can use your education for a greater good.

The sad reality is that education in many ways now follows a consumerist model. You probably know what I'm talking about. The joys of kindergarten and grade school, where you got to explore and create, have been replaced by a lot more stress. The focus in education seems to have changed from intellectual exploration and risk-taking to the mindless pursuit of grades, tests, and elite college acceptances. Examples? One New Hampshire school has replaced its summer reading list of great books with a course on drafting Common Application essays. Goodbye, love of literature. In 2014, a New York elementary school made headlines for canceling an annual kindergarten show so that the five-year-olds could make better use of their time to prepare "for college and career with valuable lifelong skills."[1] Five-year-olds!

Adding to this loss of learning is the heightened anxiety in what seems to be a shrinking playing field in a zero-sum game of college admissions. As spots in first-year classes remain static for many elite universities, the number of applicants continues to climb. You look at the numbers, your counselors show you the statistics, and your family members share tales from their friends and their friends' friends. Getting in seems impossible. And when you ask admissions officers how the selective process works behind the scenes, you probably get the answer: "holistic admissions." This blanket term allows admissions officers to make decisions based on any or all information as they so choose. The majority of admissions teams do so with integrity and care, yet the reality is that there are countless other competing priorities and mechanics that are completely out of your—or your parents'—hands. You're left wondering: What does it all really mean?

Given this seeming lack of transparency about the college admissions process, many students and their concerned ones do almost anything to crack the code and figure out the "secrets to getting in." Many turn to the internet, which is loaded with misinformation. Others pay hefty sums to get a "leg up" from so-called experts. Some of you may have even picked up this book hoping to find the secret sauce.

Moreover, as much as you might sometimes think your teachers are simply exhausted bureaucrats, most of them teach because they love it. They truly, genuinely (stop the eye-rolling) want to instill a love of learning and strength of character in you. They're not in it for the money, most certainly. But they're battling the same pressures you are—standardized testing and performance evaluations. Many face pressures of being evaluated based on how many of you get into college, or even into a certain "tier" of colleges. Some of your parents may have shelled out a lot of money to live in your current zip code area because your high school was ranked to be "the best" according to *U.S. News & World Report*, or to send you to a private school where your annual tuition is higher than your teacher's salary (how many of your teachers actually live in your neighborhood?). Others of you may be attending a school where you haven't even met your counselor, or where you may not even have one. In short, everyone is under a lot of pressure to "get in."

Your well-meaning teachers and parents, who are as human and as susceptible to external pressures as you are, watch you and your friends transform from naturally curious kindergarteners to fearful fifth graders and anxious high schoolers. Some of you now hesitate to take risks because you think one bad grade means no Harvard, and others of you don't even want to try. One young man from a top private school known for building "young men and women of character, curiosity, and courage" asked me once in private, "I really want to go to College X, but I heard its admissions rate is below 10 percent. That means it's really hard to get in. Should I not even bother?" It is true that a 10 percent admissions rate doesn't work in your favor, and it is wise not to apply *only* to schools with a 10 percent acceptance rate. However, that doesn't mean you should not try. That young man chose not to stray from a prescribed path of extreme academics and extracurriculars for fear of failure. Sleep and dinner are bonuses.

Sound familiar?

Students like you feel pressure to play the part of the happy overachiever. Social media suggests that success and happiness equate with money, fame, and selfies. Such pressures not only negatively impact true learning but also mental, socioemotional, and cognitive health. A 2015 NYU study showed that nearly half of high school students surveyed reported a "great deal of stress," with 26 percent reporting clinical-level depression. Over two-thirds of surveyed high school students manage stress with substances like alcohol and marijuana.[2]

Fantasizing about yourself as one of the fun-loving, relaxed California college students you see on TV? Over 40 percent of U.C.L.A. first-year students reported feeling overwhelmed.[3] Even the most idealistic of you may strain yourselves to get into the "right" schools with the idea that once you get there, *then* you can change the world. This idealism is often shrouded in anxiety and autopilot living—succeeding for the sake of achieving. Many of your peers are under intense pressure to put on a happy, overachieving face but are really feeling terribly lost about who they are or who they want to be. As Yale professor and author of *Excellent Sheep* William Deresiewicz[4] noted,

Our system of elite education manufactures young people who are smart
and talented and driven, yes, but also anxious, timid, and lost, with little
intellectual curiosity and a stunted sense of purpose: trapped in a bubble
of privilege, heading meekly in the same direction, great at what they're
doing but with no idea why they're doing it.[5]

In the current paradigm, many of you often turn into lost adults
who then become the individuals who make up the almost 70 percent
of U.S. workers disengaged at work.[6] Even those who make it up the
corporate ladder are not immune to disengagement. As an executive
coach, I work with high performers who struggle mightily because,
while they were given the tools to get the corner office—the same tools
that earned them the 4.0—they were never given the tools to live with
authenticity. Many hit middle age with blinders on, trying to "make
it" without paying attention to mental or emotional health. Desperate
to find out who they really are and to discover their purpose, they are
now willing to invest time and money to step off the hamster wheel to
explore mindfulness and emotional intelligence. Those who do so have
often seen enhanced productivity and performance, leading me to the
belief that these practices can benefit young people before they get to
that desperate stage.

The reality is this: Some of the schools you are looking at have an
under 5 percent acceptance rate. The odds *are* against you, regardless
of who your daddy is or what sport you play. No one is entitled to an
acceptance, not even if you have given up so much for the A+ or 0.10
gain in your GPA to demonstrate your IQ. That doesn't mean, however,
that you don't or shouldn't try. However, getting in is not a game.

If I told you that you had a 5 percent chance of winning a car if you
completed a series of complicated math equations and then put your
name in a jar with thousands and thousands of others who also completed them correctly, would you do it? Would you likely consider that
it's worth the long shot? Probably. Would you actually expect to or feel
entitled to win? Probably not.

My experience in competitive college admissions within the Ivy
League and other selective institutions has led me to the conclusion
that the current climate is untenable, with overwhelmed young people
growing up to be underwhelmed adults. I believe it is possible to regain
control of this wayward ship.

This is not a "secrets to getting into your dream college" guide.
Instead, I propose that emotional intelligence (EI) may help you thrive

during the process—and afterwards. Given the highly competitive nature of the selective admissions process, instead of focusing on just "getting in," consider preparing yourself with the tools needed to build your resilience, awareness, and mental strength to more than simply navigate life but to *live* it, and maybe even do some good. Consider this book your companion counselor. It articulates the general metrics currently used as part of the review process at many selective institutions, framed in ATLAS 1.0,[7] and offers a more expansive path for lifelong growth with ATLAS 2.0. Many of you are already familiar with ATLAS 1.0 from your counselors, guidebooks, and other resources. I will help explicate it further, particularly for those of you who are new to this. However, I am suggesting that there is more to "getting in" than traditional metrics. With ATLAS 2.0, I introduce multiple dimensions of mindfulness and emotional intelligence as a way to address the points of pain that currently exist in college admissions and beyond. By promoting inner wisdom, character, and awareness, ATLAS 2.0 may help you navigate the competitive process with greater grace and balance, rediscovering a love for learning, and a way to step into your future with renewed wonder and excitement.

Who am I to suggest that this path may offer longer-term payoffs than just surviving a stressful college application process? I cut my teeth in management consulting before working in competitive and Ivy League college admissions over the course of nineteen years.[8] Through

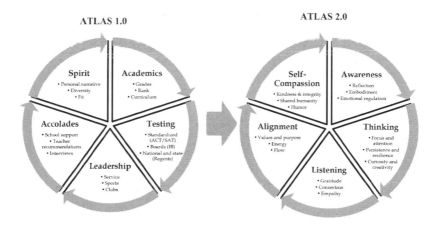

Figure 0.1. ATLAS 1.0 and ATLAS 2.0

these experiences, I have been part of entire admissions cycles, from meeting students at their high schools, to interviewing them, to debating over them in committees. I have also served as an alumni interviewer, sat in committee rooms, been part of the strategic decision-making processes, and have had the privilege of working with many thoughtful colleagues around the world trying to honor you and your stories.

Throughout my travels, I have spoken to thousands of students, families, and counselors, all trying to remain mentally healthy but often getting caught up in the groundswell of keeping up with others. I have been yelled at by angry parents whose child was not accepted. Outside the earshot of well-meaning, hypervigilant parents, I have comforted many students who break down in tears, overwhelmed by the pressure and feeling cheated that school is no longer a place to learn.

I also conduct research on EI and mindfulness, and have presented with colleagues around the world from Puerto Rico to India. I have the great fortune of working with individuals such as Dr. Daniel Goleman, the "godfather of emotional intelligence," and organizations such as the Google-born Search Inside Yourself Leadership Institute (SIYLI). In my work outside of higher education as a leadership coach and trainer for Fortune 500 companies, I have seen the parallels between corporate leadership and college admissions. Corporate leaders are often imprisoned in golden handcuffs (the trappings of success), stressing out their stressed-out teams or living on complete autopilot. Instead of trying to compete for a spot at a given university, they are competing for some other metric of "success," sort of like an older version of what you might be feeling right now. Many of these adults find that the technical skills that got them in the door are insufficient to enable them to lead effectively. Fortunately, emotional intelligence and practices based on mindfulness have been shown to shift paradigms of engagement to wiser leadership, productivity, and engagement.

Incorporating such knowledge and practices may help you navigate this tough college process and equip you to find your way through what will be the even trickier waters of "adulting."

Instead of rewarding and pushing smart, mindless sheep into the world, I suggest an alternative path. Your brains are primed right now for either a lifetime of chronic anxiety or one of curiosity and compassion. By building your emotional intelligence muscles, you might increase your cognitive ability for attention and focus as well as your capacity to build connections, challenge assumptions, and break barriers. Get off the hamster wheel to nowhere. Now.

It is *then* that you can change the world.

I

From Anxiety to Awareness: The Case for Emotional Intelligence

You may have surmised that this isn't your typical "how to get in" book. This book is about helping you thrive in life.

There is an increasing call to reconfigure what has become an industry of frenzy and fear, where in some communities, lawnmower parents and zombified teens run amok. It is no wonder that Frank Bruni's book, *Where You Go Is Not Who You'll Be*,[1] struck a chord around the world, articulating that how well you do in life is not dictated by where you go to school. While many readers responded positively to this wake-up call, it didn't necessarily change people's behaviors ("Yes, I knew it! It doesn't matter where my child goes to school . . . but they will be *really* happy and have more advantages if they get into Columbia. Then they can save the world.") Around the same time Bruni's book came out, a group of university admissions deans signed on to a coalition that published the report "Turning the Tide,"[2] which included broad recommendations to reshape the process and promote students' ethical and intellectual engagement. While the report received much attention and praise, stress levels continue to rise and acceptance rates continue to plummet as the more complex question of "how" to turn the tide remains unanswered.

Many of you are desperate to find more balance, improved mental health, and a sense of well-being. Yet no one seems to know or agree on how to put a tourniquet on the pressure hose of competitive admissions that threaten mental, physical, and emotional health. I don't have the answer either. If I knew how to stop this frenzy so you could find instant relief, I'd tell you. What I *can* offer is the proposition, and some evidence, that tools based on emotional intelligence and "hacking" your brain with mental practices may bring you closer to a more meaningful and joyful future.

Emotional intelligence (EI) can alleviate some of the points of pain encountered in the competitive world of college admissions. This section begins to equip you with an expanded model for greater mindfulness, self-awareness, and intention for a successful journey through the process and beyond. In an ideal world, it doesn't matter where you go to college, but the reality you face is that it likely at least *seems* to matter. You probably feel the pressure that it matters a lot to somebody, and you don't want to let that somebody down.

I have watched you and your families breathe a sigh of relief when folks like me mention the importance of sleep rather than grades and your IQ. It is like a temporary reprieve to know that admissions officers truly care about you and your well-being. Then panic behind the eyes sets in at the mention of "admit rate." Instantly, well-being gets buried under the constant strain of test scores and class ranks. Guidance counselors commiserate as they watch you and your peers buckle under the chronic stress of what seems to be a lifetime of college application planning. Despite universities boasting wellness programs and therapy dogs, when all is said and done, it appears that admissions officers only seek perfection, prompting parents to move mountains for their children, educators to battle the demands of external metrics of learning, and students to keep it all together.

In this section, I introduce emotional intelligence (EI) and the neuroscience behind how your brain works and why sometimes it seems like your emotions are taking over.

However, before even talking about *how* to get in, I discuss the importance of knowing your *why*, that is, your true motivation for pursuing higher education. After all, just getting in is not enough. A college degree isn't an automatic right or simple passage of young adulthood. I then discuss how there is growing awareness that the current pressure cooker of achievement is harmful and unsustainable, and that awareness and kindness have critical roles to play in your learning.

Chapter One

Will Meditating Help Me Levitate?

How might a book about college admissions have *anything* to do with emotional intelligence (EI) or mindfulness? After all, isn't EI that squishy thing people talk about if they don't have "real" skills? Isn't mindfulness that thing that yogis do to levitate? And isn't college admissions about getting ahead and competition? Aren't these concepts completely in opposition?

On the contrary; mindfulness and awareness are the foundations for cultivating the emotional intelligence you need to "get in" and to navigate life successfully. For those who question the use of mindfulness in what may seem a selfish manner, as the peace activist Thich Nhat Hanh says, "we need not fear that mindfulness might become only a means and not an end because in mindfulness the means and the end are the same things."[1] Even if you picked up this book hoping for some magic secret to getting in (spoiler alert: there is no magic secret), if you actually start practicing mindfulness with true intention, you may see benefits that will last way beyond your college acceptance.[2] Dr. Jonathan Kabat-Zinn, credited for bringing secular mindfulness to the West, sees it as being useful if applied to and practiced in real life. He views "mindfulness as a love affair—with life, with reality and imagination, with the beauty of your own being, with your heart and body, and with the world."[3] This book is about helping you rediscover that love.

Obviously, if you're reading this, you're curious about what mindfulness is, and you likely suspect that the many existing perceptions about mindfulness are *mis*perceptions. I'm going to hopefully address a few of your burning (and not-so-burning) questions here: What is emotional intelligence (EI)? What misconceptions exist? What is mindfulness? Is mindfulness just a passing trend? Who benefits from it? And why bother when you're already so busy trying to achieve so that you can actually get into college?

WHAT IS EMOTIONAL INTELLIGENCE (EI)?

You have likely spent most of your time focusing on one type of intelligence, as if only one type of intelligence is valued. Ever since you were a kid, you knew the game: you get the A+ and you get the pair of shoes or praise from adults. It seems that the only type of intelligence that matters is measured in terms of how well you perform on a test. Yet many of you recognize that you have different types of intelligence, and you wish others would recognize and value those as well.

Howard Gardner wrote a seminal piece on different types of intelligences: visual-spatial; linguistic-verbal; and body-kinesthetic.[4] Whether Gardner's model is comprehensive remains a question, but it nonetheless makes the important acknowledgment that there is more to you than your cognitive intelligence and IQ. Psychologist Matt Lippincott notes that two of Gardner's intelligences—interpersonal intelligence (ability to understand others) and intrapersonal intelligence (ability to understand oneself)—are connected closely to EI.[5]

What exactly is EI? First coined by John D. Mayer and Peter Salovey, EI has since been studied as something that is learnable and allows us to navigate our worlds and other people in it effectively. One way to understand emotional intelligence is to see it as "solving problems and making wise decisions using both thoughts and feelings or logic and intuition . . . the ability to monitor one's own and others' feelings and emotions, to discriminate among them and to use this information to guide one's thinking actions."[6] If we're not aware of or know how to manage our emotions, we are more likely to react impulsively to everything happening around us and to us. You have a lot of talents and skills, but you might not be utilizing them as effectively as you could be. EI gives us the emotional aptitude to "use whatever other skills we have."[7]

There is also increasing evidence that suggests that EI is the big difference-maker in determining your success, not how high your IQ is or what grade you earn on that English paper. Research shows that teaching young people how to manage the ups and downs in life is critical to their long-term ability to cope successfully. In 2014, a study of low-income preschool kids showed that when they were taught to better manage their emotions, they didn't just demonstrate better behavior, they also demonstrated greater problem-solving and executive-functioning skills—skills necessary to handle academic rigor.[8] There are longer-term benefits. For example, one study of fifteen global companies found that 85 percent of leadership success was linked to high EI. Insurance sales agents with high emotional intelligence sold policies worth an average of twice the amount as those who were deemed lower in EI.[9]

Such research suggests that building your emotional intelligence is just as important, if not more so, than building your academic intelligence. Emerging studies suggest that EI plays a role in academic achievement, from rural students in the United States to students in Sri Lanka. For example, medical students with higher EI skills, such as well-being and sociability, have been reported to have stronger GPAs,[10] as well continuous and final assessments,[11] than their peers. Beyond the classroom, numerous studies have been conducted with similar results indicating that EI is the differentiator between good and great leaders—those who have stronger communication skills, team performance abilities, and decision-making capacities.[12] According to Daniel Goleman, who expanded on Mayer and Salovey's research, it is the secret weapon of superstars. Goleman expands on the original concept to propose that there are four main competencies within the emotional intelligence framework, and that you can practice and build on each one to enhance your EI. While I will look at these more in-depth later, let's take a quick peek so you can become more familiar with them (and they may also help you manage your adults):

1. Self-Awareness—your ability to understand your emotions and how they affect you;
2. Self-Management—your ability to check your emotional disruptions and impulses when you are under stress, set challenging goals for yourself and persist through obstacles, see a bright future, and be flexible;
3. Social Awareness—your ability to sense others' feelings and points of view; and

4. Relationship Management—your ability to positively impact others, support others to grow, manage conflict, inspire others, and work in teams.

The more you are emotionally intelligent in these areas, the less likely you are to get overwhelmed by your emotions and be distracted from your goals and greater purpose. To better regulate your emotions, you have to be able to accurately track your responses, and learn how to cultivate the healthier emotions and manage the less healthy ones. It sounds easier than it is. At this stage in your physical development, your brain isn't yet fully developed and you are still subject to raging hormones. Yet you might be surprised how much more effective you become at handling all the things that come at you, whether it's a classmate brushing you off or the impending SATs, when you start to learn and practice the EI competencies.

Some of you might have had EI training already in your schools. Often known as SEL, or social and emotional learning, it teaches young people like you how to apply EI to navigate everyday life, your school, home, and community. First introduced by the Collaborative for Aca-demic, Social, and Emotional Learning (CASEL), SEL works in schools to help you develop the EI knowledge, skills, attitudes, and behaviors you need to make wise decisions through emotional regulation, healthy relationships, conflict management, and taking responsibility. In addition to the four EI competencies, SEL adds a fifth one, "Responsible Decision-Making," which is the ability to set and achieve positive goals. All these are critical to your current success in school and, certainly, in life.

IS EMOTIONAL INTELLIGENCE WORTH LEARNING?

Handling all those things coming at you during a most sensitive period in your life is no small feat. In 2014, the American Psychological Association found that 42 percent of teens are not doing enough to manage the increasing stress in their lives.[13] Think about you and your classmates—does that statistic seem to ring true?

Elementary school was (hopefully) sort of fun, middle school added more pressure and stress as you focused on social acceptance and tougher classes, and now high school seems like a dump truck unloading tons of additional stress. From your family putting the pressure on you to get into a good college, to your teachers scrambling to get you ready for the AP tests, to the demands of work and activities and schoolwork, it's not easy. Throw in the stresses of fitting in and being accepted by your peers—I know this matters even if you pretend it doesn't—and it can sometimes seem like you can't keep your head above water. Or perhaps you've adopted the "duck approach," where on the surface, everything is seemingly calm and serene. But just below the surface, you are frantically paddling to stay afloat.

When you're feeling high levels of stress day in and day out, you are more likely to develop chronic stress. Chronic stress leads to poorer physical health later on as well as greater likelihood of depression, anxiety, and poor academic performance. In fact, when you're stressed, your access to the part of your brain that is responsible for social and higher-order executive functions is compromised. When those connections are compromised, you become less open to new ideas and information, "which makes learning almost impossible."[14] If getting straight As is putting so much stress on you that you are sacrificing your mental and physical and emotional health, that's not going to serve you in the long run.

Does EI help people better manage all the stresses around them? Evidence suggests so.

A study of Dutch teenagers showed that the greater their emotional intelligence, the less likely they were to experience depressive thoughts. But there is more to what EI can do for you. In the same Dutch study, the more the teenagers demonstrated EI, the more their classmates saw them as leaders and cooperative individuals. These same teenagers were therefore more likely to be elected into positions of leadership.[15] Those who ended up as class or club leaders didn't necessarily have higher IQs or better grades. Rather, their higher EI led others to perceive them as having stronger qualities of leadership and confidence.

Other studies have found that children with stronger emotional awareness are perceived as more popular by classmates and more intelligent by teachers. In a study of sixty kindergartners, the kids with stronger EI were better able to detect the nonverbal cues of other people by naming the emotions exhibited in photographs of adults.[16] More of their classmates wanted to sit and play with them, building a more secure sense of self-worth and self-esteem. More of their teachers treated them favorably due to what they perceived to be greater intelligence. The preferential treatment continued into middle and high school.

EI training appears to have tangible benefits. The Collaborative for Academic, Social, and Emotional Learning (CASEL) ran a meta-analysis of SEL programs for kids from five to eighteen years of age. Children who participated in SEL showed a jump in state testing scores from 11 to 17 percent, a 70 percent drop in suspensions, and improvements in prosocial behaviors such as self-management and relationship skills.[17] Social and emotional learning pioneer Dr. Roger Weissberg studied over 270,000 students who went through SEL training and found a 10 percent increase in prosocial behaviors, such as school attendance, and a 10 percent decrease in antisocial behavior, such as bullying. Academic achievement test outcomes went up 11 percent.[18] Other meta-analysis studies support the evidence that SEL can improve achievement scores and GPAs.[19]

SEL and EI may boost academic achievement by helping students find greater resilience and intrinsic motivation. Having higher EI means having greater emotional balance and regulation, which relates to how persistent you are. Are you someone who gets derailed the first time you get a less-than-perfect grade or do you bounce back to keep learning and improving?

According to the VIA Institute on Character, "in terms of achievement in work and school, perseverance appears to be the most robust character strength, emerging in most studies conducted in areas related to life success. Perseverance, love, gratitude, and hope predicted academic achievement in middle school and college students. After controlling for IQ, strength of perseverance, fairness, gratitude, honesty, hope, and perspective predicted GPA. In another study, those character strengths that predicted GPA in college students were perseverance, love of learning, humor, fairness, and kindness. Higher hope levels are related to greater scholastic and social competence and to creativity."[20] In college students, those with higher resilience self-report fewer issues with problem drinking and a higher sense of well-being.[21]

So you want to be president of MUN (Model United Nations) or go for valedictorian? Try working on your *emotional intelligence* rather than trying to show off how well you can rattle off world capitals.

EI isn't important just to get into college. Sure, your GPA and board scores may matter now. Depending on the universities to which you are applying, the overwhelming majority of applicants will be academically competitive so it's confusing why some get in and others don't. You probably have heard countless examples about former classmates with "perfect" GPAs and board scores getting rejected from their dream university while the dark horse in English class got an acceptance offer. EI matters in this process because admissions—and college *and* life—aren't simply about having the best grades or the highest IQ. Five years from now, even one year from now, very, very, very few people will ever ask you what you got on your SATs or ACTs. To thrive during this stressful process and beyond, you need to develop this other type of intelligence, your emotional intelligence.

Leaders in the corporate world recognize the value of emotional intelligence as a desired quality for career success. According to Robert Half, one of the largest staffing agencies in the United States, two-thirds of human resources (HR) managers believe that EI is as important, if not more so, than IQ when it comes to doing well in the workplace.[22] Emotional intelligence has also been shown to "improve relationships via sustained attention to interaction partners, which improves communication and increases the capacity to communicate emotional information . . . through greater *empathy* and *compassion*."[23] When it comes to getting a job and getting promotions, it's going to matter less where you went to college or what your GPA was. What matters more is your ability to regulate and balance your emotions, build healthy relationships with others, and communicate well.

Such benefits carry into adulthood, regardless of where you went to school or how well you did on the organic chemistry exam or even how many years you've been on the job. A study of 515 senior executives suggested that those with high EI had a greater likelihood of succeeding than even those with more relevant work experience. Numerous studies, from Johnson & Johnson to AT&T managers, corroborate that leaders with greater emotional awareness are reported to be more productive, to achieve greater performance results, and to develop stronger capacities for complex decision-making, problem-solving, and crisis management.[24]

To do well in college and beyond requires not only time in the library to build IQ, but the persistence and awareness of EI.

HOW CAN EMOTIONAL INTELLIGENCE BE DEVELOPED?

Just as studying for the SATs may increase your vocabulary intelligence, there are also ways you can build your emotional intelligence. As with all things, mastery requires practice and patience. Simply reading this book or going to a yoga class isn't going to cut it. EI training, such as SEL programs, are critical to exercising these muscles. Philosopher Alain de Botton notes that "emotional intelligence isn't an inborn talent. It's the result of education, specifically education in how to interpret ourselves, where our emotions arise from, how our childhoods influence us and in how we might best navigate our fear and our wishes."[25] To separate ourselves from our own emotions and not let them get the better of us so that we can be more present for others, we have to raise awareness. This is where mindfulness practices become important in developing your EI.

Professor Peerayuth Charoensukmongkol studied over three hundred respondents in Thailand and found that those who practiced one form of mindfulness—mindfulness meditation—improved their EI in three ways: understanding one's own emotions, recognizing emotions in others, and controlling one's own emotions. Practitioners also demonstrated less perceived stress, greater self-efficacy, and the ability to know when to use which emotion appropriately and effectively.[26]

These changes aren't just born out of feeling good; there is brain science behind it. Mindfulness practices, such as mindfulness meditation, engage the *insula*—a part of the brain integral to self-awareness—which helps us to make sense of bodily sensations and subjective emotions that are happening in the present moment. When we habituate the practice of awareness, it becomes a trait. The embodiment of a trait can build the gray matter (part that helps us think) of our brains. Practitioners also show activation in the regions of the brain associated with emotional self-management and memory, such as the *anterior cingulate cortex* and *temporal lobe*. One study suggests that a mindfulness practice "alters an individual's emotional self-management capacity . . . and also chang[es] the way their brain processes emotional experiences."[27] In fact, mindfulness is not simply one type of activity; rather, it encompasses a family of practices. Just as you would go to the gym and use different machines for a particular part of your body (biceps versus triceps), mindfulness practices range from meditation to mindful eating, depending on what you want to cultivate. Warrior Mind Training founder Sarah Ernst teaches those in the military to use mindfulness practices, calling them "mental push-ups."[28]

As Goleman says, "mindfulness practices, or meditation generally, are essential practices of self-awareness. That's the first part of emotional intelligence."[29]

WHAT IS MINDFULNESS?

Mindfulness, in its most simple description, is "being present." It is the practice of paying attention to our attention, our awareness, and our present moment.

You know how sometimes you can't focus on one thing, or there are so many thoughts swirling in your mind that you can't make heads or tails of them? Well, imagine your mind is like a snow globe with a really cool little figurine in it that, if you could see what it was, would allow you to figure out the answer you're searching for or help you to be ready for that test you have to take. But it seems like someone keeps shaking the snow globe so that every time you almost make out what that figurine is, everything around you—your billion inside-head thoughts and the external pressures from parents, teachers, friends—clouds it with whirling snowflakes. What mindfulness helps you to do is pause the shaking so that all those little flurries settle to the bottom. Mindfulness doesn't mean those little white flurries disappear forever; like your thoughts and external pressures, they don't disappear—they are still there. But mindfulness settles them and allows you to see with greater clarity that figurine you've been trying to see.

Mindfulness and awareness can help us get to know our brains better. When we get to know our brains better, we become more aware of how we think, feel, and behave. Otherwise, we may move through life on our whims or act blindly. Mindfulness serves like an inner rudder for our actions, guiding our decisions and behaviors.

The good news is that there is a lot of emerging science that suggests mindfulness has potentially powerful benefits. You don't become Yoda. Like anything else worthwhile, you have to work for it.

Psychologist Ellen Langer's forty-plus years of research underscores how mindfulness allows us to pay attention to everything around us, and by doing so, "it makes you more sensitive to context and perspective . . . and it's energy begetting,"[30] reducing stress, unlocking creativity, and enhancing performance. How useful mindfulness may be for you! Not only for better managing stress but also for improving your focus and concentration, all things you need to strengthen your cognitive and technical intelligence and be "successful," at least in the traditional sense, at school. It may also energize you to be more innovative, more productive, and more aware of what is happening. It may decrease your anxiety and your tendency to ruminate—that is, worry about what you coulda, shoulda, woulda. It may help strengthen your immune system and help you get better sleep. It may help you be a better friend, child, and student.

It is useful to understand the science behind mindfulness so that you can put it into practice in a way that works for you. There are many different types of mindfulness practices to raise your awareness, and they may have lifelong impact. Evidence from emerging research suggests that mindfulness meditation can enhance self-regulation (your ability to manage your thoughts, emotions, and behaviors) and train your brain to: 1) improve attentional control and ability to focus; 2) limit self-referential thinking (your tendency to focus on yourself); and 3) enhance your capacity to recognize and regulate your emotions.[31] It has been linked to greater capacity to lead teams and develop more satisfying relationships.[32] These powerful tools can help you find greater calmness in your stressful world, and to grow as a leader, global citizen, and friend. Mindfulness may help you to achieve greater focus and react less impulsively and strongly to those things that irk or bother you. It may make you be more pleasant to actually be around.

If you're thinking about these mental practices in the pursuit of an end goal, say, a better GPA, you might be surprised at the results. One study showed that a two-week mindfulness training course actually improved GRE (Graduate Record Examinations) reading scores and working memory.[33] Does that mean mindfulness can help you improve your SAT scores and raise your GPA? It might, as studies suggest, but not in the way you think. While your GPA may or may not improve, your approach, attitude, and actions will likely see positive impacts, which in turn may make you a more interested and interesting student. To really start seeing the benefits, it takes practice, time, and dedication. Mindfulness is not a means to an end or a way to "get something." Real impact happens when you move to practicing it as part of your lifestyle—a way of being that may transform and prepare you for your life.

Imagine that—a fuller and happier life, and perhaps improvement in test scores and memory as pretty neat by-products.

WHAT ARE SOME MISCONCEPTIONS ABOUT MINDFULNESS?

When you first heard the words "meditation" and "mindfulness," what crossed your mind? When you picked up this book, did you hide it away lest your friend from AP biology see it and laugh in your face for wanting to shave your head and become a monk?[34] As self-proclaimed mindfulness skeptic Dan Harris, author of *10% Happier*,[35] notes, meditation has a public relations problem.

Mindfulness *cannot* help us levitate, escape our stress, or get rid of all thoughts. Unless you know something that I don't, gravity is real, stress is a part of being human, and (over)thinking is natural. While mindful meditation *may* be one reason why Luke Skywalker was able to transport himself elsewhere to fight a battle with his own hologram, sorry to say that's likely not going to happen for you. Mindful meditation is not about sitting still without any thoughts and forgoing all ambition. It is not a panacea that will get you into your first-choice college or clear your acne. It is not a religious conversion ritual that will make you a Christian or a Buddhist or a Muslim. It doesn't mean you have to eschew fun.

Mindfulness does not mean you should "let it go" in the Disney *Frozen*-Elsa-sense, hiding away from the world in an ice castle. According to Evan Thompson who spoke at the 2016 Mind & Life Institute, mindfulness is not just about you. It's not just about what's happening inside your brain but rather "it exists in the social world of human life."[36] It is impossible to separate what is happening in our brains from what is happening outside of us. Mindfulness is not simply accepting everything that happens to you without standing up for yourself. Mindfulness isn't the secret to getting into your top-choice college—did I say that already? Mindfulness is a cornerstone to building your emotional intelligence.

IS MINDFULNESS JUST A FAD?

Some suggest that mindfulness is "new" or a "fad" that will eventually go out of fashion like banana clips and jelly shoes (you probably have no idea what those are, but trust me, they were fads that should remain in the past). You probably are aware that many enterprising folks have jumped on the bandwagon and slapped the word "mindful" in front of everything, peddling it as mindfulness—mindful toast, mindful mints, mindful gloves.

But buying a "mindful smoothie" doesn't make you mindful. Mindfulness is neither new nor a fad. It isn't just a label. It has been practiced for thousands of years across all cultures and religions. It has been broadened and secularized as it evolves without adherence to any particular religion. You can believe in anything or nothing and still gain benefits from mindfulness practices.

To give you a bit of its more recent history, Kabat-Zinn created the Mindfulness-Based Stress Reduction (MBSR) Program at the University of Massachusetts in the 1970s to treat depression and stress. MBSR's eight-week course has now reached over 22,000 people. Kabat-Zinn did a follow-up, three-year study and found that the initial results of decreased depression, anxiety, anger, and stress, and increased positive mood and cognitive function, were ongoing and maintained.[37] Around the same time, other prominent U.S. teachers, such as Jack Kornfield, Sharon Salzberg, and Joseph Goldstein, founded the Insight Meditation Society (IMS) to offer mindfulness meditation to a more general population in the United States.

Mounting evidence suggests that mindfulness has a real and well-documented impact in all sectors—business, healthcare, education—and with different populations. Increasing evidence (a great research project for those of you fascinated by neuroscience) suggests that long-term mindfulness practices have profound benefits, such as improved attention and focus, relationships, and immune systems. Since the last decade or so, we have seen studies on the impact of mindfulness explode from a handful in the 1970s to over one thousand in 2016—in English alone.[38] Psychologists Daniel Goleman and Richard Davidson note in *Altered Traits* that much of this emerging science suggests that mindfulness practices can decrease stress, improve emotional regulation and self-awareness, and make sustained changes in our socioemotional and physical well-being. For example, fMRI (functional Magnetic Resonance Imaging) scans of experienced meditators suggest that they have a greater capacity to hold attention than non-meditators do.[39]

Mindfulness may also increase the capacity for empathy and optimism. And guess what? Optimism has been demonstrated to be a stronger predictor of first-term college grades than SAT scores. While this isn't something testing prep companies emphasize, your attitude plays a huge role in how you'll fare in college and beyond—more on this later.

WHO DOES MINDFULNESS HELP?

The benefits of mindfulness are so promising that *10% Happier* author and journalist Dan Harris is convinced that mindfulness is poised to become the next public revolution, much as exercising and teeth brushing have become.

In other words, it can help a lot of people, including you.

Mindfulness continues to spread in the West because there is undoubtedly a need. We now live in what is known as a VUCA world— "volatile-uncertain-complex-ambiguous." It's a confusing world in which we don't know what will happen at any point, and there is no clear answer or path that we can simply follow. You feel the stress— that's why you're reading this. That uncertainty you often feel about what's going to happen to you or to the people you care about—or even to people around the world? You're not alone. As a result, many people from all walks of life have turned to mindfulness for a healthier and more sustainable way to manage this stress.

More folks now agree that mindfulness is a "must have . . . way to keep our brains healthy, to support self-regulation and effective decision-making capabilities, and to protect ourselves from toxic stress."[40] As a mainstay of well-being, mindfulness now has a commanding presence in the marketplace. The Global Wellness Institute values the overall wellness industry at $3.72 trillion, of which mindfulness-related activities comprise $1.1 billion.[41]

Let's take a look at how it's helping.

The government. The United Kingdom has taken mindfulness and well-being to another level. Recognizing the damaging effects of isolation, it has even appointed the world's first minister for loneliness. At a systemic level, mindfulness now is being integrated into education, work, health, and criminal justice systems. The UK Parliament explicitly articulates that mindfulness may help build its citizens' resilience to raise self-awareness; recognize signs of stress; discern what activities nurture or deplete; support positive relationships; and boost creativity.[42]

The private sector. Leading corporations, such as Google and LinkedIn, have embraced mindfulness practices as a way to enhance employee productivity and performance. They recognize that rising stress levels are resulting in lost productivity, absenteeism (folks not showing up for work), and rising healthcare

costs, adding up to $300 billion a year in costs to U.S. compa-
nies alone.[43] Many of these companies are turning to mindfulness and meditation, now a $1.1 billion industry, as companies
are catching on that mental health is directly related to performance and productivity.[44] A National Business Group on Health
and Fidelity Investments study showed that 22 percent of companies offer meditation at work. And the evidence is mounting.
Aetna, a leader in providing mindfulness training, has shown a
$3,000 increase in productivity per employee, a 28 percent de-
crease in stress levels, and a $2,000 decrease in medical costs
per employee due to the program in which over 50,000 of their
employees already participate.[45] General Mills offers a "Mindful
Leadership" program, with 80 percent of senior executives reporting better decision-making capabilities, and 89 percent better listening capabilities.[46] Mindfulness programs are no long
seen as woo-woo, fun-to-have perks but as essential to preparing
employees for high performance and for improving the bottom
line.

The kids. Mindfulness programs haven't just become "in demand"
within corporations; they are growing in schools as well. Some
of you may have participated in these, such as the well-known
Mindful Schools program which has already worked with over
1.5 million youth and 25,000 educators. An increased sense of
self-compassion and efficacy and reduced stress for educators
has been measured, and educators have seen significant increase
in focus, emotional regulation, compassion, and engagement in
their students following implementation of such programs.[47] In
one study of over 1,300 students from grades 1–12, mindfulness-
based interventions showed improved cognitive performance
and resilience to stress.[48]

The teenagers. These programs aren't simply focused on younger
students. Mindfulness has been shown to be correlated with increased empathy and decreased volatile behaviors in teenagers.
For example, a longitudinal study involving youth who participated in five-day, intensive meditation retreats run by Inward
Bound Mindfulness Education (iBme) has shown this training to
have had a serious impact on teenagers, particularly in stress
reduction, less depression, improvement of well-being and happiness, greater self-compassion and satisfaction—even three
months after the retreat.[49]

The college students. Many universities, from San Diego to Brown, have recognized the benefits of mindfulness on student mental well-being. In addition to yoga classes and therapy dogs, many now offer courses to positively impact athletic and academic performance, while reducing antisocial behaviors such as binge drinking. Increasingly, universities are adding mindfulness and meditation to reduce the overwhelming stress that university life can offer, and these come in many different forms, from retreats to courses on flourishing.

WHY PRACTICE MINDFULNESS WHEN I'M BUSY APPLYING FOR COLLEGES?

The last thing you probably want is to read a book on which you are not going to be tested. You might have even skipped to the pages that talked specifically about the college application process. However, it is important to better understand *why* you want to go to college and how to go through the process with greater effectiveness, success, and, hopefully, less stress.

You're busy, but imagine if you can get through this stressful college application process ready to fully engage in your next adventure, instead of depending on high-energy drinks and lacking sleep. You can.

Most of the time, you're probably sleepwalking through life. Have you ever gotten to school and wondered how did I get here? It happens to all of us; particularly when we habituate to something, we don't pay attention to what is around us. This is autopilot living, "whereby we are sleep-walking into our choices."[50] When you don't pay attention, you can miss a lot of opportunities. You might end up doing things "just because" without a whole lot of thought or purpose behind them.

You're not alone. Adults do this a lot. In fact, 96 percent of the Britons who participated in a survey by Marks & Spencer admitted to making multiple decisions on autopilot daily, including answering emails.[51] I know you've had that experience of writing a text or email and then, once you press "send," you panic because you didn't *really* mean to do that. When you function on autopilot, you actually may end up making decisions that are not the most appropriate. In the same Marks & Spencer study, almost half of those surveyed said they say "yes" to things they actually didn't want to do. When you sleepwalk through life, you are more prone to passively acquiesce than to take conscious and deliberate action.

Think about your day yesterday: How many times did you just act without giving much thought to what you were doing? How many times did you do something because it was easier than trying to figure out something else? Some of us tend to move on autopilot because we like to please everyone so much that we forget to please ourselves. Others of us do so because we're just so busy—or we do things for the sake of being busy, or because of FOMO (fear of missing out), or to avoid looking like we're lazy and unproductive. And then there are those of us who would rather play it safe and move on autopilot because we're overwhelmed by the information coming at us. But living on autopilot means that you're not actually conscious of what you're doing—whether it's taking a test, or conversing with a teammate, or signing up to work on the yearbook—and often you are not giving whatever you're doing your full attention.

Much of the time, your brains are off somewhere else. You might be sitting in AP English, and your brain starts to think about your upcoming pop quiz in calculus. Your brain wanders *a lot*. Mind-wandering is the tendency to think ahead (that quiz next period!) or to ruminate about what has happened (that quiz last period!) instead of focusing on what is right in front of you. You may miss out on what you're doing and possibly a whole lot more. Psychologists Matthew Killingsworth and Daniel Gilbert conducted a study which revealed three key findings: 1) 47 percent of people surveyed said they "mind-wander"—for almost half of the day, people think about something other than what they're doing; 2) people are less happy when their minds wander; and 3) what people think in the moment is a stronger predictor of happiness than *what* they are doing.[52]

However, people with deep mindfulness meditation practices have brains that wander less. In one study by Judson Brewer, those with a mindfulness meditation practice showed less activation in the main areas of the brain known as the default mode network (DMN), so named because, when you're supposedly not doing anything, your brains are dancing around like jumping beans.[53] Mindfulness may actually help you strengthen the connection between your prefrontal cortex (PFC), the part of the brain behind the forehead that is associated with higher executive functioning and decision-making, and the parts of your brain associated with making sense of the world to keep you alive. The stronger the connection, the less your mind wanders and the less you react without thinking. An Emory study, for example, showed that Zen meditators with three or more years of practice have less activation in DMN when focusing on breathing.[54] Mindfulness may help you to notice when your mind wanders and to bring it back, and that may offer you a greater sense of well-being and happiness.

What might this mean for you? First, if you're spending half your day not concentrating, you're less likely to perform well. Second, if you're not focused on the present, you might not be as happy as you could be. Finally, how you feel and what you think about being president of MUN can impact your happiness level more than actually being it. The good news is that you can train your brain so that you can be more conscious about what you do as well as more aware of when your mind decides to take unnecessary detours.

Hopefully, you are not just blindly applying to colleges because you're "supposed" to do so but are instead thinking carefully and thoughtfully about *why* you want to go to college. And if you want to go to college, particularly a highly selective one, presumably you're keen on having greater attention, focus, and control of your emotions. You're not alone if your brain is constantly moving in what seems like a million-and-one directions and you can barely keep it together, even though you pretend you do. While the overscheduled world you live in likely won't help you to build your concentration and your emotional balance, mindfulness might prepare you for the college application process and for life.

HOW DO YOU PRACTICE IT?

There is no one "right" way to practice mindfulness, whether formally or informally. Informal practices refer to how we can cultivate our awareness in the moment. Formal practices require more sustained periods of attention. One common practice, which we have already introduced, is meditation. Meditation isn't one single thing but, rather, a collection of mental practices that "aims to improve an individual's core psychological capacities."[55] The four basic elements of a mindfulness practice involve: 1) focusing on one thing; 2) mind wandering; 3) taking notice of wandering mind; and 4) shifting attention back to the original thing.[56] Just like there are different ways to train different parts of your body, there are different practices to train different parts of your brain. For example, there are different practices depending on whether you want to improve your ability to be in tune with your emotions (body scan) or your capacity for creativity (open monitoring). Don't worry about memorizing these (this is not a test nor will there be one). What is important to know is that meditation is not about sitting on a mountain with a blank mind; it is a myriad of practices. Virginia Commonwealth University professor Kirk Brown defines it as "a state of consciousness of awareness and attention" with four key parts: 1) clarify of awareness; 2) ability to increase or decrease level of attention without judgment; 3) orientation to the present; and 4) ability to discern focus on the inner and outer world.[57] Lippincott notes that it is "a receptive state of mind that enables the practitioner to experience reality in a nonreactive manner, free of interpretations, or emotional responses that are influenced by past experiences, beliefs, or preconceived filters.[58] Goleman and Davidson note that mindfulness is not about a blank mind but rather the capacity to "simply [note] without reactivity whatever comes into mind . . . and then . . . let [it] go."[59] Their research shows that mindfulness practices, such as meditation, can have a physiological impact on the actual brain. Your brain is not fixed but rather constantly changing due to neuroplasticity. Neuroplasticity is the ability of the brain to rewire itself in structure and function by making changes in neural pathways and synapses depending on repeated experience and attention to particular areas. Like any muscle, your brain gets stronger where you focus.

There are four ways that the brain responds to meditation: 1) ability to recover from adverse events; 2) capacity for compassion and empathy; 3) ability to focus; and 4) sense of self.[60] Giving awareness to our awareness can help bring greater focus on what is in front of us.

Different practices will be outlined for you throughout the book so you can pick and choose the ones that speak to you for the appropriate moment.

WHY IS MINDFULNESS IMPORTANT TO ME NOW?

While it is easy to think, "all this sounds good, but I don't have time," you don't want to waste time by *not* practicing. Mindfulness practices can help cultivate your emotional intelligence. The more you chase an external goal on a hamster wheel, the more stress and anxiety you're building now and for life. Step off the hamster wheel now.

This is not easy. It takes courage. Recently, I had a conversation with a gentleman with a long-standing mindfulness practice of his own. With his wealth, he has invested in meditation companies to help create a world that values a different perspective on success. He spoke about the deep impact meditation has had on him and his ability to become a billionaire. Inspired by his vision, I wondered how, as a parent, he was able to balance the desire to help others redefine success while his teenage daughter attended a pressure-cooker high school.

He said: "She'll be fine because she's a Harvard legacy."

Despite his cognitive awareness that Harvard isn't the solution for world peace and his good intentions, his daughter may be getting the message that many of you are getting: Do everything you can to get a leg up and get into your dream college; be mindful later. He is making a huge impact on others, but he is still human. He is still a father who wants the best for his daughter. Mindfulness and well-being would have to come later. For someone who prides himself on being on friendly terms with His Holiness the Dalai Lama, when it comes to his daughter, a Harvard acceptance letter still came first.

What I am saying is: Do not wait. Mindfulness may help you now, and for a lifetime.

Chapter Two

The Brain Behind the Brain

Your brain is pretty phenomenal. It is wired in fantastic ways to help you maneuver in your world. Yet it doesn't come with a manual of how to optimize it so you can think, act, and feel your best.

Now that you know a little more about what mindfulness is and isn't, let's take a look at how it actually works. Mindfulness isn't a bunch of yogis walking around feeling good (though mindful yogis *do* likely walk around feeling pretty good), but it can offer you a greater sense of well-being, and help to improve your performance and your relationships.

If mindfulness practices are mental training practices, you would hope that they are grounded in some sort of researched and documented scientific data. And they are. What I'll do in this chapter is share more about how our brains work. Once you understand your brain better, you might not be so hard on yourself when you have one of those days where you're so stressed that you lash out at your little sister or blank out during a test. You might cut yourself some slack *and* understand how to train your mind so those moments of stressed-out reactivity happen less. It will help you be better equipped throughout the college admissions process and beyond.

In this chapter, let's address Brain 101; triggers, unconscious thinking, and brain reactions; neuroplasticity; the impact of meditation on the brain; and the teenage brain.

BRAIN 101

For those of you in AP biology, the next few paragraphs might be a review. Let's take a look at the brain and how it works. (Don't worry about memorizing this; there is no quiz.)

Your brain was designed to keep you alive so that you can keep the species going. In so doing, it prefers to keep you in the happy place of *homeostasis*, such as having a 98.6°F body temperature. For a long time, it was understood that your brain has a "thinking" brain and an "emotional" brain. More recently, professor and Guggenheim Fellow Lisa Feldman Barrett has revived the argument that, in fact, your brain isn't separated in such a way.[1] Instead of a "lizard" brain governed by the emotional *limbic system* and "reasoning" brain governed by the *cerebral cortex*, the many various parts of your brain play multiple roles and are deeply integrated. (Disclaimer: I am not a neuroscientist by training so this is a *very* basic layman's overview.[2])

While scientists continue to debate which parts of the brain perform what functions, it is generally accepted that a bunch of interdependent units of the brain are associated with emotional processing. These units alert you to new information that might knock your balance off, whether good (smell of pizza: yay!) or bad (smell of old sneakers: yuck!). Your mind then quickly (and usually unconsciously) assesses the situation based on past experiences to give it meaning and decide how to react. For example, imagine way back in the day you ran into a hungry saber-toothed tiger; parts of your brain noticed something new and big in the way and sent a message to get your heart racing, just in case you had to act. Your brain quickly remembered how a hungry saber-toothed tiger had eaten your best friend and, well, you preferred not to get eaten. So your brain gave meaning and sense to your racing heart as a signal to experience fear and got the parts of your brain associated with motor control moving so that you could . . . RUN! While saber-toothed tigers no longer exist, the parts of your brain that protect you from perceived threats (like a disappointed mom—RUN!) still do. Four parts of the brain that are commonly associated with this processing[3] include: the *hypothalamus, amygdala, thalamus,* and *hippocampus.* Let's take a peek:

First is the *hypothalamus*, which triggers your hormones like adrenaline and plays a role in regulating your drive, need for sleep, and hunger. It also helps to regulate your *autonomic nervous system* (ANS), which in turn regulates the parts of your body that you don't really have a lot of control over, such as your blood flow and digestion. Two parts of your ANS work together to help you survive. When your brain perceives something to be a threat, what is known as your *sympathetic nervous system* kicks in to manage your body so you can escape the threat, often referred to as the fight-flight-freeze response. Several things happen physiologically: your pupils dilate (see the tiger chasing you so you can RUN); you get dry mouth (ever happen in the middle of a class presentation when you want to RUN?); you breathe more heavily and your heart rate goes up (more oxygen to RUN!); and you release adrenaline (energy to RUN!). On the other hand, when you don't perceive any threats, your *parasympathetic nervous system* regulates your body to get rest. Physiologically, your bodies slow down because you don't have to RUN.

Second is the *amygdala*, two little knobs that act as the brain's 911-alarm system. When a new piece of information comes in, it tells the brain to pay attention because it might need to act so that your body maintains its balance. While it traditionally has been linked with fear, the amygdala is more a signaling device, such as helping you to make sense of other people's facial expressions and other visual cues to see if they are a threat or not.[4]

Third is the *thalamus*, two big lobes that sit behind the amygdala. The thalamus acts as a relay station, directing information you take in and relaying sensory signals to appropriate areas of the body.

Fourth is the *hippocampus*, a curve-like structure that plays a role in converting short-term memories into long-term ones. If you're learning a new language, for example, your hippocampus helps to convert the verbs you're cramming for a pop quiz into your longer-term memory. If you damage this part of your brain, you may remember what you did when you were five but not remember the person you just met.

These four units are connected to the executive functioning area, your *prefrontal cortex* (PFC). Your PFC sits right behind the forehead and is responsible for higher-order executive functioning, such as processing language and information, solving problems, making decisions, and managing your behaviors in different social settings. This area is also the last to develop in the human brain. So guess what? The younger you are, the less developed your executive functioning area is. In other words, the younger you are, the less able you are to *think* before you *act*. While this is not an excuse for bad behavior or judgment, it might offer some explanation as to why you sometimes do things that don't seem to make a whole lot of sense (although I doubt your teachers will accept this as an excuse for not doing your homework. Sorry). Throughout your brain is also a network of neurons. Neurons are cells that are responsible for your thoughts and feelings of sensations. Each neuron is made up of three key parts: the *soma* (the body), the *dendrites* (tentacle-ish extensions that branch off from the soma that transmit signals), and the *axon* (the tail of the neuron). What happens in your brain is that a stimulus, let's say the smell of pizza, stimulates the dendrite. The dendrite receives this information—the smell of pizza— and if it's strong enough, it travels through the axons, activating them and connecting them to other neurons.

Of course, there are many other parts of your brain that are important to note. Ever wonder why a certain smell evokes intense memories? Perhaps the smell of books brings you back to a childhood library or the smell of butterscotch candies reminds you of your grandmother's house. Your sense of smell is processed by the *olfactory bulb*, which starts at the nose and goes to the bottom of your brain. This area is connected directly to the *amygdala* and the *hippocampus*. Both of these areas are associated with sense-making and memory. So want to imprint a memory? Smell it.

TRIGGERS, UNCONSCIOUS THINKING, AND BRAIN REACTIONS

Our complex brain structures give us information as to why we react to things the way we do—and sometimes, overreact. Let's take a look at the amygdala hijack, unconscious thinking, and left-right brain activity.

First, your brain gets triggered—a lot. Triggers are a stimulation of some sort that evoke a response. Your brain can be triggered by stimuli happening outside of you (a speeding bus that startles you) or something internal (a memory that sinks your stomach). When your amygdala notices something that might disturb your body's desire for equilibrium, it goes into action and tries to send a message to your prefrontal cortex in hopes that it can make sense out of it and send a message back to your amygdala to tell it how to appropriately respond. For example, a graded paper with a red D on it might trigger your amygdala to get your heart to beat faster. If your brain interprets the racing heart as an indication that your identity as a "smart" person has been threatened, you may experience the emotion of anxiety. But if you pause, your brain may be able to sort out that neither your racing heart—nor the grade—is a threat. If your amygdala is happily talking to your PFC, the conversation might go something like this:

Amygdala: Oh my gosh—a D! Never seen this before! I have to get the heart moving fast because our identity is being threatened, and we need to escape this threat!

PFC: Take a breath. It's not the grade we'd hoped for, but let's take a look to see what we can learn from it. We're going to be fine.

Amygdala: Whew, OK, it's not the end of the world. Let me slow the heart rate and calm down.

However, sometimes, you can get *so* triggered that the communication channel between your amygdala and PFC gets short-circuited and your amygdala takes over. The message never gets properly communicated to your PFC, and you go into fight-flight-freeze mode, often known as the *amygdala hijack*, where you "can't think straight." So instead of that civil conversation between your amygdala and your PFC, the conversation might go something like this:

Amygdala: Oh my gosh—a D! Never seen this before! I have to get the heart moving fast because our identity is being threatened, and we need to escape this threat!

PFC: . . . .

Amygdala: You're a failure, you're never going to get into college, you're going to end up penniless and homeless and no one will love you. You suck! AAAAAAAA!!!!!!!!!!!

This ever happened to you?

The good news is that emotional regulation can help you reframe what is happening and open those channels of communications.

Second, your mind makes all sorts of decisions without you even being conscious of them. "Of the 10 million bits of information that each of our brains process each second, only about 50 bits are devoted to deliberate thought—in other words, 0.0005%."[5] Your mind doesn't have the capacity to be conscious about every decision you make; instead, it "leaves it up to our unconscious to make the vast majority of choices about our behaviors."[6] Your decisions are usually a mixture of both logic and intuition—your gut feelings. Regardless of how many pros and cons you list, you're influenced by your instinct as to which response "feels" right, regardless of whether you end up there or not.

Third, different parts of our brains get activated depending on whether we are experiencing positive or negative emotions. Functional magnetic resonance imaging (fMRI) studies suggest that your left and right brains engage differently with specific emotions. If you're having a grand day, let's say winning the 200-meter sprint or being elected class president, your left hemisphere is activated more, enhancing feelings of sociability and joy. If you're having a not-so-grand day, let's say receiving a disappointing test grade or finding out that you've been cut from the spring musical, it's your right hemisphere that lights up, with accompanying feelings of isolation, fear, and depression.

Given your brain structure, is there anything you can do to help your amygdala and PFC have better conversations with each other or to be more aware of your unconscious thinking? Yes.

NEUROPLASTICITY

Neuroplasticity is the capacity of your brain to change in its structure and function in response to experience. Just like you can build up different muscles depending on what type of exercise you do, science suggests that you can actually change the strength of information flow depending on what you pay more or less attention to. This phenomenon may help you with memory and learning, and even in recovery from brain injuries. Your brain has its biggest growth when you're a wee little baby and when you're a teenager, but it doesn't just stop changing and growing (or shrinking) the rest of your life. What you pay attention to, you strengthen.

Remember neurons? The spaces between neurons where specialized connections are transmitted are the synapses. With neuroplasticity, you might actually change the number of synapses you have or the structure of target cells. The brain can also build synaptic connections—the strength and flow of communication between neurons—by "sprouting" (growing) or "pruning" (losing) the number and complexity of dendrites. Where your neurons fire a lot, you might develop more synapses or neurons with longer or more complex networks of dendrites with receptors that are more sensitized to certain stimuli. Where they are not used, you may end up with shorter and simpler neurons with less-sensitive receptors, or you may even lose the entire neuron if it is no longer needed.

Where your neurons fire, they rewire. What you don't use, you lose. Neuroplasticity is particularly noted with people who have suffered brain injuries. If you have ever had a concussion or know someone who has, it's not easy bouncing back. If your brain didn't have the capacity to rewire itself, you would never recover. Moreover, if you keep your brain active and focused now, your brain may shrink less—and more slowly—as you age.

IMPACT OF MEDITATION ON THE BRAIN

Given the way your brain works, is there anything you can do to get it to work in your favor? Yes. Mindfulness meditation is one tool to use to focus your attention. In a meta-study of twenty studies conducted by the University of British Columbia and the Chemnitz University of Technology, researchers found at least eight different regions of the brain impacted by meditation. One area is the *anterior cingulate cortex* (ACC), located behind the brain's frontal lobe, which is associated with your ability to direct attention, behavior, and self-regulation. Meditators demonstrate a greater ability to resist distractions and regulate their emotions and impulses. Another area is where *cortisol*, your stress hormone, finds receptors. Mindfulness strengthens the part of the brain's capacity for resilience to stress.

Researchers have also found a correlation between mindfulness training and a thickening of the gray matter in your brain, *cortical structures*, associated with attention, working memory, empathy, self-reflection, and regulation.[7] A 2014 study showed that an eight-week practice of mindfulness meditation, known as mindfulness-based stress reduction (MBSR), increased the gray matter concentration in different parts of the brain associated with greater psychological well-being.[8] In a study of fourteen K–12 mindfulness training programs, not only did students demonstrate benefits in attention and memory but their teachers who implemented the programs also benefited by being better able to handle work-related stress and having improved executive-functioning ability. Regular mindfulness practices may boost IQ *and* EI.

In particular, mindfulness meditation can affect the parts of your brain related to how aware you are of your body, how you regulate your emotions, your sense of self, your capacity for complex thinking, and even your tolerance for pain. For example, meditators see changes in the *frontopolar cortex*—the part of the brain related to complex, higher-order behavior—enhancing meta-awareness (your ability to notice when your awareness wanders and to bring it back); *sensory cortices* and *insula*—enhancing body awareness (your ability to notice what your body is trying to tell you about what you're feeling); *hippocampus*—enhancing capacity for the processing of memory; *anterior cingulate cortex, midcingulate cortex, orbitofrontal cortex*—enhancing your ability to regulate your emotions; and *superior longitudinal fasciculus* and *corpus callosum*—enhancing the communication between the two hemispheres of your brain.[9] In particular, mindfulness training is consistently linked with alterations in the *anterior cingulate cortex* (ACC), which helps you to self-regulate so you're not flying off the handle. On tests of self-regulation, for example, those who regularly meditate "demonstrate superior performance . . . resisting distractions and making correct answers more often than nonmeditators."[10]

Your brain also has only so much capacity to hold cognitive resources; it simply can't hold all the information that is coming at it. Mindfulness has been shown to support *attentional efficiency*, in other words, helping your brain to more economically utilize its limited resources. One phenomenon, *attentional control*, refers to how your brain directs attention appropriately, even though there are many demands competing for your attention. Emerging studies suggest that "mindfulness has been associated with improved attentional stability (sustaining attention on a current target with less mind-wandering), better control of attention (selecting appropriate targets from among a field of potential targets), and attentional efficiency (economical use and allocation of attentional resources)."[11] It has also been associated with *flexible cognition*, your brain's ability to adapt to new or novel perspectives—great news for your creativity abilities.

Jonathan Kabat-Zinn's research suggests that meditation and mindfulness training can increase activation on the left frontal activity of the brain, associated with the capability to approach problems and situations with greater resilience.[12] Other studies show that meditation can reduce effects of stress on working memory capacity, which enables us to learn information and make wise decisions.[13]

Daniel Goleman and Richard Davidson argue that meditation can lead to new characteristics that endure beyond the practice and alter our traits, shaping "how we behave in our daily lives, not just during or immediately after we meditate."[14] If we are under constant stress and perceived threat, our amygdala is on constant high alert, gets enlarged, and becomes more easily triggered. Brain scans of people with years of ongoing stressful work histories reveal enlarged amygdalas and weakened connections with the PFC.[15] The researchers note that even your working memory—your ability to hold information that you need—requires executive functioning and is compromised.[16]

Awareness practices can help counter this.

You don't, however, need to devote years to training. In fact, studies have shown that even eight weeks of mindfulness-based stress reduction (MBSR) training can improve attention and give you greater attention to consciously select attention.

Mindful meditation may also help you build resilience. Consider this: You have been given five minutes to prepare for a presentation but, before that time is up, your pen and paper are taken away. Then you have to deliver a five-minute presentation as if you were interviewing for a job while all the judges are staring at you stone-faced. Next, you have five minutes to complete a math problem. This is known as the Trier Social Stress Test (TSST), one of the most reliable ways to trigger your brain's stress circuits. If you're like most people, you will struggle mightily on that math test. Studies have shown that participants who undergo mindful meditation training have lower levels of cortisol, or stress hormones, during the test. In other words, they were better able to regulate and balance their emotions during these difficult challenges.[17] They were also able to tolerate and recover from the stress more quickly after the test was completed.

Mindfulness practices may also increase your capacity to hold information. *Attentional blink* is when "the mind's ability to notice goes blind and attention loses sensitivity."[18] We can get so caught up in one area that we miss what else goes on because humans are terrible at multitasking. Most of us are switching from activity to activity. On the other hand, if we build our cognitive control, we can "focus on a specific goal or task and keep it mind while resisting distractions."[19] This helps us to actually expend less effort in trying to stay focused. In other words, "the brain of a novice works hard while that of the expert expends little energy."[20]

But even beginners to meditation with as little as two weeks of practice show less amygdala reactivity to stress, greater focus, less mind-wandering, and better memory.[21] Certainly, long-term meditators see even greater benefits, such as lowered reactivity to stress, lower levels of the stress hormone (cortisol) and inflammation, and stronger prefrontal circuits to manage distress. Meditators who practice compassion may see greater neural attunement with those who are suffering and enhanced ability to do something to help. When it comes to attention, benefits include: stronger selective and sustained attention, heightened readiness to respond to whatever arises, and decreased attentional blink, mind-wandering, self-obsessed thoughts. It can also help you shift to a slower breath rate, indicting a slowing of the metabolic rate.[22]

THE TEENAGE BRAIN

Before you celebrate that you can lifehack your way into hyperfocus, remember this: Your brain isn't fully developed yet when you're a teenager, even if you're valedictorian. Because you do not have as much activity in your frontal lobes as adults do, you are less able to make sense of all the stimuli coming at you or to solve problems as readily. As such, some of you might not yet be ready for college-level courses (I'm sure you and your parents don't want to hear this).

Moreover, your sense of identity is still being formed so there is a constant "endeavor to define, over-define and redefine [yourself], and each other in ruthless comparison."[23] One day you have blue hair, the next no hair. Guess what? Your teenage brain is trying to figure it out.

Your brain is adaptable and moldable, and this is one of *the most critical times of your life* when your brain is going to make, reinforce, or get rid of neural connections. When you are chronically anxious, you risk elevated levels of stress hormones, which then have a "domino effect that hardwires pathways between the hippocampus and the amygdala in a way that might create a vicious cycle by creating a brain that becomes predisposed to be in a constant state of fight-or-flight."[24] You might think that the anxiety you have now will simply go away in college, but the science suggests that the greater occurrence of your anxiety, the more likely that your brain may alter into a default mode primed for chronic anxiety with a greater chance of a lifelong tendency for depression and anxiety. Goleman even posed that "how popular a child was in third grade has been shown to be a better predictor of mental-health problems at age eighteen than anything else,"[25] including IQ scores and even psychological tests. A child who faces ostracism or bullying may suffer longer-term mental health implications. Those who are constantly fearful of failure and overly sensitive to stress may "simply tolerate the humiliation and shame associated with what *they* experience as repeated failures [but] with their increasingly depressive mind-sets, some contemplate suicide."[26]

By being more aware of your awareness, known as meta-awareness, you may be more able handle these internal and external triggers. Doing so can help you strengthen your cognitive control during a particularly intense period of your life.

So don't despair. It's normal to have emotions sometimes get the best of you. There are tools you can learn to better regulate them.

Chapter Three

Educating My Emotions

Have you ever started crying when you see other people cry? Have you ever "snapped" and said something mean to someone and then regretted it later? If you've answered "yes," congratulations—you're a human being.

Let's take a look at the teenage brain and emotions, the competencies of emotional intelligence and balance, the role of the body in offering information about emotions, and the role that sleep and digital addiction play in emotional intelligence and balance.

YOUR BRAIN CAN'T HELP IT

You're born with a lot more neurons than you'll need in life. Over time, your brain goes through a process of "pruning" whereby it discards the neural connections that you don't use. It also strengthens the ones that you do use. While this happens throughout your life, your brain goes through two major times of growth—the first is from birth to about three years of age, and the second is when you're about thirteen or fourteen years old.

Remember your friend the amygdala (the brain's 911-threat detector)? The amygdala alerts your brain to information it needs to know so that it can prepare your body accordingly. Threat? Run! Reward? Celebrate! Since, from an evolutionary and developmental perspective, the amygdala develops faster than the prefrontal cortex (PFC), this means that as a teenager, your primary response to the world is often "driven by emotion, not reason."[1]

For example, if you get the "happy feels" from social acceptance (most of us do) or when you earn a great grade (most of us do), parts of your brain light up and say, "more please!" That may also mean that if you get a good feeling by doing something foolish, you might still go for it even if it's not the wisest thing to do. For example, if your friends tell you to steal a shirt from the store because "it's cool," there may be a part of your prefrontal cortex that says, "dude, not a good idea!" But the other part of your brain that wants to be accepted says, "but these people will like you more," so you might slip that shirt under your jacket. Or if you get an adrenaline rush from speeding on the highway, the executive decision-making part of your brain may not be as quick to kick in and so you risk your life and the lives of others around you by going 75 in a 60 mph zone. It might explain how 70 percent of the 13,000 teen deaths each year result from car crashes, unintentional injuries, homicide, and suicide.[2] It isn't that you're not able to distinguish what's risky or safe. It's that you might not be as able to make the right choice in the moment.

The neurocognitive skills needed for critical and analytical thinking—what you need to get into and thrive in college—lie in the prefrontal cortex (PFC), which, of course, is the area which develops last.[3] The PFC is associated with learning and mastering modulating skills, and it doesn't even fully develop until a person is in their mid-to-late twenties—for some, into their thirties. So if you find yourself having a hard time managing your high sensitivity to stimuli, or even keeping up with organizing your schedules, your backpack, and your room, your brain might have something to do with it. (Next time your teacher asks, "Where's your brain?!" when you do something idiotic, you can respond with some accuracy that your PFC isn't quite ripe yet.) Your desire to get the "good feels" may take precedence over your rationality.

TEENAGE DREAM: WHY ARE YOU SO SENSITIVE?

Have you ever spent an entire day or week ruminating about why that girl from English class walked by you without smiling? Was it something you said? Something you wore? Has she now gone and told her friends to exclude you from the lunch table? Chances are that she didn't even notice she wasn't smiling at you; chances are she was too worried about why you were staring at her. And off both of you go down the rabbit hole, creating stories about the other.

Your identity is being formed. This process, as you know, is not easy. The teen brain is more sensitive to external and internal stimuli. You are intensely evaluating yourself by what others say. You are constantly comparing yourself to others to understand. You are self-conscious about your self-worth, your body, your voice. It's not easy, but it's normal. This ongoing sense-making may impact how you feel about someone else or even influence what you're guessing someone else is feeling. For example, imagine you see a classmate down the hall. If you're holding a warm cup of coffee, you might have warmer, fuzzier feelings toward them and even feel more generous toward them. If, on the other hand, you're holding an iced coffee, you're more likely to have cooler, distant feelings toward them and perhaps feel less inclined to be generous.[4] In other words, how you react or what emotions you experience toward someone may have nothing to do with them.

As much as we like to think we are logical, thinking creatures, we're strongly influenced by how we feel. Scientists continue to discover new things every day about emotions and how they work in the brain. According to professor Lisa Feldman Barrett's theory of constructed emotions, emotions are not expressed or even recognized universally. Rather, they are embedded in social and cultural realities.

This theory poses that your brain is constantly trying to make sense of what's happening externally (contextually) and internally (physiologically) and to guess what will happen next based on previous experiences to help you achieve a certain goal. In so doing, you brain constructs an emotion to let you know how to act. For example, suppose that your heart is racing. By itself, it's a condition without meaning. It could simply be that you just raced up a flight of stairs. But let's say you sit down for an exam. Your brain is trying to predict what to do to keep you alive and well given the context (exam) and what it senses (heart racing). If your previous experience was positive—the last time your heart raced during an exam, you were excited at knowing the answers and sailed through—your brain may construct an emotion of excitement. On the other hand, if you blanked on your answers the last time, your brain may construct an emotion of fear. Either emotion gives meaning to the sensation of your racing heart to keep you alive and well (e.g., excitement > engage; fear > avoid).

As Barrett says, you are the "architect of your experience."[5] Emotions don't happen to you; you create them. In other words, you have more control over your emotions than you think. Multiple parts of your brain engage to constantly construct emotions in the moment so it really is your whole brain at work.[6] Stanford's James Gross studies emotions and suggests that they can be both our best allies and worst enemies. In general, we tend to regulate our emotions in two ways. The first method is *suppression*, where we try and just pretend they aren't happening. Have you ever needed a good cry because something really upset you or made you sad, and a well-intentioned friend or family member said, "oh, stop crying, let's get some ice cream instead!" or perhaps you pretended that you weren't upset and slapped on a plastic smile over the hurt like a Band-Aid over a gaping hole? When we try to minimize and pretend like this, we actually are not addressing the issue at hand. What usually happens is the opposite of what we're hoping for because suppressing can actually diminish a person's ability to be resilient, to solve problems, or to build a sense of self-efficacy and self-esteem. Instead of successfully squishing them away, we can actually stimulate our sympathetic nervous system, triggering our fight-flight-freeze response and lessening our cognitive capacity for memory. According to research, suppression will make it harder for you to transition to college with new roommates and professors and classes. Suppression is also associated with compromised memory and problem-solving abilities,[7] making exams even more difficult.

For example, if you're anxious about the upcoming SATs and you try to pretend or suppress that anxiety, you might not only be *more* anxious, you also may not retain information as well; consequently, you won't do as well on the test. In other words, you might not only feel worse about the experience, your actual performance may suffer.

The second way we tend to respond to our emotions is *reappraisal*, whereby we try to reframe our emotions and contextualize them. Studies show that when we reframe, we may decrease activation of areas of the brain associated with generating emotions and, as a result, they either have a neutral or positive impact on exam performance.[8]

Want to do better on the SATs? Accept that anxiety and reframe your perspective on it. Instead of allowing the anxiety to cripple you, perhaps you can use it to motivate you to focus. Building your emotional intelligence allows you to fine-tune your emotional awareness and management to reappraise.

WHAT DOES THE BODY HAVE TO DO WITH IT?

There is a constant feedback loop between what we experience in our bodies and what emotions we assign to these sensations considering context and previous experiences. Sometimes, we can even trick our bodies into experiencing an emotion. Try this: Hold a pencil between your upper lip and your nose. You are naturally going to frown, and if you hold that position for too long, either someone's going to be very concerned about you and/or you might start feeling a bit angry or down. Now try this: Hold the pencil between your back teeth. You are naturally going to grin, and if you hold that position for a while, you might just start feeling cheerier.

Given the strong connection between your body and your emotions, the more aware you are of your body, the better you can become at managing your emotions—a key part of EI. In a study known as the Iowa Gambling Task, researchers gave people four decks of cards that they had to turn over one by one. They could choose from two red decks, which had little chance of winning, or two blue ones, which had better chances. One by one, participants unknowingly started favoring the blue decks, even though they weren't cognitively aware that they were doing so. It took fifty cards before participants expressed a hunch that the red cards were landmines. It took eighty cards before they could verbally articulate that idea with certainty. That is a lot of time between when the unconscious behavior got to the conscious brain.

There was another twist. Participants were also hooked up to polygraph tests to detect the uncontrollable sweat the body makes when doing something uncomfortable, like lying. On average, people's palms started sweating by the tenth card. In other words, by the tenth card, their bodies were telling them to stay away from the red cards and, in fact, many unconsciously started to favor the blue ones. But the conscious mind didn't catch up until seventy more cards had been chosen.[9]

Your body holds a whole lot of information that your conscious brain doesn't even know. The more heightened awareness you have, the more able you are to manage your emotions. If someone says something triggering to you, your impulse might be to react and punch them. However, if you pause, you might notice how fast your heart is beating and how hot your face feels. Knowing that you are about to erupt may give you a moment to count to three, slow your breath, and cool your body temperature so that you can respond in a more effective manner.

For now, keep this in mind: The more you can bring awareness to what's happening, the faster and better you can regulate yourself.

HOW DOES MY SMARTPHONE HAVE ANYTHING TO DO WITH IT?

Have you ever gotten too little sleep and the slightest thing sets you off in a bad way? Say your little sister adoringly asks you to fix her breakfast and, instead of seeing her adulation of you, you snap at her to get out of your face. Your moody reaction doesn't mean you're a terrible human being. It means that you didn't get enough sleep. Even temporary sleep loss can lead to temporary changes in your emotional balance, behavior regulation, cognition, and ability to make wise decisions. A 2008 published study showed that sleep loss resulted in lower EQ (emotional quotient) scores, lower intrapersonal functioning (ability to have self-regard), lower interpersonal functioning (empathy towards others), lower stress management (ability to control impulses), and lower behavioral coping (capacity for positive thinking and action).[10] In other words, when you don't get enough sleep, you're more of a jerk and probably a less able student. Sleep deprivation impedes your ability to pay attention to and manage your emotions.

Then there is technology.

You and your friends are trying to multitask—watching TV, texting while doing homework—and we now know that scientific evidence suggests that our brains are not built to multitask: *No matter how well you think you are doing it, you're not.* Half of teens admit that they are addicted to their mobile phones (parents aren't much better).[11] Studies show a correlation between teenagers' addiction to technology and mental health. A longitudinal study published in 2018 of teenagers fifteen and sixteen years of age who didn't initially demonstrate any significant ADHD symptoms showed more symptoms after twenty-four months of higher frequency of digital technology use.[12]

Digital addiction also impacts relationships, safety in driving, and, of course, academics. In a 2018 survey of college students done out of San Francisco State University, researchers found that those who used their phones the most reported higher levels of depression, loneliness, isolation, and anxiety.[13] You've noticed it before. You've walked into a lunchroom and rather than hearing people chatting, they're all on their cell phones. The other finding the same study noted was that those students who used social media the most frequently when they were in a crowd of people reported the greatest degree of loneliness. Lack of human connection impedes our ability to cultivate EI.

All the pings you get on your phone and your automatic need to peek are similar to an addiction to nicotine—you get a quick flush of relief and reward, but that only leaves you wanting more. The Pavlovian responses our smartphones elicit from us make us beholden to an electronic device versus relying on our own agency to react and reply.

For those of you stuck on Fortnite and Snapchat and other ways of "connecting," keep this in mind—the people *creating* those apps you're on usually don't even allow their children to be online. Athena Chavarria, who was an executive assistant at Facebook before moving into Mark Zuckerberg's nonprofit, the Chan Zuckerberg Initiative, didn't let her children have cell phones until high school. She has been quoted as saying, "I am convinced the devil lives in our phones and is wreaking havoc on our children."[14] This is coming from a person who works for the very company pushing you to stay on social media. Tim Cook (Apple CEO) and Bill Gates (Microsoft) limit their young family members' social media, cell phone, and iPad use. The former CEO of Mozilla teaches his son that such technology is done in a way to manipulate people, and it isn't always for the positive.

Digital addiction can also decrease emotional intelligence by immersing us in a virtual world. Many teenagers move through a "narcissistic bubble" where everything is about them; they ignore what others are feeling, have limited awareness of the world and people around them, and are desensitized to the plight of others. When we indulge in overusing our smartphones, we spend less time understanding our own minds and what our bodies are trying to tell us. We become more susceptible to amygdala hijacks. We may become less able to regulate our emotions or to develop the social and coping skills we need to maintain good relationships. We may not learn compassion, and we risk losing the motivation to do anything that takes us away from the comfort of a screen.

Keep in mind that not all technology is bad. In a large cross-sectional study in Korea, researchers found that school performance was positively associated when the internet was used *for study purposes* such as academic research. Unsurprisingly, the opposite was true of those who primarily used the internet for more random searches, social media, and entertainment.[15]

What does this all mean? By being more aware of your emotions, you can build your emotional intelligence, which is critical to your short- and long-term potential for achievement and success. It also means that you need to sleep and put that phone down—you might do better on that test, and you might also be less of a jerk to others.

It can be a win-win.

Chapter Four

It's Not Just About You

Emotional intelligence is not a new way for you to "get in" your dream school, but it may make a difference in your future success, well-being, and happiness. It may also raise your awareness of what is important to you and why you do what you do. It may remind you that pursuing higher education is not just about earning a fancy diploma, but a worthy pursuit all its own and a pathway to becoming a more useful and contributing citizen for the betterment of society.

WHAT DO YOU WANT TO MAJOR IN?

You're probably getting a lot of questions: "Where do you want to go to school?" "What do you want to major in?" "What do you want to be?" While everyone around you seems to know exactly what they want to do, the "secret" part of you screams, "I have no idea!"

You might be stressing out already about which medical school to attend or the investment banking job interview. You might be the one asking at the college fair, "what percentage of your graduates get into medical school?" Rein in the horses; focus on the present. For those of you who are convinced that you know what you want to study, keep in mind that in the United States only 27 percent of college graduates actually end up working in a profession that is related to what they majored in.[1] That means that you are extremely likely to have a career in a field that is unconnected to whatever major you choose in college. So relax and stay open-minded to the possibilities.

The rapid change of our workforce is yet another evidence point as to why you should spend less time worrying about your major and more time understanding why you're hoping to study in the first place. In 2013, an Oxford study estimated that by 2033, almost half (47 percent) of all jobs are going to be obsolete due to technological advances.[2] Without an education to prepare you for whatever may come, you might also become obsolete. If your goal is to become an actuary, you might believe that the only major you should focus on is accounting. But how can you be sure that the future of actuarial work will look as it does now? You can't be.

To be truly ready for the unexpected, you need to build your EI and resilience.

WHY IS HIGHER EDUCATION GOOD FOR YOUR BANK ACCOUNT AND YOUR WELL-BEING?

You probably know at your core that you're not pushing yourself to get the As just to buy the university bumper sticker for bragging rights. At some level (even though it might not seem like it sometimes), your folks push you to pursue higher education because they understand that getting a good education will prepare you for a better future and help you to contribute something worthy to the world. According to the National Center for Public Policy and Higher Education, 84 percent of Americans believe that higher education is important in order to get ahead.[3]

The Bureau of Labor Statistics showed that with every level of education, average income rises (except for those with PhDs) and unemployment drops. In 2017, 4.6 percent of those with a high school diploma were unemployed, versus 1.5 percent of those with a professional or doctorate degree. Those with a high school diploma earn an average of $712 a week compared with $1,836 for those with a professional degree. Those with a bachelor's degree earn an average of $1,173 with an unemployment rate of 2.5 percent.[4] Project that over your lifetime, and you're more likely to recoup your costs and then some as opposed to going straight to full-time work after high school.

If you're a college graduate, you're going to earn $1.2 million more over a lifetime of employment compared to nongraduates.[5] You're more likely to have job security. You're 72 percent more likely to have retirement benefits[6] and you'll contribute more in taxes. You're far less likely to live in poverty—statistics contrast 15 percent of those with a high school diploma in this category versus 4 percent of college graduates.[7] A report from the Center on Education and the Workforce at Georgetown showed that 95 percent of jobs created from 2010 to 2016 went to Americans with more than a high school education. At the same time, those with a bachelor's degree gained 4.6 million jobs compared to 80,000 for high school graduates.[8] Going to college means you're more likely to have a job in the future. You're more likely to live with greater stability, which may allow you to be of greater service to others.

There are also nonmonetary benefits to the pursuit of higher education. You are 44 percent more likely to enjoy better physical health.[9] In a study of fifteen countries, a thirty-year-old man who has a college education is expected to live eight years longer than one who does not.[10] If you go to college, you're 17 percent less likely to smoke, thus decreasing your risk of cancer.[11] You're less likely to be obese, which reduces your risk of death due to various conditions associated with obesity. You're more likely to wear your seat belt, exercise, and go to the doctor. You're 47 percent more likely to have health insurance. You're 4.9 times less likely to go to jail.[12] You're more likely to be a strong communicator and critical thinker. You're more likely to enjoy better mental and emotional health, and positive relationships, which might also be why you're 21 percent more likely to be married, and 61 percent less likely to be divorced or separated.[13]

What about benefits right now? The College Board, responsible for your SATs, articulates that the benefits that may help you now include the realization of passions, greater meaning and purpose of work, sense of accomplishment, personal development, well-being, and happiness.

WHY IS HIGHER EDUCATION GOOD FOR SOCIETY?

This might also be a good time to ask yourself: Are you pursuing higher education for the sake of learning, for the corner office, or maybe for a bit of both? Or is there something more to this frenzied push for a shot at the top universities?

It is easy at this point to be so caught up in the details of *which* school to attend (urban? rural? public? private?), *which* major to choose (biology? business?), or *which* SAT subject tests to take (French? English?) that you forget to ask yourself *why* you're putting yourself through all this stress. It might seem to you that the only thing your family, teachers, and peers care about is that you get into the "right" school. It's almost as if your job is to get into a particular college. Your own "why" and your own motivation for higher education seem to be irrelevant in a game to grab the Ivy ring. You're not alone. Whereas 58 percent of adults identify job prospects as the primary motivator for a college degree, only 23 percent report it is for the pursuit of knowledge.[14]

The pursuit of learning is not just about you, however. Aristotle argued that education is a moral obligation for the well-being of individuals and society. John Dewey noted it is to prepare young people to live a useful life in practical ways, and "to cultivate deep-seated and effective habits of discriminating tested beliefs from mere assertions, guesses, and opinions . . . and to ingrain into the individual's working habits methods of inquiry and reasoning appropriate to the various problems that present themselves."[15] UNESCO presents education as "a means to empower children and adults to become active participants in the transformation of their societies."[16]

Society benefits from the pursuit of knowledge. You don't live in a bubble. From school shootings to government inefficiencies, there are big issues that need your and your peers' contributions to address. These big issues require a broad and diverse representation of expertise and experience. In a Knight Foundation/Newseum Institute study, less than a quarter of those surveyed believe Americans are good at seeking out differing views.[17] Education is critical for preparing us to understand how to approach controversy with deliberation and critical thinking, and for fostering our abilities to argue and debate different points of view with more fully developed communication and analytical skills, thereby enhancing the lives of everyone in society.

As professor Anne Bert Dijikstra said, to create "a peaceful, strong and vibrant society, differences can only exist if there is sufficient common ground."[18] Author Lorelle Espinosa makes the case that regardless of politics, "higher education can lead to a more tolerant society."[19] She shares the example of Derek Black, godson to David Duke and heir to a white nationalist movement. Black was on his way to becoming the next voice of white supremacy when he went to study at New College of Florida, a liberal arts school, to study medieval European history and German. There he met a classmate, an Orthodox Jew, who invited him to Shabbat dinner, and that was the beginning of his transformation supporting diversity and inclusion.[20]

THE GREATER PURPOSE OF HIGHER EDUCATION

Hopefully, one of the reasons that you're pursuing higher education is to be a contributing member of society. Many of you will write your college essays on how you want to "save the world," with evidence from your volunteer hours. For a few of you, volunteering is done to "look good," rather than for genuine purposes. The reality is that college admissions officers can "sniff out" inauthenticity. They are trying to determine whether you sense that there is something bigger than you, and whether you are bringing meaning and purpose to their universities.

Father of positive psychology Martin Seligman offers insight into how having a larger sense of purpose and meaning is important to sustained well-being. Seligman argues that there are three types of "happy lives" that give us some sort of pleasure and joy. These three lives include: the "pleasant life"—having those things that give us pleasure such as a fancy car or ice cream; the "good life"—having a sense of engagement and flow with our work and values; and the "meaningful life"—having a sense of purpose larger than ourselves and which leverages our strengths. While these lives may intersect, they may not. For example, you might one day decide to join the Peace Corps. During this time, you might not have easy access to running water. But the work you are doing is extremely meaningful to you.

Those who pursue higher education are more likely to find themselves living the good and/or meaningful life. Partly it is because, as we have learned, they have greater financial freedom to pursue what brings them meaning, and partly it is because they will have spent time with peers and professors grappling with ideas as to what might be possible.

When admissions officers ask about your service or civic engagement, they are not counting your hours or asking you to simply check off a box. They want to learn how much you think about other people and want to make a real difference. Top colleges are not looking for the straight-A student whose primary focus for college is a fancy diploma. If they were, these institutions would be full of self-serving individuals, and you probably wouldn't want to study at such a cutthroat, unhappy place. You likely would rather surround yourself with people who are excited about creating and innovating to help others, and who are enthusiastic about supporting each other.

Studies show that the pursuit of higher learning impacts how one sees one's responsibility as a citizen. The Organization for Economic

Cooperation and Development (OECD) found that the more education people have, the more likely they are to vote, volunteer, and take part in community and political affairs. In twenty-seven OECD countries, 80 percent of college graduates reported a willingness to vote compared to 54 percent of those who had not completed upper secondary education.[21] In the 2012 U.S. presidential elections, 73 percent of college graduates voted as compared to 42 percent of high school graduates. College graduates are also twice as likely to be more knowledgeable about current political issues (45% versus 21% of high school graduates)[22] and 3.2 times more likely to serve in a leadership role in community, religious, and service organizations.[23]

College graduates are more likely to volunteer (42% versus 17% of high school graduates).[24] They are also more likely to be employed in the nonprofit sector and 3.4 times more likely to give to charities.[25] Those who give not only tend to serve a broader community, they also seem to be happier individuals. In his book, *Give and Take*, Adam Grant actually found that people fall into the three main categories: those who like to give more than get; those who like to take more than they give; and those who like to give appropriately without self-sacrifice. He found that givers were the most successful, even in the most cutthroat of environments. A giver who gives too much may compromise their well-being. But successful givers are able to mitigate negative impact on themselves when they recognize the bigger impact they have on others. They tend to have more supportive networks, inspire those around them, and gain the most out of negotiations due to their generosity, collaboration, and ability to motivate others.[26] Research shows that caring for and helping others reduces the negative impact of stress. This may be attributed to the fact that when we care for others, we release oxytocin, the hormone behind maternal behaviors, which helps to reduce the release of cortisol. University of British Columbia researchers even found that acts of kindness helped to reduce social anxiety.[27]

Additionally, working with others for the betterment of society may offer you a healthy sense of humility. You may be more open to admitting what you don't know and more curious and motivated to learn from others. You may more willing to forgo the perfect GPA for the pursuit of a fascinating research project. While you may very well end up as valedictorian, if all you do is focus on yourself, you may also experience great stress and not-so-great relationships.

When you start pursuing knowledge for the sake of learning and making a positive impact on others, you actually may end up doing better. Stanford researcher Tenelle Porter noted that the lack of intellectual humility stymies discovery, learning, and focus, finding that "the more intellectually humble students were more motivated to learn and more likely to use effective metacognitive strategies."[28] In other words, those who believed themselves to be super smart actually took fewer chances to discover, had less motivation to learn, and showed less focus. Those who were more willing to appreciate how their intellectual life connected to something bigger than themselves actually earned higher test scores.

The pursuit of higher education carries with it a responsibility and opportunity not to be squandered. Some of you may have heard of Mister Rogers. He believed that those who are more generous are happier, and those who are happier are healthier. In his commencement speech at Dartmouth College the year after 9/11, Mister Rogers didn't tell the newly minted Ivy graduates they had now "made it," but spoke instead about their larger responsibilities:

> I'm talking about that part of you that knows that life is far more than anything you can ever see or hear or touch. That deep part of you that allows you to stand for those things without which humankind cannot survive. Love that conquers hate, peace that rises triumphant over war, and justice that proves more powerful than greed.[29]

Mister Rogers made a point that education instills a sense of greater responsibility to leverage love and justice to make the world a better place.

Chapter Five

A New Education

By now, you've figured out that this book views college admission as more than simply getting in; it is an opportunity to pursue knowledge so that you can go into the world and make it a better place. Yes, your grades and tests matter. They matter not because they reflect your value as a human being but because they are indicators of your ability to persevere, follow through, and manage impulses—all skills that will help you to be a decent human being.

Despite whether you feel like your teachers only care about how well you perform on the AP tests, you're not the only one who craves greater meaning in education. Many of your teachers and school leaders believe in that greater purpose. Otherwise, they wouldn't sacrifice monetary comfort and personal time to constantly think about how to support your learning.

The first part of this book focuses on the neurological, cognitive, and emotional benefits of emotional intelligence and mindfulness. This chapter will explore how the future of education is rejecting the old model of rote memorization for one whereby emotional intelligence and mindfulness are integral to the learning process in order to help students develop as more complete humans.

TEACHERS UNDERSTAND THAT THE EXISTING
EDUCATION PARADIGM NEEDS A REBOOT

Many current and former teachers express frustration that, in the United States in particular, the educational system isn't working (we won't get into the lack of funding that forces your teachers to spend their personal funds to buy you notebooks or the not-so-hidden inequities of funding depending on which zip code area you live in). Many bemoan the fact that "instead of letting children explore ideas and explore themselves, they're force-fed information and placed under a strict set of guidelines as to how they are supposed to learn. . . . The purpose of the educational system used today is to eradicate the genius of our children, quash their curiosity, and train them to become good soldiers for the corporations they will eventually work for."[1] All the preparation you are doing right now seems focused on SATs and GPAs.

As "edupreneur" Ted Dintersmith says, "our education system is stuck in time, training students for a world that doesn't exist."[2] He argues that U.S. education seems to "rank human potential, not develop it."[3] Such prognostications are not simply made by entrepreneurs and CEOs seeing the lack of preparation for the "real world" in some young people. Historian Yuval Noah Harari, author of *Sapiens*, argues that from an expansive historical analysis, "much of what kids learn today will likely be irrelevant by 2050. At present, too many schools focus on cramming information. In the past this made [sense], because information was scarce . . . in the 21st century we are flooded by enormous amounts of information . . . in such a world, the last thing a teacher needs to give her pupils is more information. . . . Instead, people need the ability to make sense of the information, to tell the difference between what is important and what is unimportant, and above all to combine many bits of information into a broad picture of the world."[4] In other words, much of what you are learning to "get in" might not be that useful when you "get out."

This sentiment is pretty much agreed upon by leaders in the "real world." Evidence is mounting that how you perform in the classroom isn't a strong predictor of how well you will do in your job.[5] Author Adam Grant argues that your transcript tends to measure how well you spit out what you crammed into your head, but success in real life requires you to go beyond addressing problems and question what needs to be solved.[6] For example, you may spend months redesigning the most amazing trash can. But if you haven't questioned whether a new trash can is even needed, you've spent hours creating something beautiful and irrelevant.

In fact, valedictorians tend not to be the disruptive visionaries who ask those questions but instead maintain the status quo. Educator Sir John Jones argues that the world does not need any more stressed-out premed/engineers who stay up until 3:00 a.m. cramming. Rather, he articulates five key characteristics that determine one's efficacy and success: creativity, ingenuity, agility, adaptability, and sociability.[7] In an era where innovation and empathy are critical, the future belongs to those who see possibilities rather than just checkpoints of "success." It belongs, as author Daniel Pink says, to the right brainers.[8] Innovation lies not only in the realm of logic and intellect, but also requires the integration of the brain and heart—and emotional intelligence and awareness helps us to strengthen both. Yet as Daniel Goleman noted, "even though a high IQ is no guarantee of prosperity, prestige, or happiness in life, our schools and our culture fixate on academic ability, ignoring *emotional* intelligence, a set of traits—some might call it character—that also matters immensely for our personal destiny."[9]

Sociologists Richard Arum and Josipa Roksa researched 2,300 students at twenty-four colleges to measure their critical thinking skills, the capacity for self-directed, active thinking. This kind of thinking requires the analysis, conceptualization, evaluation, application, and synthesizing of information. Arum and Roksa's study showed that after the first two years of college, 45 percent of these students showed no gains in this area.[10] In other words, while you or your family are paying a lot of money for college, almost half of you are not learning the skills you actually need. How are you supposed to help find cures to chronic diseases if you don't know how to think?

To its own surprise, Finland is ranked number one in reading, math, and science in OECD rankings. Finland never set out to become number one, but they have two key distinctions from other school systems. First, unlike in the United States where teachers can't afford to live in the same town as their students and recess is being cut from the school day, Finland elevates their teachers to the same professional level as lawyers and doctors, and they are financially, professionally, and socially rewarded for their work. Second, Finnish schools integrate three criteria into their teaching: the importance of failure, well-being, and play. Celebrating failure leads to innovation, well-being leads to healthier bodies and focus, and play leads to creativity and empathy.

Albert Einstein knew what mattered in effective teaching: "I never teach my pupils, I only attempt to provide the conditions in which they can learn."[11] A classroom that supports emotional intelligence can help to create such conditions. In many countries, including the United States, teachers may have less freedom to craft lesson plans. Instead, they are given a script and evaluated by how well their students do on exams, not how creative they are. All these conditions negatively impact the class conditions conducive to learning.[12]

The good news is that there are educational models that seem to be countering this trend. The Aspen Institute established the National Commission on Social, Emotional, and Academic Development, recognizing that students require more than test-taking to thrive. Some U.S. states are planning to submit under the federal Every Student Succeeds Act a requirement that schools measure student success with "nonacademic" measures in addition to traditional academic ones.[13] Your teachers know that the current way of learning is not preparing you fully, and they are working to transform the antiquated models to dynamic and relevant ones.

In the United States, more schools are adopting an inside-out approach[14] that goes beyond teaching to the test. While there are different emerging models, let's take a quick look at three:

1. The Building Blocks for Learning for Children[15] focuses on:

    a. Stress management and self-regulation
    b. School readiness, self- and social-awareness
    c. Growth mindset, self-efficacy, sense of belonging, relevancy of school
    d. Perseverance, resilience, academic tenacity
    e. Independence, curiosity, civic identity

2. Model of Psychological Well-Being by Carol Ryff[16] focuses on:

    a. Self-acceptance
    b. Personal growth
    c. Autonomy and independence of thought
    d. Ability to handle challenges in life
    e. Positive relationships and trust
    f. Life purpose and meaning

3. PEAK[17] focuses on:

    a. Global impact by addressing important challenges
    b. Mindset and skillset

Notice how none of these models speak specifically to GPA or SAT scores. Rather, they look at how you can grow and what skills you'll need to not only improve your capacity to get better grades but also to build the skills and habits that will give you a clear advantage throughout your lifetime.

EMERGING RESEARCH SUGGESTS SOCIAL-EMOTIONAL LEARNING (SEL) AND MINDFULNESS WORK IN SCHOOLS

Many schools, both public and private, now offer meditation or reflection rooms. If you attend one of two City Charter Schools in Los Angeles, you may have participated in "peace corners" or begun four days of your week with an advisory period discussing a topic with your teacher and classmates. You may have learned about how a restorative justice approach to discipline can help build a healthier campus culture. If you attend a school in the Medford, Massachusetts, system, you may have worked on social change projects grounded in social and emotional learning with the Center for Citizenship and Social Responsibility. Such initiatives are not just trends; they are grounded in emerging research.

Even though the research is in its infancy, SEL programs have been shown to have modest benefits to overall well-being *and* capacity for intellectual engagement.[18] A meta-analysis of 213 studies and 270,000 students shows that SEL programs saw a 10 percent increase in positive social behaviors, a 10 percent decrease in emotional distress, and an 11 percent increase in academic performance.[19] A University of Exeter study looked at mindfulness-based interventions (MBIs), reviewing four meta-analyses of forty-three individual studies. Though the sample size was still relatively small, the study found that short, focused, classroom-based MBIs have a small-to-medium positive impact on social and emotional skills, psychological well-being, and mental health, including reduction in child and teen depression, anxiety, and stress. A small-to-medium positive impact on prosocial skills, such as caring and compassion, self-perception, self-care, relationship skills, empathy, and emotional regulation, as well as physiological health, was also noted.

Additionally, there was a small-to-medium positive impact on cognition, learning, executive functioning, attention, focus, grades, and metacognition—thinking about thinking.[20]

Studies also reveal that when your teachers integrate SEL into your academic learning, you're more motivated to learn and more committed to school, and less likely to act out in class.[21] The Common Core State Standards now actually require you to demonstrate greater focus and rigor. For example, the Common Core in English will require you to handle more complex texts so that when you recognize that you don't understand something, you're willing to ask for help. When you get stuck on a problem, you have to learn to regulate your emotions so your frustration doesn't send you into a tailspin. All of this requires emotional intelligence.

There is also the positive impact of SEL and mindfulness training for you as you learn to recognize and manage stress. Whether the stress arises from a long daily commute to school, not having the resources to take advanced courses, or the pressures of your peer group to "be perfect," chronic stress can actually change your brain structure and function. Recall our discussion of your brain? Your amygdala is your brain's 911 system, alerting you to information that you might want to know in case of a potential threat. Your hippocampus is associated with learning and memory and helps to regulate your amygdala. Your prefrontal cortex—the part of your brain that is likely not yet fully developed—also helps to regulate your emotions and behaviors, and helps you to make wiser (less stupid) decisions. Researchers at Harvard have shown that the toxicity of chronic stress can negatively impact how active your hippocampus and prefrontal cortex are. Mindfulness can counter this by strengthening the connection between your amygdala, hippocampus, and prefrontal cortex.

Mindfulness training and SEL can help mitigate the negative effects of chronic stress. In one study comparing a twelve-week social emotional learning (SEL) program to a social responsibility program in Canada, those trained in SEL scored higher in math, demonstrated 24 percent more social behaviors, and 20 percent fewer aggressive behaviors, as well as greater attention, memory, emotional regulation, optimism, ability to cope with stress levels, and empathy.[22] Studies on meditation training retreats with teenagers showed improvement in emotional functioning, such as positivity and gratitude, self-regulation, and working memory.[23]

MANY HIGH SCHOOLS ARE CATCHING ON THAT MINDFULNESS WORKS, THOUGH INEQUITIES REMAIN

Over the last decade, there has been a lot of movement in K–12 schools and universities toward understanding how mindfulness can positively impact students personally and help them to do good in the world. Yet a word of caution is needed. As with many things, it can be easy to overstate claims or jump on the bandwagon; "mindfulness" isn't a panacea for all the evils of the world. Programs that offer mindfulness and EI in schools should be grounded in evidence and rigorously researched. For every one that is ill-conceived, there are many more that are robust and evidence-based.

For those of you fortunate to attend schools with resources, you likely have greater access to such programs. If you attend a private school, your teachers may have more freedom to be innovative in their teaching methods, including incorporating mindfulness. For example, multiple independent schools have come together to host the Northeast Independent Schools Mindfulness Conference. In 2016, conference members, well versed in the levels of toxic and chronic stress their students face, shared how to support the most up-to-date mindfulness practices to promote health and well-being.[24] For example:

> Lawrence Academy promotes mindfulness throughout school, including starting all faculty meetings with a mindfulness practice and conducting research;
>
> Phillips Exeter Academy offers a mind/body program on resilience, potential, and peace;
>
> Pomfret School offers a course based on mindfulness-based stress reduction and contemplative practices;
>
> Northfield Mount Hermon conducts a weekly meditation class and staff/faculty training—mindfulness is part of its mandatory first-year health class;
>
> The Spence School supports mindfulness in an urban environment and at on/off-campus retreats;
>
> Ethical Culture Fieldston School incorporates a pre-K–12 mindfulness program; and
>
> Middlesex School has a dedicated, full-time mindfulness faculty member, requires new students to take a mindfulness class, and sponsors annual retreats for parents, faculty, staff, and alums.

Sounds pretty good for some of you. Because schools and communities are unequal in resources and opportunities, some of you may never get access to these types of programs. If you live in a community with fewer academic opportunities, it may take more effort to bridge the gap, but the good news is that mindfulness training can help.

University of Chicago professor Amanda Moreno studied mindful-ness in more than thirty high-poverty Chicago public schools over four years, focusing on approximately 2,000 students in kindergarten through second grade. As the largest mindfulness study funded by the federal government, it assessed academic achievement for young kids of color from low-income families. Her hypothesis was that the bene-fits would be greater for these students who are already living in high-stress environments. She also hypothesized that students exposed to toxic stressors early in their development become more susceptible to academic and achievement gaps. The results of her study show that students who spent even 10–12 minutes a day on mindfulness practices improved their self-control, emotional regulation, and ability to focus. It wasn't testing but emotional intelligence that primed the students to learn and engage, closing the achievement gap.[25]

There are a growing number of programs for students who attend an under-resourced school or who live in under-resourced communities. For example, at New Haven Academy, the entire freshman class is required to take yoga, and studies show that the three-day-a-week requirement reduces students' measured levels of the stress hormone cortisol.[26] In a San Francisco middle school where fights and gunfire are not uncommon in the neighborhood, students participating in a program called "Quiet Time" (which emphasizes meditation) demonstrated some compelling findings: double the number of students scored as proficient on the state achievement test in English, reduced suspensions by 45 percent, increased attendance rates 98 percent, and high happiness levels.[27] Low-income, urban, elementary schools that use "Move-Into-Learning" programs have also found less student hyperactivity and ADHD.[28]

While these programs are not all created equal, many are being evaluated and demonstrate a positive impact. Let's take a look at a few:

Mindful Schools, founded in 2010 with a program modeled on mindfulness-based stress reduction (MBSR), has reached thousands of teachers and over 300,000 students to build attention, self-regulation, and empathy. An assessment of their Oakland, California, program's effectiveness for low-income, minority, elementary school students studied over four hundred students who went through the five-week curriculum. Although the study didn't have a control group, it showed that there were four long-lasting improvements in: 1) attention; 2) self-control; 3) classroom participation; and 4) respect for others.[29]

Inward Bound Mindfulness Education (iBme) is a nonprofit started in 1989 to develop self-awareness, compassion, and ethical decision-making. Its retreats have been shown to reduce rumination and to improve attention and sense of well-being.[30]

Holistic Life Foundation, founded in 2001, seeks to nurture children in economically disadvantaged neighborhoods and to help them develop their inner lives and sense of well-being. In conjunction with Johns Hopkins and Pennsylvania State, research shows individuals in communities served by the nonprofit organization have improved stress reactivity and less rumination and emotional arousal.[31]

MindUP, developed in 2003, is now taught in over twelve countries to six million kids to reduce stress and anxiety. A new $3.3 million federal grant will research its efficacy.

Brain Power Wellness focused on New York City schools to prepare teachers and schools with short, accessible activities to help energize and focus the classroom environment through physical and mental brain breaks, mindfulness, and social emotional learning. Survey results show 93 percent of educators with better stress management, with over 94 percent seeing a more positive and engaged classroom with more emotionally balanced and focused students.

Inner Explorer was developed in 2007, based on MBSR, to teach mindfulness in over 250 schools across ten states. A nonrandomized, controlled study of eight low-income third grade classrooms showed reductions in behaviors such as suspensions and classroom disruptions, and improved reading and science grades.[32]

Resilience Kids was developed in 2009 to teach self-regulation and balance, self-confidence, and focus, and to promote healthier communities and prosocial behaviors. An internal program evaluation showed a 30 to 50 percent reduction in behaviors requiring discipline, reduction in stress, reduction in violence, and improvements in self-confidence, emotional regulation, and school climate.[33]

Still Quiet Place is a mindfulness program developed in 2004 to teach peace and stress management. A nonrandomized, controlled study of family-based interventions showed less emotional reactivity and depressive symptoms, improved parental mood and anxiety and self-efficacy, and greater child compassion and self-judgment.

Wellness Works in Schools training has been incorporated in the classrooms of over 11,000 students since 2001. Since then, teachers report positive impacts of the curriculum, with 94 percent citing improved focus and attention, and 76 percent noting better stress and emotional management in their students.[34]

Many of these programs move beyond simply making participants more aware of their brains; they help them to be more conscious of who they are and how they relate to the world. As we discussed, higher education is not just about having a line on your resume—it's about the opportunity to become a responsible global citizen. For example, one program called "Project Wayfinder" works with schools and students like you to connect greater self-awareness to purposeful action.

It's not just about feeling good. It's about doing good.

CHANGING THE EDUCATIONAL SYSTEM REQUIRES MANY VOICES

If you don't attend an institution with a homegrown mindfulness program, you might want to consider how to introduce such a program at your school. Education is not simply about state standardized test scores or admission to a prestigious college; it's about how you think, grow, and engage with others.

At the time of this writing, there are a few notable larger initiatives underway attempting to shift the conversation from a focus on GPA and ACT scores, despite the fact that they still get their fair share of criticism for being pretty packages perpetuating an unequal playing field for the elite. One is the Mastery Transcript Consortium (MTC), proposed by a network of schools working to transform the high school transcript to adopt a rubric based not on rank but on the traits that support student success across eight metrics: 1) analytical and creative thinking; 2) complex communication; 3) leadership and teamwork; 4) digital and quantitative literacy; 5) global perspective; 6) adaptability, initiative, and risk-taking; 7) integrity and ethical decision-making; and 8) habits of mind. The member list joining this effort is growing although, as critics point out, they are primarily private institutions. While the reality is that private schools can be more nimble than public ones in making such a drastic change, critics suggest that the Mastery Transcript is yet another way for the elite private schools to obscure grades so that their students "look better" on paper. Is that true? It's too early to determine. The interesting point is that there is commitment to changing an imperfect system to incorporate emerging research on what actually predicts future success.

Individual admissions offices are also taking the lead to review applicants beyond traditional measures. At Trinity College in Connecticut, admissions officers use metrics called "predictors of success," such as "delayed gratification" and "risk taking." No longer requiring SAT or ACT testing, their admissions officers seek evidence about these traits in your file, such as in a letter written by your guidance counselor. As a result, Trinity has seen the diversity of its first-year class expand. Instead of a one-on-one interview, Olin College of Engineering in Massachusetts puts applicants like you together in small groups for two days to complete design challenges. Their admissions officers aren't obsessed with your class rank but want to see how you think, collaborate, and manage tough problems. MIT (Massachusetts Institute of Technology) offers students the opportunity in the application to create a "Maker Portfolio" to demonstrate their different talents in a nontraditional way, and faculty and alumni evaluate them.[35]

More institutions would like to see greater change, as the traditional focus on rank and grades is insufficient. Yet, as universities tend to be risk-averse, many look to industry leaders to start the trend. Until then, the admissions process will continue to evolve and change.

Artificial intelligence (AI) will eventually provide universities with even more ways to evaluate you than just your GPA. AI also means that the world will look very different by the time you graduate, and you will need to be ready for whatever that future looks like. Circling the right bubbles will be insufficient. You must learn to be comfortable with ambiguity and change. The most successful of you will be resilient, innovative, and creative. College is but one possible step on your path. As Sir John Jones says, "the true joy of life is the journey itself; the station is only an illusion. Regret and fear are the twins that rob us of today, life must be lived."[36] Emotional intelligence and mindfulness can help you, your family, and teachers shift the tide to be more learning-ready and to better manage the stress that impacts your well-being.

II

Inside the Ivy Tower:
The Myth, the Legend, the Truth

While there is hope that educational institutions and organizations are beginning to see the benefits of a more holistic approach that nurtures students intellectually and emotionally, this section will discuss the harsher realities of competitive college admissions.

The ever-increasing levels of stress that many of you and your peers face, and some of the myths as well as the truths surrounding the competitive college admissions process, will be examined. An overview of what enrollment management is and what you can and cannot control in this process will be presented. Understanding that many things are outside of your control is important in determining where to best focus your attention. We will also discuss the human component of the college admissions process.

Chapter Six

It's Only Getting Worse

I can share all I want about these programs on emotional intelligence and mindfulness, but that doesn't really help you if you don't have access to them. Even if you do, they don't magically make the untenable stress you feel disappear. If you weren't stressed about this process, you probably wouldn't be reading this book.

Whether you're in ninth or twelfth grade, ask yourself: How much stress do you typically feel? From where does this stress come? If you answer "a lot" and "from everyone," you are not alone.

You probably get confused at the two contrasting messages coming out of the mouths of people you trust and respect. Well-meaning people tell you to be yourself and follow your dreams. Everyone else around you, from online forums to parents' friends, is saying that you have to take forty-five AP classes, start a nonprofit, and play three sports in order to have a shot. It can be confusing, but most people are just trying to be helpful and don't really understand the admissions process. Instead, individual cases get confounded as general rules and rumors fly unchecked around the internet. To make it worse, while your rational mind understands that there are many incredible institutions where you will find not only a fit but a place where you can thrive, there is likely a little part of you—the sensitive part that is naturally susceptible to what your peers are doing—that is telling you something else. That little voice says to get the best grades possible and get into the "best" university possible—and there are only a few worth attending—or you're a loser. Again, if you hear that voice, you are not alone.

There are other factors that exacerbate your stress levels. Let's take a look at a few: technology, substance abuse, lack of sleep, familial pressures, school pressures, the business of college counseling, and the deterioration of adolescent mental health.

TECHNOLOGY IS MAKING YOUR LIFE BETTER – AND MORE MISERABLE AT THE SAME TIME

Your days are probably filled with a million texts and emails, not to mention Instagram and Snapchat updates. You belong to the iGen generation, born between 1995 and 2012. You of the iGen differ from the oft-maligned millennials because you grew up with the internet 24/7. The majority of you own some sort of smartphone, which means the majority of you also spend a lot more time on it than any previous generations. Members of the iGen don't "hang out" in person; you hang out online instead. Psychologist Jean Twenge studied how overdependence on digital devices as a social outlet has resulted in you being more comfortable in your bedroom than in a car or at a party. There are also more hovering parents who don't want you running around town unsupervised. As a result, since 2000, "hanging out" has declined among teenagers by 40 percent.[1] On the positive side, you're probably less likely to drink and drive than your predecessors. On the other hand, you're less likely to be independent or to know how to talk to people in person.

Technology can be a great thing, but technology addiction is not. For many of us, technology is a way to fill moments of "boredom," handle stress, or connect with others without the need for any face-to-face time. More than just causing a misaligned neck from staring down on your phone all day, technology overuse impacts the areas of your brain associated with pleasure and reward. Similar to substance abuse or sugar, technology can give your brain a sense of pleasure and reward, which leads you to want more and more. The cycle of addiction continues. You stay up reading BuzzFeed, so you lose sleep, which makes you more cranky and less able to connect with real human beings, which makes you avoid face-to-face interactions. All of these behaviors may end up causing you to lose your edge in sports or academics.

The National Institute on Drug Abuse's annual survey for eighth through twelfth graders found that those who spend more time in the virtual world are unhappier than those who spend more time in the analog world. Eighth graders who spend more time online are 27 percent more likely to report depression than those engaged in non-online activities—even homework! This study also found that "as teens have started spending less time together, they have become less likely to kill one another, and more likely to kill themselves."[2] If you spend three hours or more on your iPhone, you are 35 percent more likely to have a risk factor for suicide. And if you're a girl, you're more likely to engage in cyber bullying and/or to feel excluded on social media. You're twice as likely as boys to show depression.[3]

So while technology can be awesome and let you research papers a lot faster and more comprehensively than your parents could, if you're not careful, it can make your life far worse.

YOUR BRAIN IS NOT HAPPY ON DRUGS

Some of you might have seen the famous "this is your brain, this is your brain on drugs" ad from the 1980s of a cracked egg in a hot pan. You may have giggled and laughed, but didn't think it applied to you. Even if you're (hopefully) not on heroin, substance abuse, another form of addiction, is ever rampant, and it cuts across class and race among young people. You likely have seen it among your peers, or perhaps you have an addiction yourself.

In addition to opioids, heroin, cocaine, ecstasy, etc., that have probably found their way into your school, you and your peers have likely been exposed to other substances. For some, substance abuse might not even be seen as a way to "fit in," but is instead a means to manage the overwhelming pressures or to try to get a boost of energy or focus or stamina to pull those all-nighters. Unfortunately, what may seem a short-term, harmless solution (it's just once or twice) has far more damaging consequences that you may think. Remember, your brain is still developing so you're less likely able to make wise choices, more susceptible to addictions, and more vulnerable to longer-term impact on brain growth.

While tobacco use is on the increase, alcohol continues to be the number one most commonly used substance among teens. Among twelfth graders, almost two-thirds have tried alcohol. Much of the drinking among young people is not a glass of wine at dinner but binge drinking. Twenty percent of twelfth graders have used someone else's prescription medication.[4] Researchers at Johns Hopkins found that the majority of those who use Adderall without a prescription get it from family or friends.[5] You may know at least one person who has convinced a friend with a prescription for Adderall to give them a few pills as a "pick-me-up" to help them focus better on their exams.

Some of you might think you're not a "real" substance user because you don't drink or do "hard drugs." Rather, you simply inhale some flavored water and vapor, thinking that vaping is relatively harmless. After all, they aren't cigarettes, right? And it looks like a flash drive that you charge just like your phone so it seems more like an interactive digital game. Almost five million young people now use some kind of tobacco product, the most common of which are e-cigarettes, particularly flavored e-cigarettes. The 2018 National Youth Tobacco Survey found an increase in tobacco usage by middle and high school students. From 2017 to 2018 alone, there was a 78 percent increase (1.5 million) in students in the United States using e-cigarettes. Some of you might have started even younger. Among middle school students, there was a 48 percent increase. This isn't just one-time usage. The frequency of usage has also increased.[6]

The reality is that many teenagers think that vaping is just using a few cool flavorings and are unaware of its dangers and addictive properties.[7] While it may have seemed like some harmless puffing of "cool" flavors like fruit medley (how harmful can fruit be?) at first, you probably noticed your friends (or you) were unable to stop. E-cigarettes deliver heated nicotine liquid, and each one actually has the same level of nicotine as one pack of cigarettes. That's like smoking a pack a day. In December 2018 Surgeon General Jerome Adams declared vaping among youth an epidemic. Contrary to misperceptions that vaping is harmless, studies show that teenagers who vape have higher levels of chemical toxins[8] and inflamed lungs.[9] Beyond the growing evidence of physical damage (immunity, heart, etc.), there is also suggestive evidence that the activity in the brain's frontal cortex, associated with processing sensory inputs, is impacted, which may lead to other mental conditions.[10] It may also lead to greater susceptibility to other addictions, slow your brain's development, and compromise your memory, focus, attention, ability to self-regulate, and mood.[11]

While you may think alcohol, your teammate's Adderall, or fruit medley vapors give you greater focus and alertness—or at least a reprieve from the stress—you actually become more at risk of compromising your cognitive capacity, well-being, and physical health, now and in the long run.

LACK OF SLEEP IS NOT SOMETHING TO BE PROUD OF

You've always been told "no pain, no gain." It has become somewhat of a badge of honor in some areas whereby "chronic stress [has] been cited as the new 'cultural currency' in highly competitive private schools where students often equate their schools' level of rigor with the amount of stress [they] experienced."[12] The harder you work—or make others think you do—the more awesome you appear.

While persistence and grit have been shown to have a longer-term impact on success, there is a difference between persistence leading to resilience and overwork leading to burnout. Many of you have probably heard classmates (maybe yourself?) boast to each other how little sleep they get, as if the less sleep you get, the more important, intelligent, and hard-working you are. The reality is the complete opposite. Happiness gurus Shawn Achor and Michelle Gieland note that staying up until three in the morning finishing a science fair project is a "distortion of resilience."[13] They argue that overwork and exhaustion are diametrically opposed to resilience because without the capacity to strategically stop and rest, you cannot get the necessary internal and external recovery periods to be resilient. Staying up until 3:00 a.m. might get that project done, but it might not be done well, not to mention how impaired you might be for the rest of the day or week due to lack of necessary rest. The most successful students are those who can boast eight hours of sleep.

The American Academy of Sleep Medicine (AASM) recommends that teenagers get 8–10 hours of sleep, and those from ages five to twelve need 9–12 hours. Yet only a quarter of twelve-year-olds get more than nine hours, and that number gets smaller as students get older.[14] The National Sleep Foundation estimates that only 15 percent of teenagers get eight-and-a-half hours of sleep a night.[15] (If you are secretly priding yourself on the fact that you don't need 8–10 and can function on 3–4, you're likely fooling yourself.) If you spend three or more hours a day on your iPhone, you are 28 percent more likely not to get enough sleep.[16] This doesn't improve in college, where fewer than 10 percent of undergraduates get eight hours of sleep.

Studies have found that teenagers who get eight or more hours of sleep show fewer symptoms of depression, less nodding off in class, and the greatest achievement gains. However, those who get less than eight hours of sleep a night report greater depression, use of substances like caffeinated energy drinks, and risk of making poor choices. Lack of sleep can result in compromised thinking and reasoning, behavioral problems, poor school performance, weight gain, lower immune systems, and greater risk of self-harm and thoughts of suicide. It is associated with poorer academic performance and greater likelihood of a car crash.[17] A study conducted in Norway of teenagers (16–19 years old) showed that those with the shortest sleep habits had the greatest risk for poor school performance and of achieving the lowest quarter of GPAs, while those going to bed between 10:00 and 11:00 p.m. had the best GPAs. And if you think you can put off your sleep until the weekend, think again. Those who try to "save" their sleep for the weekend also were associated with poorer academic performance[18] compared with those who did not.[19] This lack of sleep is everywhere, not just with young people. Arianna Huffington, champion of sleep after she broke her cheekbone falling from exhaustion, notes that "we sacrifice sleep in the name of productivity, but ironically our loss of sleep, despite the extra hours we spend at work, adds up to 11 days of lost productivity per year per worker."[20]

Your brain is always making connections. Sometimes those connections are no longer necessary, and sometimes they need strengthening. Remember that your brain is constantly in a state of "synaptic pruning," removing connections that are just taking up space, and strengthening those you need. Better to remove from your limited memory capacity David Bowie's shoe size and retain the SAT vocabulary words. In a 2018 study at Baylor's Sleep Neuroscience and Cognition Laboratory, students who averaged eight hours for five nights during final exams week performed better on finals than those who did not.[21]

If you really want to do better in school, get eight hours of sleep per night. Sleep is critical to the retaining of desired information. When you are in deep, REM sleep, your brain is in optimal remodeling mode to convert short-term to long-term memories. But when you don't get enough REM sleep, your brain never gets a chance to absorb useful information and remove the useless. So that test you studied for all night? Instead of bragging about what little sleep you got, you *might* be lucky enough to remember just enough to get by the next day. But you'll likely forget it soon, which means you have to restudy for the end-of-year cumulative test.

As a teenager, your natural circadian rhythm is to wake up later and go to bed later than at other times in your life. Studies show that delayed school start times improve student sleep patterns. Those schools that begin at or after 8:30 a.m. report over 60 percent of their students getting a full eight hours.[22] Another study showed that by moving the start time from 8:00 to 8:55 a.m., absences and tardiness dropped. Incidences of car crashes decreased by 13 percent.[23]

If you think boasting about your lack of sleep is a good thing, what you're actually doing is telling your friends that you don't know how to manage your time, that you're not performing as well as you could in class, and that you're probably all the sadder for it.

FAMILIAL PRESSURES CAN DO MORE HARM THAN GOOD

One of the most commonly reported sources of teen stress is parents and family. In general, your parents and families are well-meaning and sincerely want the best for you. Some go over the top. You probably have heard the term "helicopter parent" (referring to the parent who hovers around, not letting their kid out of their sight). That was the early 2000s. Then emerged the "Velcro parent" (the parent who won't leave their child's side). The year 2018 saw the rise of the "snowplow parent" (the parent who removes anything in their child's way to make sure they see only rainbows and unicorns). Recognize anyone you know? You are not alone.

As much amusement that those names offer, such phenomena may add tremendous stress and might be more harmful than helpful to your future potential for success. As psychologist and author of *Emotional Agility*[24] Susan David argues, when your parents or family members try to shield you from all things bad or do not allow you to figure out tough things for yourself, you are not going to be equipped to handle real life—even if your IQ is Mensa-level (the Netflix series *Black Mirror*, season 3, eerily takes this subject on). If your parents or family members don't allow you to take charge of your college search process and, instead, call your counselors on your behalf to fight for a grade or call your admissions officer to set up an interview (pretending to be you— yes, this happens), you're not going to learn how to stand up for yourself. Additionally, the universities you are looking at will make note that you might not have the maturity to make it at their institution. These institutions will question whether your application was even truly written by you or crafted by a watchful, overly invested parent.

Regardless, show a little kindness for your stressed-out parents and family members. They are human and as susceptible to pressure as you are. They too have grown up being measured on "performance." While there is no grading system for parents, some crave the same external validation that you might. Where you get into school then becomes a grade on their parenting. If you get into Harvard, your guardian is A++ material. If you don't, your guardian is a loser. Such self-imposed pressures are a reality. As *The Secrets of Happy Families* author Bruce Feiler[25] notes, for a certain group of overinvested parents, where their kid gets into college is a benchmark of whether they're a "good" parent or not.

For other families, the process of applying to colleges has become a whole family endeavor, as if your parents or guardians are going to move into the dorm with you. (Trust me, people have tried. I recall one mother calling our office extremely upset and angry at our institution because we did not allow her to sleep in the dorm with her daughter and her roommates the first three nights of freshman orientation.) In certain communities, Facebook has become the platform whereby parents proclaim their children's college searches and/or acceptance offers. Instead of referring to "my child," the conversation becomes "we're looking at" or "we're going to." This kind of living vicariously through you adds to your already high levels of stress.

This form of familial pressure impacts your schools and teachers, which also adds to your stress. A 2019 *Washington Post* article reported some no-no behavior on the part of some parents who attempted to sabotage their children's classmates in order to "help" their own child's chance of admission.[26] Some teachers get bullied by intensely involved parents and desperate students who will take nothing less than an A grade. I remember a colleague who told me the dad of a college sophomore flew in from a different state to "have a discussion with the dean" about why his daughter received a B+ and not an A in class. Does the idea of having your family member fly across the country to argue for a better grade that you didn't deserve make you cringe? It should.

For some families, anything less than an admit letter is unacceptable. I recall a colleague who mentioned that not even thirty seconds had passed after decisions were released when a well-meaning, overzealous parent made her daughter's college counselor call the admissions office because her daughter did not get the admit letter. The mom was extremely engaged in both the high school and university community, and so automatically presumed her daughter would be admitted. Needless to say, she was upset. The barrage of subsequent emails and additional recommendations sent directly to the college president, deans, and anyone who would listen wasn't unheard of, sadly (nor was it effective). While admissions officers are used to this behavior, I couldn't help wondering: What must this young woman have thought to see her mom so adamant that she "get in"? Did she think she was a failure for disappointing her mom who had expected her to be a "shoo-in"? Even if she was eventually accepted, did she always wonder that she wasn't "good enough" on her own without her mother's work behind the scenes? No person should feel that pressure.

Such pressures can also lead to a mismatch of ability and fit. The unhealthy push to load up on a million challenging courses means that some students are taking on intense schedules that they simply are not ready for. This kind of stress has fueled accusations of cheating. Studies suggest that "80–90% of high school students report some form of cheating in the last year, and many of these students view cheating as trivial or don't see it as a problem at all."[27] Admissions officers sometimes receive anonymous letters about a cheating applicant, and some universities face claims of college students paying other students to take the exams they are not ready to do on their own.

This is not to say all pressure is bad. There are certain "parenting" books out there that argue that tremendous pressure is the key to getting your child into Harvard. While *some* pressure and stress is beneficial (it probably takes a bit of prodding by your family to get you to clean your room or study for that test when your favorite show is beckoning), such approaches examine and compare harmful stress with productive stress. Professor Kelly McGonigal researches this very subject and notes that it's your mindset about stress that can actually help you be smarter and happier.[28] The right kind and amount of stress motivates us to act. McGonigal's colleague, Stanford professor Alia Crum, along with Peter Salovey and Shawn Achor,[29] explore how being honest about stress and perceiving it to be a helpful experience and natural part of life means you're more likely to use that stress to your benefit. On the other hand, trying to pretend stress doesn't exist can actually increase your longer-term risk of not-great outcomes like depression, and perceiving stress as harmful can lead to unhelpful coping mechanisms like drinking.[30]

Author Donald Gleason notes that even though some parents may see pressure as necessary for a short-term "win" (for example, getting you into Harvard), "it is well documented that excessive stress activates the human nervous system and puts its entire metabolism on high alert, leading to temporary compromises in attention, memory, and learning, as well as to increased risk of anxiety and depression."[31] If you're under chronic stress, that pressure can be toxic to your teen brain's proper growth during this vulnerable period. You might not actually get the chance to become a fully self-actualized human being and the truest best version of yourself, instead finding yourself a ball of nerves and anxiety caught up in competition and fear of failure.

Being faced with contradictory messages—"Be yourself" and "You'd better get into Princeton"—can cause your brain's stress reactions to go through the roof. You're told to "be yourself," as long as that "self" is an approved and winning edition; even for a seemingly high-functioning overachiever, that veneer can wear thin.

SCHOOLS ADD FUEL TO THE STRESSORS

Your teachers may also face similar pressure, feeling that, if their students don't get in the Ivies, "we'll lose our standing as an elite school."[32] While this is more an issue in private schools, there is still pressure on public and charter institutions to boast about their list of college admittances.

While such college acceptances may genuinely reflect the strength of the teaching and curricula, the pressure for these acceptances can go overboard. Education has in many ways adopted a consumerist model. With rising tuition costs, why should one shell out that much money if not to guarantee a perfect GPA? It can seem as if the focus is on how many students get glowing reviews so that they can get into the right schools and avoid unhappy parents. One result is the not uncommon practice of grade inflation. Teachers confess it is often easier to inflate grades for fear of losing their jobs.[33] As a result, we now see phenomena like having 25 percent of high school seniors being valedictorians.[34] Aside from the fact that that figure defies the definition of valedictorian, schools now are pressured to focus more on what will make them look better to parents and families hoping to get their students into elite schools than on education.

At one prestigious private school on the West Coast, where there are almost as many Teslas as there are yoga mats, teachers and counselors, with the added pressure of tuition-paying parents, move students from harder classes to less challenging ones if they start getting grades below an A−. These less-challenging classes still have "honors"-type-sounding names so that college admissions officers can't easily tell the difference. The result is that the majority of the class has a 4.0+ GPA in "honors"-level classes while, in reality, many are actually not ready for the far more challenging coursework they will face at university.

You may feel bombarded with other people playing a game of chess with your education. As Gleason quotes, "the college admissions process can induce feelings of inferiority in students [as it] forces [them] to deal with unwanted advice, shame or invasion of privacy brought on by external influences, such as high school administration, admissions boards and their peers."[35] Instead of being taught how learning can be exciting or that life is a constant challenge and that collaboration can be useful, you learn how to play a zero-sum winning game where competition is key. Instead of instilling a love of learning, "academic achievement is squeezing the lifeblood out of children . . . [fostering] the common [belief] that one must earn top grades *now* in order to have the best opportunities *later*."[36] Instead of being present, you're always thinking about what will happen later. How will you get to medical school or law school?

The excitement of learning and exploring often gets lost in the frenzy of trying to grab the golden ticket into Stanford, followed by the brass ring of the big paycheck and the corner office. One California high school student told me that the majority of her classmates feel pressure to follow a prescribed path to "success": 1) get into a University of California school; 2) suffer through the coursework and maybe attend a class or two; 3) graduate as quickly as possible in four years; and 4) get the highest-paying job possible. Nowhere in this process is mentioned a desire to learn, to be part of a community, or to make the world a better place. Going to class isn't even part of the plan! The path is to get in, go through the motions, get out, make money, post photos of awesome life.

PEOPLE MAKING MONEY OFF OF YOUR FEAR
ARE STRESSING YOU OUT MORE

The return on investment (ROI) of your education has sometimes be-come more of a measure of quality than learning itself. *Town & Coun-try* estimated that the total cost of getting a child through college was a sizable $300,000 in 1973. In 2017, this number skyrocketed to over $1.7 million for some students—particularly those who have the re-sources to indulge and "ensure" that their children have the best shot at the best schools possible. This $1.7 million figure includes $11,000 for six months of music classes for infants and toddlers, a $450-an-hour coach to get kids into preschool, and a $47,000 annual fee for nursery school itself.[37] That's just for preschool!

The amount of money some families are willing to pay and the amount of pressure schools face open up the window for enterprising individuals to make money by playing off of their fears. In seven years, from 2005 to 2012, the number of independent college consultants has exploded from 4,500 to 14,000. The Independent Educational Consul-tants Association estimates it to be a $400 million industry and grow-ing. In China, it is not unheard of for parents to pay $42,000 a year to send their children to the United States for a boarding school in order to get a "better" chance to get into a prestigious university. One New York outfit charges up to $3,000 an hour to get children into schools. In Boston, the average cost for an independent consultant is $4,800, but "star consultants" can charge $80,000 and more. One company helps students curate their online presence. (Have you thought about NOT posting anything that you don't want your future employer/college ad-missions officer/grandma to see? Or how about being yourself instead of pretending to be someone else on a college application?)

The good news is that many independent counselors have signifi-cant experience on the college and/or high school side, providing ethi-cal, thoughtful, and beneficial advice to students who may not other-wise have access to assistance at their high schools. These counselors help students reflect on their interests and values and find a "right fit" so that they can thrive wherever they eventually attend. They often serve as a supportive ear for students who feel more comfortable shar-ing their true selves with them than with their parents.

Yet for every experienced counselor, there is one who overstates claims and experience. Some boast 95 percent acceptance rates for their clients getting into a "top college of their choice." Others who claim "inside knowledge" might actually mean that they held a short-term admissions job, got a degree from an Ivy League institution themselves, or have a child who was accepted into a top-ranked institution. While there are laudable attempts on the part of the National Association for College Admission Counseling (NACAC), the governing body of U.S. counseling personnel, to extend some form of legitimacy to independent counselors, the industry is not monitored. The lack of oversight means that, unfortunately, some have figured out that preying on the anxieties of students and parents is far more lucrative—and legal—than dealing in subprime mortgages.

One New York private consultant urges their clients to "be inauthentic." Another student reported that her consultant gave her incorrect information about the requirements. One family paid an independent consultant over $2 million to help their child get into Harvard, but their child did not get in. The parents sued and the consultant was eventually sentenced to five years and ordered to pay over $800,000 in restitution.[38] Another company has a starting fee of $40,000 for guaranteed admissions. Using an algorithm not unlike making bets in the stock market, some families pay for a money-back guarantee package of $600,000 to $1 million.[39] While the claim is that such companies have "cracked the code"[40] of college admissions, it may be more a code of fear that you might not "get in."

More than a quarter of you now pay someone to help you get in. For every qualified counselor with the background, expertise, and ethics to do well by you, there are others who offer advice without any qualifications. While more universities are engaging with independent counselors so that these consultants are better informed, the most highly selective institutions prefer that you ask them directly to ensure that you receive accurate information.

GETTING INTO COLLEGE DOESN'T SOLVE EVERYTHING, AND TEEN MENTAL HEALTH IS DETERIORATING

While independent counselors may help you get into the college of your dreams (imagine how many lives you could save by spending that money buying mosquito netting?), getting into college isn't a cure-all. If you experience anxiety and depression now, they don't "go away" just because you're sleeping on extra-long bed sheets. You don't gain resilience just because you wear a college sweatshirt. The 2016

American College Health Association survey of 28,000 college students found that over 60 percent said they experienced extreme loneliness, even though they were surrounded by thousands of classmates.[41] The most recent and world's largest survey just conducted by the BBC showed that sixteen- to twenty-four-year-olds make up the loneliest age group.[42] Unlike the generation before you, you're likely to arrive on your college campus with all your friends from high school (even virtual friends) already tucked away in your iPhone. This means that instead of going to the dining hall, you're more likely now to stay in your room and Snapchat with your old friends. Without having the tools to cope with feelings of loneliness and isolation, it is easier to stay tethered to the past or isolated than to embrace the unknown present.

In the United States, the rate of suicide attempts of those ten to fourteen years of age increased 135 percent from 2001 to 2014.[43] Singapore saw a 70 percent increase over five years from 2012 to 2017 in suicide prevention calls, from children as young as five.[44] Can you imagine? Five-year-old children are calling into the hotline because they are contemplating suicide. In China, suicide is the leading cause of death for those aged 15–34, and of elementary and middle school suicides, 92 percent of those cases are related to school-related stress.[45] In 2018, a sixteen-year-old California student who was a seemingly happy high-achiever took his own life. In his suicide note, he bemoaned the fact that no one ever paid attention to the kid who simply has "great character . . . so much pressure is placed on the student to do well that I couldn't just do it anymore."[46] This pain is happening around or within you. *Note: If you ever have such feelings, please, please tell a trusted adult immediately.*

Chronic stress has other longer-term consequences. The Child Mind Institute states that 20 percent of children suffer from some sort of mental health disorder, and 80 percent of chronic mental disorders begin in childhood. If a first grader is at risk, there is a 5 percent drop in academic performance in only two years. A twenty-year longitudinal study in Ontario showed that a third of surveyed teenagers exhibit moderate to severe symptoms of psychological distress. This distress is exacerbated by the external pressure of "keeping up" and by the limited face-to-face interaction with others, as 25 percent of teens spend over five hours on social media. By twelfth grade, Ontario teenagers have reduced the amount of sleep and exercise they get by one-third since they started high school, all of which have detrimental consequences.[47] In the United Kingdom, 25 percent of surveyed girls are clinically depressed by the age of fourteen.[48] In the United States, the American Psychological Association (APA) reports that over a third of teenagers feel overwhelmed, depressed, sad, and experience stress-induced fatigue,[49] and almost half report high daily stress. Teenagers report clinical-level depression at four times the rate of the national average.[50]

New York University researchers studied juniors attending a competitive private high school, where going to the "right" college had practically been imprinted as a must as far back as when they were in their mothers' wombs. These researchers found that over half of these juniors reported feeling a "great deal of stress" on a daily basis, and over 25 percent reported clinical-level depression.[51]

Stressed-out high schoolers become stressed-out college students, and universities are seeing the overspill onto their campuses. This stress doesn't end just because you "got in." Rather, "every achievement is a temporary high, which has to be followed by another achievement."[52] This never-ending hamster wheel is taking its toll. The APA reports a 30 percent rise in college students seeking mental health support from 2009 to 2014. Over 60 percent of those students who actually get appointments—there is a waiting list at many universities because the demand is higher than the availability—report anxiety, and almost half report depression and/or stress.[53] The UCLA Higher Education Research Institute has conducted a freshman survey every year since 1966, and with the 2016 incoming class, the call for mental health services was at an all-time high, with almost 12 percent reporting "frequently" feeling depressed.[54] The statistics from university health centers are disheartening. According to the American Psychological Association, in 2013, almost one-third of U.S. college students reported difficulty functioning due to depression, and almost 50 percent reported overwhelming anxiety.[55] And it's not just difficulty functioning; over 30 percent of students seeking mental health services have seriously considered suicide—and those are just the students who report this.

THE STRESS AROUND COLLEGE ACCEPTANCE AND ATTENDANCE CAN BE ADDRESSED

In a heartbreaking op-ed, Palo Alto student Carolyn Walworth writes, "We are not teenagers. We are lifeless bodies in a system that breeds competition, hatred, and discourages teamwork and genuine learning.

We lack sincere passion. We are sick. We, as a community, have completely lost sight of what it means to learn and receive an education."[56]

The good news, as we've seen in previous chapters, is that there are skills that you can learn to help counter the stress coming at you from so many different directions. As Daniel Pink put it, "there is a mismatch between what science *now* knows, and what *some* schools do."[57] If more schools recognize the neurodevelopmental stages of the teen brain—as well as how the plasticity of your brain to grow can support your learning—then they can help. In so doing, we might be able to reach what Aristotle coined *eudaemonia*, a "quality of flourishing,"[58] rather than the fleeting, "I got into X school"—and we might find joy in learning and discovery.

You deserve it.

Chapter Seven

The Rumor Mill and the Gossip

Finding joy in learning and discovery is tough when everyone around you is telling you different "truths" about what it takes to get in. Everyone seems to have something to share, some "secret" they can offer you, usually for a price. And in a process that seems oh-so-mysterious, you're ready to pay almost anything to get an insider's scoop.

Let's take a look at some of these myths surrounding the college admissions process.

MYTH #1: THE TRUTH IS FOUND ONLINE AND FROM PAID CONSULTANTS

Many of you turn to other people—other than admissions officers—to find how to get in. Independent consultants, anxious parents, and stressed-out peers have convinced you that the information coming from the people who are actually making decisions regarding your candidacy is incomplete. They tell you that admissions officers "won't really tell you the truth, but I have the inside scoop." So many of you turn to each other. But is this information helpful or harmful?

One of these sites, College Confidential, had over 40 million unique viewers in 2016. Before decision release dates, the site buzzes with activity from anxious students and parents. Students spill their entire lives to complete strangers to ask for someone else to "chance" their likelihood of gaining admission into a particular institution. Before you do that, think carefully. From whom are you actually asking advice?

You have no clue whether the person answering you is a peer trying to play with your mind; an independent counselor trying to toy with your confidence; a sixty-five-year-old adult trolling you; or a bored ten-year-old boy living across the world. Who is *not* "chancing" you? The admissions officers you are trying to impress.

A chance rating from an unknown source cannot be very accurate, especially when you're simply listing grades and testing, along with what *you* think is important in your activities and recommendations. Do grades and testing matter? Absolutely. But remember that admissions officers are truly looking for more than that. Seeking wisdom from a crowd of people who don't know what they're talking about or who may not have your best interests at heart seems to be a flawed tactic that might only lead to more anxiety.

MYTH #2: *YOU NEED A HOOK OR TO CURE CANCER TO BE COMPETITIVE*

The word on the street is that you need a "hook"; otherwise, you have no shot at getting into the top universities. What does it mean to have "a hook"? The public generally buzzes about "hooks" that include being: 1) an athlete (so you don't have to be that smart); 2) a legacy student (so you don't have to be that smart); 3) an ethnic, cultural, or sexual minority (so you don't have to be that smart); 4) a poor, first-generation American student (so you don't have to be that smart); 5) a VIP (so you don't have to be that smart); 6) an heiress (so you don't have to be that smart); or 7) a survivor of something horrible (so you don't have to be that smart). If you don't have one of these "hooks," you'd better be really, really smart, or have been saving dolphin babies since you were in utero.

Meanwhile university admissions officers are telling you to "be yourself," and you're suspicious that just being yourself isn't going to cut it. In 2013, Suzy Lee Weiss penned a piece that was published in the *Wall Street Journal*: "For years, [students like herself] were lied to. Colleges tell you, 'Just be yourself.' That is great advice, as long as yourself has nine extracurriculars, six leadership positions, three varsity sports, killer SAT scores and two moms."[1] She continues by wishing she could put on a headdress to present herself as Navajo, start a fake charity for homeless people's pets, and "scoop up some suffering child in Africa." While some viewed the piece as satire, it is important to be mindful when satire promotes stereotypes. An athlete can be a scholar. A scholar can be an heiress. An affluent kid can be smart—so can a less affluent one. No one is entitled to or guaranteed admissions. What the article does point out is the contradictory messages you likely receive. "Be yourself!" but "take as many APs as you can." "Take what interests you!" but "take the toughest curriculum you can." Which is it? Check off the boxes or do what you really want? Both.

Many students who are accepted into these institutions are "hookless." You know, like that kid who got into a dream college from your school, and you're scratching your head because they weren't a star volleyball player, or the kid of a movie star. They're pretty smart, but overall, just "kinda nice." Guess what? Nice kids get into top colleges.

Highly selective universities look for thoughtful, bright young people with potential to contribute regardless of "hook." Is it challenging to get in if you're "un-hooked"? Yes. It is also challenging to get in if you're "hooked." Just ask the thousands of angry alumni and donors whose kids get turned down each year by their beloved institutions.

Remember this: If you have a strong interest in attending a school, do your best, share your story, and be authentic. Hooked or not.

MYTH #3: *YOUR SATS ARE REALLY WHAT MATTERS, NOT YOUR ESSAYS*

In 2013, the University of Pennsylvania dean of admissions set off a flutter of anxiety when he said that his office found that only one out of eight essays made a difference in the admissions decision.[2] Students and parents around the country flew into a frenzy trying to focus on test prep with the understanding that their essays would be afterthoughts.

Here is the secret formula on how most highly selective universities count SATs and ACTs: *more than you want . . . and less than you think.*

Remember that your test scores are only one part of your file. At these highly selective institutions, your essays *do* matter. Most of these officers will tell you that at least 70 percent of their applicants are academically qualified. In other words, at least 70 percent of your "competitors" have the GPAs and SAT scores to make the cut. So how do you stand out?

It's not about "standing out," at least not in the way most people think about it. Unlike what many students (and parents and independent counselors) think, your story does not have to outshine all others. It just has to be yours. Your essays don't have to be overly dramatic. Some students bemoan the fact that they haven't had any real obstacles or traumas in life—if that's true in your case, be grateful. There have been more than a handful of cases where independent consultants have advised students to make up or exaggerate their stories. Most of these get sniffed out. Even if you *do* get in, as you will see later in the book, your essay is likely not the *only* reason you got in. There are other compelling factors.

Take time in writing your story, but—Do. Not. Overthink. It. There is not a particular topic or subject that admissions officers want to hear. If you start contorting yourself, you are not only being disingenuous in your application but to yourself as well, and that does even longer-lasting damage. We will talk more about tips later on but, for now, remember this: Your words matter.

MYTH #4: *YOU HAVE TO HAVE A MILLION AND ONE EXTRACURRICULAR ACTIVITIES TO HAVE A SHOT*

Many students believe that if they don't have that one thing that they are clearly extremely talented at (Olympics? *New York Times* bestseller? Oscar winner?), they *have* to have a novel-length's worth of extracurriculars. Some parents attempt to curate their children's activities from age two to be "ready" for college admissions; how sad that these children might not have had the chance to explore what they love.

It isn't that you have to enjoy every minute of every activity to feel that it's worth doing. After all, some things require lots of hard work and sacrifice. For example, if you're really into tae kwon do, it takes years of practice and pain. If you love it and keep at it, you grow in your mastery of it. But that is different from suffering through piano practice—which also takes years of practice, hard work, sacrifice, and pain—when you absolutely dread it. You play on autopilot with little passion, just to make your teacher and your mom happy. You do it because you want to show colleges that you don't give up. But the minute you get into college, you're going to burn that sheet music and be tempted to toss the piano out the window (don't do that, please). It takes a level of self-awareness to discern between the two.

One student a few years ago asked my colleagues and me, "I really hate MUN (Model United Nations), but everyone tells me I have to do it to get into the Ivy League. Is that true?"

Resounding NO!

Imagine if you went to college where everyone was president of MUN, it would be a pretty boring place. Colleges are not looking for cookie-cutter kids. This isn't to say you should change your mind about an activity every three months and chalk it up to, "That's just me!" It might be you, but if you flitter too much, you're also indicating to universities that you might not have the stamina or perseverance to see things through. Some stick-to-itiveness gives an indication of how committed you can be to a cause and a team.

Admissions officers may roll their eyes when they see an over-achiever compile a five-page resume with all of their activities. If you actually calculate the hours-per-week time commitment, it often comes out to be something like 60 hours a week—and that doesn't include homework, going to class, eating, showering, sleeping, going to the bathroom. In other words, admissions officers question whether or not you're really doing all of those things, or at least how meaningfully you're doing them. Jotting your name down just to be added to the club roster doesn't count.

It is also important to recognize that when schools say "leadership," they don't necessarily mean you have to be captain or president of everything. American society—and yes, your teachers and admissions officers—tends to have a bias toward extroverted and vocal individuals. Yet we know that some of the most successful leaders—Bill Gates, J. K. Rowling, Warren Buffet—are introverts. Your leadership may be at the front of the room—or in the back. Your title matters less than your impact on the group or in the community around you. Admissions officers will be seeking information to back this up—your letters of recommendation, a quick Google search (yes, shocking, they have the capacity to search the internet), and your essays. Does the club you founded consist of three best friends sitting around for an hour a week catching up, or does the club you belong to give you the opportunity to help a senior citizen become less lonely over the course of a year of volunteering? Do you lead by being the unofficial mentor of a group or by captaining a team and helping its members to stay positive despite a season of losses? Admissions officers aren't looking so much for what you do but why and how you do it.

Being a "club founder" isn't the be-all and end-all. Many independent consultants have recommended students create clubs to demonstrate "initiative" and "leadership," two things many top colleges state they look for. Unfortunately, just starting up a club is not going to do it.

There have been more than enough cases where an applicant has said that they founded a nonprofit for some poor kids in [insert developing nation name here], perhaps selling cookies to pay for sneakers overseas or collecting pencils for an underprivileged school. Regardless, there is an impressive-sounding name AND a website. Admissions officers do a Google search and see a fancy webpage, but they also know that it doesn't take much time or effort to set up a website. The people reading your file are often experienced and savvy.

If you are doing these things because you believe it's the right thing to do, great. But if you're doing it because it makes you look good, you're moving with the wrong intention. Trained admissions officers tend to sniff those out pretty quickly.

The point is this: You don't need to be the next Einstein, the captain of captains, or have a ten-page resume (PLEASE don't have this). You simply have to pursue those things you enjoy. When you do, you are more likely to be engaged and committed (even with 6:00 a.m. practices). When you are more engaged and committed, you are likely to do well, even if you experience a few failures. When you are doing well, others will recognize you. When others recognize you, you can make a bigger impact. It's a virtuous cycle.

MYTH #5: *YOU HAVE TO DONATE A LOT OF MONEY OR GET A RECOMMENDATION FROM THE PRESIDENT*

It might seem that the only chance you have is if you come from a lot of money. Famous cases of people who got into top-tier institutions with shaky transcripts don't help. So do you only really have a shot if you donate a lot of money?

Not so much.

While it is true that big donors may have some impact, it's not as simple as many may think. While the public likes to pooh-pooh the preferential treatment of large donors, the reality is that these institutions also have budget considerations. They are not flush with cash. In fact, every year, it seems budgets are cut and people's jobs are lost, which means fewer services for you as a student and more unhappy parents and faculty. For example, Hong Kong venture capitalist Gerald Chan gave the largest gift in Harvard's history with a $350 million donation to the School of Public Health. Coca-Cola's Robert Woodruff donated $105 million to Emory. Sanford Weill donated $215 million to

Cornell's medical school, now named after him. These are all alumni of their respective institutions. Chan's $350 million is going to pay for a lot of research, faculty, students, facilities, etc.—all of which will enhance the student experience. Will their offspring get an automatic "yes"? No. Might their offspring get a careful review? Likely. Is it completely fair? No.

It is true that many of the top colleges have more students from the top 1 percent of income scales than from the bottom 60 percent.[3] That reality is impacted by a whole host of factors including disparities in access to preschools, safe neighborhoods, and family income. But it doesn't mean that your family has to donate millions—or any money at all. The vast majority donates nothing at all. These very few cases (very few people have or will offer $100 million+ to any one organization) should not be generalized as regular practice.

Many people believe that if they don't have the money, they should seek powerful assistance in other forms. Parents call upon old classmates and buddies who "know someone." Maybe it's a trustee, or a state senator, or the CEO of a big company writing on your behalf. The majority of the time, these letters are unhelpful. Well-meaning people who owe your folks a favor, but who may have met you only once or twice, often write either a form letter or a nice but bland letter about how you are great. We trust you are great, but if there is little true engagement between you and that person, it simply is another way to try to impress without substance.

That said, some of you may have worked with pretty famous people. Perhaps you were the intern for a director's production company or the one high school intern at your councilperson's office and you got to fully engage with the team. Those individuals might be able to share great detailed information about you and your impact. Keep in mind, though, admissions officers aren't so impressed by the name as by what they say about you.

It's not about who you know or your bank account, but what you do and how you do it.

MYTH #6: *TOP COLLEGES ARE TOO EXPENSIVE*

Regardless of whether your family is in the comfortable upper-middle class or in the struggling lower, you might be writing off some of these highly selective institutions because you don't think you can afford it.

It is true that many selective, private colleges are expensive. With tuition at many of the ones you are looking at topping $75,000 a year (wow!), it can seem that it's not worth it. However, don't just write these opportunities off. Many students don't pay the full price tag because they are able to secure financial assistance.

You may have heard the term "need-aware" versus "need-blind." At institutions that practice "need-aware" admissions, your request for financial aid may impact your decision. At institutions that practice "need-blind" admissions, your need for financial aid makes no difference in the decision on your candidacy. However, it isn't that one is better than the other. Some schools are "need-aware" to ensure that they are able to meet your full financial need. Because these schools have more limited budgets, they cannot promise that everyone will receive 100 percent of their demonstrated need. These schools remain need-aware so that if they offer you admission, they can meet however much you need. For example, if your family can afford $5,000 out of $65,000, they take that into account before offering you admission and $60,000 in financial aid.

Not all institutions that practice need-blind do so equally. Some might not take your financial need into consideration, but they also might not be in a position to meet your full need. In other words, the school will let you in, regardless of your ability to pay. Hooray! But when it comes to financial aid, they might not have the resources to cover you. Your family might be able to afford $10,000 out of $50,000. The school accepts you and gives you a $25,000 financial aid package. If you do the math, that's only $35,000, leaving a "gap" of $15,000 that you have to meet through a job or loans.

Only very few universities in the country are need-blind *and* meet 100 percent need. These few schools will not consider your financial need during the admissions process, and they will also meet 100 percent of whatever your need is. Need $1? You get $1. Need $70,000? You get $70,000. What this means is that many of the most highly selective institutions may actually end up being more affordable than in-state universities, depending on circumstances.

Financial and Terminology Cheat Sheet

Need-blind: Colleges that do not consider financial need as part of the evaluation

Need-aware: Colleges that take into consideration financial need as part of the evaluation

Scholarships/grants: Financial support that is given that does not need to be paid back

Loans: Financial support that is given that needs to be paid back

Need-based: Financial aid given on the basis of demonstrated family need (e.g., income)

Merit-based: Scholarships given on the basis of some measure of merit

Athletic scholarship: Scholarships given on the basis of athletic talent and commitment

Gapping: Financial aid that is given but does not cover the full demonstrated need

The important thing is to have a conversation with your family now about what is realistic and what to expect. There are many resources that can help your folks estimate what they might be able to afford. Federal law now requires that every institution has a Net Price Calculator to help you figure out what your EFC (Estimated Family Contribution) might be. Doing your homework may take the mystery out of the process and allow you to see that perhaps these institutions are not out of reach financially after all.

MYTH #7: WHERE YOU GO TO HIGH SCHOOL MATTERS

You might suspect that where you go to high school matters a lot. I recall a parent calling me to ask me which zip code they should move to so that their daughter would get into the right preschool to get into the right Ivy. I advised her to pick the community she wants to raise her daughter in, the house that felt like a home, and a community that was inviting. She didn't like my answer. She wanted me to tell her the exact zip code for the proper schools. She's not alone.

There are plenty of well-meaning parents willing to do anything to get their kid into the "right school." Thomas Jefferson High School for Science and Technology, a perennial *U.S. News & World Report* top darling for high schools, is highly sought after. Their curricula are pretty impressive. It is also a high-pressure environment in which some students thrive and others wilt. Yet countless families bend over backwards to get their kids in. One mom asked when her child was eight years old what programs she should put them in and spent every weekend and afterschool (summers included) doing Kumon to prep them for admission to the high school. Her child spent summers not exploring and being curious, but memorizing equations for a test. This is not to say that discipline and cognitive practice are bad ideas (think Sudoku to keep senior citizens' brains sharp), but to bypass a childhood to get into a high school for college admissions is a recipe for disaster.

Where you go doesn't and does matter. It matters more what you do with what you are offered. Some schools, like Thomas Jefferson, seem to have countless opportunities for their students. But even if your school offers limited rigorous courses, admissions officers will take that into account and see what you've done with what you have.

The process *is* inherently unfair. If you attend a poorly resourced high school, you may be more likely to be battling upstream on multiple levels. You might not have access to many clubs or you may have other obligations that mean you can't participate in as many activities. You might be in an environment where the thought of leaving the state for college, or of going to college at all, is laughed upon. Up to 15 percent of low-income students who are otherwise prepared for consideration at top institutions don't actually apply to them. Twenty percent accepted into highly ranked institutions don't matriculate.[4] Many of these young people who attend spend four years feeling as if they don't belong. (The truth: you DO belong.)

Let's not pretend that socioeconomic class doesn't have an impact. A former admissions officer admits that "admissions at elite institutions can make a fool and a liar out of anyone,"[5] given the idealism and the reality of the practical goals of a university, but that "elite-college admissions is at root a story of class warfare."[6] If you attend a private school or a savvy public school, your counselor likely has more interaction with admissions offices and receives useful information (e.g., decision release dates) that a public school counselor may not know they can also get.

If you attend a lesser-resourced school, the onus is more on you to know the process. However, admissions officers at these institutions do not make decisions based on your high school. All of these institutions want and need a diversity of backgrounds and experiences in their student body. Recognizing that the information disparity is huge, many admissions offices offer different programming and information sharing to dispel these myths and demystify the process as best they can. There are also many community-based organizations that do great work to help, such as the Jack Kent Cooke Foundation and Say Yes to Education. Don't forget that admissions officers also spend weeks, if not months, of their lives going to different high schools to learn about these differences and unique offerings.

Nor do these institutions "blacklist" high schools. An alumna once informed me that her university admitted students from her daughter's high school based on a three-year cycle and was blacklisted the rest of the time. While I knew for a fact that she was wrong, she continued to scare students at her daughter's high school with what she thought was the truth. Somehow students become convinced that their school gets blacklisted because no one had gotten in during the last four years, or because last year's valedictorian declining an offer had pissed off the admissions officers too much. This doesn't happen—at all.

The *only* time an admissions office might be wary of a high school is if that high school has a record of falsifying or exaggerating predicted grades. This is rarer than an albino deer. It's not a perfect system nor a perfectly fair system, but it is one that tries to honor your context.

MYTH #8: *WHERE YOU GO TO SCHOOL DETERMINES WHERE YOU WILL BE IN LIFE*

One of the biggest myths is that you have to give up happiness and mental health to get into the "right" school. Going with this attitude is pretty much a disaster.

True, 45 percent of billionaires attended universities where the average freshman is in the top 10 percent for SAT scores. Yet, in a landmark study done in 2002, for the majority of those who go to a highly selective institution, the brand name of the university did little to boost income. In other words, graduates would have earned the same income had they gone to the state university down the road.[7] This study was reexamined in 2018, and noted some variances. For men, there was no difference in how selective an institution is and income. Women, however, earned 14 percent more and married 4 percent less for every 100-point difference in average SAT scores.[8] What the researchers found was not that women made more doing the same work, but that they made more because they tended to delay marriage and child-rearing. Moreover, a 2017 study showed that attending a highly selective institution had the greatest impact for lower-income students and minorities, primarily because they gained access to networks and internships previously unavailable to them.[9] SATs only predicted how well students did their first year in college. Other talents are what made the difference.

The 2014 Gallup-Purdue report on "Great Jobs, Great Lives" found that the key preconditions for later success, employment, and happiness in a person's late twenties were not grades or SATs. Rather they were having mentors, internships, clubs, and meaningful long-term projects.[10] In fact, one of the largest global companies, Ernst & Young, removed academic requirements for its new UK hires in 2015. The organization analyzed its selection process and found that it wasn't grades or their numerical equivalents that predicted the success of new hires at the firm. While academics are still part of the consideration, one grade doesn't keep someone out of contention for a position. Instead, the recruitment process includes assessment of different strengths needed to learn and thrive in the job.[11] In other words, it's so much more than simply these metrics that your high school—and admissions officers—are looking at. It is what you do with your opportunities and your potential to be a contributing human being.

IQs don't explain everything about how people end up later in life. Daniel Goleman notes that "one of psychology's open secrets is the relative inability of grades, IQ, or SAT scores, despite their popular mystique, to predict unerringly who will succeed in life."[12] In a longitudinal study of Harvard students from the 1940s, despite income levels, IQs didn't predict who was gainfully employed or not. An ongoing study of valedictorians and salutatorians from a 1981 Illinois class showed that, by their late twenties, the majority of these students only climbed to average levels of success. Boston University professor Karen Arnold says, "I think we've discovered the 'dutiful'—people who know how to achieve in the systems. But valedictorians struggle as surely as we all do. To know that a person is a valedictorian is to know only that he or she is exceedingly good at achievement as measured by grades. It tells you nothing about how they react to the vicissitudes of life."[13] Academic intelligence doesn't determine how resilient you are, or how you will respond to and handle the natural ups and downs of life.

Sure, where you go to school has impact. It shapes the initial network you have coming out of college, your friends, maybe even your partner for life. It shapes how you might learn or engage with the world. It shapes the new interests you find and the old ones you nurture and the ones you drop. But it's not so much about the schools themselves. There are plenty of people who go to Harvard, but engage little in the community or class. They graduate, get a good-paying job, but they aren't necessarily the leaders in their community or the ones changing the world. They are simply good human beings living a simple life. There are plenty of people who go to community college (or no college at all) who invent, innovate, and lead in a way that far outpaces what others might have expected of them. Dr. Morgan Freeman never graduated from college but earned an honorary doctorate from Boston University. Oscar-winning actor Tom Hanks went to Chabot College because it was what he could afford. Billionaire and 1992 presidential hopeful H. Ross Perot went to a junior college before graduating from the U.S. Naval Academy. More than half of U.S. senators graduated from public universities (whether you think they are "successful" or not is a different story, but they did achieve a level of accomplishment), and so did the majority of the country's top CEOs.

It matters less the name of your college, and more what you do, who you are, and what kind of positive impact you have on the world. If there is any myth to destroy, it is that the bumper sticker on your family's minivan determines the worth of your humanity.

Chapter Eight

Rolling the Dice and Betting on the House

Is admissions just a numbers game? Is everything fixed, and we're all just pawns? It's nothing quite that salacious. The deans of these institutions are not all clever statisticians who only care about numbers. But there are pieces of the enrollment management world that are more complicated than you think—or really need to be concerned about. Still, it seems like such a mysterious process that there are countless books and websites ready to share the "secrets" for a fee. Let's take a look at a few questions about the industry of admissions and enrollment management.

THE BUSINESS OF EDUCATION

Some people believe that education is an end in and of itself. Education, however, is also a business. Like most businesses in the modern world, things have become more complex as resources become scarce and demand increases.

Universities are about the pursuit and creation of knowledge, not only yours, but also faculty scholars'. As students, you are only one part of this ecosystem. Twenty years ago, universities made sure you had comfortable beds to sleep in, decent food to eat, and classrooms that kept the rain out. You considered yourself lucky if you shared a room with one instead of three others. You and whoever you tricked into helping you move in carried your XL twin bed sheets and a boom-box up several flights of stairs in the sweltering heat. Welcome to college. It didn't really dawn on most students or parents to call and complain that there was no air conditioning or elevators or VOSS water in the shared living spaces.

Things look different today. Universities are trying to outdo each other in the luxuries they offer students. High Point University in North Carolina has its own movie theater and arcade with free tickets and popcorn, and a steakhouse offering a five-course meal payable with your meal plan. Oberlin College in Ohio permits you to rent a Picasso to match your bedspread set and the use of a Steinway grand piano on campus for when the mood hits you. The University of Arizona, Tucson, has a dorm with private baths, a Keurig in your fully equipped kitchen, and a spa with a steam room and tanning beds. Washington University in Missouri makes sure you have a good night's rest with Tempur-Pedic beds. Students now seem to expect more of these luxuries, and more parents demand that their children have the best of the best.

Luxuries are not the only reason why the cost of going to college keeps rising. If you're on financial aid, you might not get the Tempur-Pedic bed. What this can create is a further separating of socioeconomic class (another topic for another day), but universities still have to pay for these somehow. The point is this: Education is also a business. As such, an admissions office has to demonstrate to the president and the board that it can contribute to the institution by bringing in tuition dollars and by continuing to improve its reputation. As vice president of enrollment and student success at Trinity College in Connecticut Angel B. Pérez says, "we don't live in a cloud—the reality is, there's a bottom line."[1]

For many institutions, money has become even more of a worry point than it was before. From 2001 to 2012, colleges increased the amount of debt they took on by 88 percent, to the tune of $307 billion.[2] Admissions offices tend to be one of the biggest sources of incoming revenue for an institution to help counter such debt (the first usually being the fundraising or development office). In other words, your tuition money helps to keep the universities afloat. Before you get all upset, keep in mind that the majority of the dollars collected have to do with providing you an education, from instruction to research to keeping the dining facilities running. While tuition prices seem to keep climbing, the average tuition discount for private institutions is 49.1

percent.[3] That means if you think $70,000 is a lot for your tuition, the true cost of your education—taking everything into consideration, including the lawn mowing of your beloved campus center—is about twice that amount.

Colleges have to figure out a way to keep everything running. With increasing demands, there are increasing costs. Most universities can't just accept more students to pay the bills, because they simply wouldn't have the space. For institutions without substantial endowments, these pressures are even greater, and they have to make sure they enroll the right number of students.

WHAT IS ENROLLMENT MANAGEMENT, AND WHAT DO ENROLLMENT MANAGERS REALLY CARE ABOUT?

Institutions have to be fiscally responsible. Because incoming tuition makes up such a big part of revenue, an institution's admissions office plays a big role. Like any business, a dean of admissions must meet expectations as part of their role. But what do they actually care about?

When most of you go to a university's website, you'll likely first go to the admissions page. Indeed, that is usually the best place for you to start. After all, you want to gain "admission" and admissions deans and their teams are looking for reasons to admit you. However, many deans are no longer simply deans of admissions but also enrollment managers.

Whereas deans of admissions focus primarily on strategies to attract, evaluate, and admit students within the context of institutional priorities, deans of enrollment management are typically also evaluated on larger metrics, such as recruitment (how many applications), yield (who accepts), marketing (vis-à-vis peers), financial health (tuition), and retention (who stays). Enrollment management began in the 1970s in the United States when Boston College was struggling.[4] Since then, it has grown to encompass using predictive models based on data to inform the strategy of institutional operations. According to the Enrollment Management Association (EMA), a professional organization supporting this work, enrollment management encompasses a broader scope of which the recruitment and evaluation of students are only two components. Enrollment managers are involved with meeting certain enrollment targets such as class sizes and student retention.

In other words, they have a lot to think about. And a lot of people put pressure on them. Presidents need enrollment managers to increase their applicant pool to make the institution look good so they can raise more money. The budget office needs them to bring in the right amount so they can meet tuition dollars. The residential team needs them to bring in the right amount so that they aren't scrambling for spots if there are too many students. The faculty needs them to bring in the "smart" students. The alumni need them to expand the applicant pool to make their alma mater look good and to admit their children. The athletic department needs them to bring in top athletes so that they can have winning teams. The fundraising office needs them to expand their pool to increase the visibility and reputation of the institution to raise more money and to help woo their high-flying donors. The student services office needs them to bring in the right students who will engage and make the community better. The offices of diversity and inclusion need them to cultivate the overall diversity of the student population to ensure an inclusive campus. The list goes on and on.

Your candidacy is being considered amongst all these (and more) factors that an enrollment manager needs to take into consideration.

According to the EMA, the top challenges of enrollment managers are fairly consistent across public and private institutions, though at varying levels. These include allocating scarce resources, navigating in an enrollment-focused culture, working with academic affairs and senior executives, keeping current with technology, generating institutional data, and making data actionable. Many enrollment managers report to a provost, who then reports to a trustee board, and so they rely on institutional data far more than ever before. At private institutions, enrollment managers focus on what the trustee board needs.[5] Enrollment managers and their trustee boards have to demonstrate that they meet "KPIs" or key performance indicators. KPIs differ by institution, and while they are not as simple as "put dollar in-get dollar out," they typically entail:

1. Enrollment (e.g., headcount—number of bodies)
2. Student quality (e.g., SAT/ACT scores)
3. Student progress (e.g., retention, graduation rates)
4. Program quality (e.g., student-to-faculty ratio, research)
5. Market position (e.g., branding)
6. Diversity (e.g., subpopulation enrollment and graduation)
7. Fiscal health (e.g., tuition)[6]

What this means is that there are a lot of considerations that come into play in weighing your application for admission, considerations that you have little control over.

DOES A GAME OF NUMBERS EXIST?

Numbers matter to institutions. As we have already seen, enrollment managers have a lot of things they must factor in, and a lot of metrics to meet. As modern-day enrollment managers rely even more heavily on data to make strategic decisions, many have the directive to continue increasing their pool while still enrolling the right number of students. This involves taking into consideration the different types of applicants desired in the class—including full-pay, middle-class, transfer, out-of-state, international, minority, and male students, to name a few—while accounting for net revenue and overall headcount. Some enrollment managers do this by individual college or academic program.

According to the Association of Governing Boards of Universities and Colleges, the five big trends that enrollment managers have to face today are: 1) shifting demographics; 2) changing economic models; 3) retention and graduation; and 4) technology and learning.[7] For example, some areas in the United States, like the Northeast and Midwest, are seeing fewer high school–age kids so that might impact geographic demographics. More enrollment managers look for nontraditional students like veterans and transfer students. They are also cognizant that, according to the National Center for Education Statistics projections up to the year 2021, the number of white, public high school graduates will decline by 9 percent, while the number of Hispanics will rise by 27 percent and Asian Americans and Pacific Islanders by 45 percent.[8] Still, white students are more likely to apply to the most elite institutions than are their peers, at a rate of 75 percent to 15 percent.[9] More attention is being placed on low-income students. While international recruitment has often been a go-to way of increasing enrollment, budget cuts, national immigration policies, and limited financial aid have placed barriers on some institutions.[10]

Enrollment managers have to be like Goldilocks. They can't over-enroll or under-enroll. When enrollment managers make a mistake, it's not great. In 2018, Purdue University over-enrolled an already record-breaking first-year class by five hundred. The result? Many freshmen moved into converted office spaces with their "dorm spaces" separated

Orange Is the New Black–style. In 2017, the University of California had 850 more enrolling students than it planned, so two months before 500 incoming freshmen were to move in, their offers were rescinded.[11] On the other end of the spectrum, in 2017, Ohio Wesleyan University saw a 9 percent dip in its incoming students and considered freezing any tuition hikes while their admissions officers pounded the pavement to drum up more interest. Concordia University in Minnesota cut its tuition by 34 percent in 2013 to increase its enrollment.

There are many factors at play. You can be the most amazing person in the world, but there is no guarantee.

HOW MUCH DO MAGAZINE RANKINGS COUNT?

Every institution likes to say, "we don't really care about rankings." As much as most admissions officers really don't like these rankings, it is almost impossible to ignore them. Suppose you owned a restaurant—of course, you'd like to aim that the critics don't matter. But if you get a one-star rating on Yelp, you're going to be pretty mad. If you get a Michelin star, you're over the moon.

Enrollment managers and university presidents don't care and they do care. Reputation does matter, and they're wise enough to know that magazine rankings are not completely accurate.

One of the most famous of these rankings is the perennial *U.S. News & World Report Best Colleges Rankings*. You probably have looked at this list. According to the magazine, it ranks colleges based on quantitative and qualitative measures, using fifteen indicators of "academic excellence." These include factors such as first-year retention rates, six-year graduation rates, peer-assessed surveys of academic reputation, class size, faculty salary, student-to-faculty ratio, professors with the highest degrees, percentage of full-time faculty, SATs/ACTs, applicant class rank, admissions rate, financial resources per student, and alumni giving. You seek out #1 as the Holy Grail. When you see an institution "jump" from a lower position to a higher position in one year, it generally is not the case that somehow that university became the "best" school, but that it did really "well" on one or more of its metrics. Enrollment managers get high praise for those jumps. When the college rankings go down, enrollment managers start worrying about their jobs.

These metrics can be tweaked considerably. For example, when admissions officers come to your school, part of the purpose is to get to know your school context. The reason why so much of the admissions budgets are spent in travel dollars is also to raise more awareness about their schools to, hopefully, get more applications. More applications mean a larger pool from which to choose and a way to lower admit rates, a key indicator in the rankings.

More recently is a trend of universities going "test-optional." While you might rejoice, you're not the only one who may benefit. Students who tend to do well on these exams will report them anyway, boosting the averages that the schools can report. Those who don't do well won't report, and more of them will apply, hoping that their other credentials might help, so application numbers rise. While it may seem like test-optional is a move toward greater equity, that doesn't always happen. What can happen is a bump in the rankings.

Another way that a few universities may tweak the rankings indicators is through what is known as "yield protection," a practice whereby an institution may reject or wait-list you because they believe that you're actually going to get accepted by and enroll at a more prestigious institution. If they accept you, they won't "yield" you, bringing down their yield rate. Institutions that can boast a "historical yield" can claim that they are such a "hot" institution that everyone wants to attend. And when everyone else wants to attend, that will likely stir up more interest the following year and boost their application numbers.

Some institutions will utilize the wait-list in different ways. According to the EMA, almost 25 percent of the 350 institutions they surveyed are increasing the number of students on their wait-list.[12] While this may be beneficial for you, it is also another way for enrollment managers to hedge their bets. Some institutions may put a larger number of students on the wait-list rather than admit them initially because wait-listed students do not count as part of the admit rate. And the admit rate is what matters on these magazine rankings. An institution may purposefully under-enroll initially and then, before the response date, contact some of those wait-listed students whom it wants and ask them to accept an offer of admission on the spot. That way, the student gets into the school they want, the institution gets the student they want, and it protects its admit rate.

Other institutions use delayed admissions for spring matriculation or a guaranteed transfer spot the following year. This way, the student still gets in eventually, and the institution doesn't have to count that student as part of the admit rate.

An institution may hire more faculty to show a higher faculty-to-student ratio, even if that faculty doesn't really teach. In a *Chicago Tribune* article, the authors noted that, to manipulate the peer evaluation of academic reputation portion, "one college president proudly proclaimed he use[s] college rankings to reward his friends and punish his enemies."[13] Other institutions shift graduation rates depending on how they measure the baseline of incoming students, whether it is during move-in day or the first day of classes. While most institutions are not beholden to these rankings, a few have taken it to a not-so-great level. In 2012, five institutions admitted to falsifying data submitted to *U.S. News & World Report*, including inflated SAT scores and class ranks.

Rankings can be useful to a degree—they can keep institutions from being complacent and ensure that they consider whether their classes are getting too big, or whether they're retaining top faculty or graduating enough students. A ranking can also help you to start your college search lists. However, it is important to keep in mind that what is "best" on a list is not necessarily best for you. Although not all enrollment managers or universities do, metrics can be tweaked to boost ratings, thereby boosting applications, thereby reducing admit rate, and thereby boosting yield rates. Even so, the majority of these institutions exist not just to look good and manipulate numbers. They exist because they believe in the transformative power of education, and they need to be selective given the limited spaces in their class.

Like you, institutions operate in a world driven by external pressures.

IS EARLY ACTION OR EARLY DECISION SIMPLY PART OF THE NUMBERS GAME?

Some schools use rolling admissions or spring enrollment. While most highly selective institutions do not, most offer different early application programs. Early action programs refer to the general practice whereby you apply sometime in the fall, and if you're admitted (you usually will be notified before the regular decision deadlines), you don't have to commit to going until a later response date. This means you can still apply to other institutions but be guaranteed a spot (unless you screw up somehow before matriculation). Early decision programs refer to the general practice whereby you apply sometime in the fall, and if you're admitted, you have to commit to that institution. So you have to really want to attend that school, as you are expected to withdraw your application from any other schools. Some institutions you are looking at practice a hybrid of both—restrictive early action. This practice refers to the general practice whereby you apply sometime in the fall, and if you're admitted, you have to withdraw from any other private institution but you can still apply to a public institution. This way you're guaranteed a spot, and you can still consider in-state options, for example, but the institution won't lose you to a "competitor."

Most of your teachers and counselors—including your private college counselor (ahem)—will tell you that one of the best strategies is to use your early action or decision choice wisely. It's not a question of whether you will apply early, but that you should be smart about it.

If you look at the numbers, they're compelling. Whereas just over 100 colleges offered early programs in the 1990s, now over 450 do, of which 37 percent admit at least 40 percent of their first-year class early. In 2016, 6.8 percent of students were admitted in the Ivy League in regular decision compared with 20.3 percent in early.[14] For Harvard's class of 2021, 14 percent of students applying via early action were admitted, versus 3.4 percent via regular decision. For the class of 2021 at the University of Pennsylvania, 55 percent of its class was admitted early. Given such figures, it looks like you'd better apply early for a better shot. Is that true?

It depends. If you are a compelling student for an institution, you will be compelling no matter what. However, it is also true that in regular decision, your chances will have been reduced just because the number of spots left open has been reduced. And the number of spots available keeps decreasing. One simple reason is that, because more students like you are applying early, institutions have more really amazing choices early on. And if they see a kid they think will want to be in the early pool, why not accept them? If they don't, they may lose that kid to another institution. They may also be sending the wrong message to that kid—"we really like you, but we'll make you wait just because." As an added benefit, if you're applying early, you're likely really interested in the school and your excitement will hopefully translate into you being a positive, contributing member of the first-year class. Everybody wins, right?

According to the late Harold Levy, former executive director for the Jack Kent Cooke Foundation, early admissions favor students of privilege. He argued that the majority of early applicants have the preparation and knowledge of where and how to apply early, including children of alumni, recruited athletes, and higher-income populations who have been primed since birth for this moment. On the other hand, many low-income students don't even know they have the option of doing so. At some of these schools, these kids might be one of 1,000 with the same guidance counselor who does not have the time or training to make sure they have taken the SATs or ACTs in time or to understand how financial aid works.[15]

Many institutions recognize this and are putting great effort into raising awareness by working with different community-based organizations like Jack Kent Cooke, to draw more under-resourced students into the process earlier on. But there is much more work to be done. In the meantime, institutions see benefits to early admit programs as they are guaranteed a percentage of their class who meet the academic standards that will keep them high on those college rankings. Yet, as Levy pointed out, the early pool tends to be skewed to those with more resources, which means these students tend to have higher test scores, lots of extracurricular activities, great grades, and well-crafted essays. This allows institutions to then "shape the class" in regular decision and round out the other pieces that are still missing.

To a critic's eye, early admissions programs guarantee yield. The larger their early admissions pool, the less they need to do later and the less uncertainty they have about yield. It is a way for them to know that you want them. And it is a way for you to tell them that.

AM I DISADVANTAGED BECAUSE I'M X OR Y? OR VICE VERSA?

Much of the uncertainty and stress about college admissions is around who gets in, who doesn't, and how fair the process is. The narrative suggests that if you're X, you have an easier chance to get in. If you're Y, you don't. The easy accusation is that admissions officers are biased and use admissions as a means of social engineering. While we will discuss further in chapter 10 how human the admissions process is, institutions as a whole do not admit (or reject) you because you fit (or do not fit) into any specific identity group. With the confusion as to why so many equally but differently talented applicants are not admitted, race is often assumed to be a determining factor. Without going into a deep discussion of affirmative action and equity, which is beyond the scope of this book, it is important to remember that universities are hoping to create a diverse community in its many different possibilities. Unfortunately, it is not uncommon to hear disparaging comments made about certain students that they only received an admit letter because of X, rather than academic qualifications. The reality is that rarely are these comments made with a full picture of the multifaceted talents that an applicant brings. Rather than letting such comments add unnecessary stress, remember that you cannot control how other people's fears lead them to speak or think in ways that attempt to diminish you.

Jonathan Zimmerman, professor of education and history at the University of Pennsylvania, argues that there is a group that *is* discriminated against: introverts. He observes that Harvard and other peer universities "favor people who are outgoing, gregarious and comfortable in the spotlight."[16] While schools seem to want the "positive" peppy types, this appears to also be an issue in the workplace, where extroversion is oftentimes assumed to imply capability. As Susan Cain, author of *Quiet: The Power of Introverts in a World That Can't Stop Talking*,[17] says, there is no correlation between being the most charismatic and assertive person and having the best ideas or natural talents. Yet the bias exists. If you're an introvert, do you dread team projects? Do you often feel pressured to show leadership by being the effervescent president? The good news is that greater attention is being placed on the different ways people communicate and learn. For example, some admissions officers train their alumni interviewers on bias against quieter students. Just because a student doesn't have all the answers straightaway doesn't mean they are not smart or a good fit. Sometimes, they're just taking the time to be thoughtful in responding.

Bias is part of being human. Scientists estimate that we are only consciously aware of our cognitive function 5 percent of the time. In other words, 95 percent of the time, what we say and do is beyond the awareness of our deliberative minds.[18] What this means is that admissions officers are also influenced by unconscious thought processes, including bias that existed even before you start the admissions process.

One study showed how teachers' expectations of students greatly affect their students' academic performance. If a student is labeled "gifted," regardless of their IQ, their academic performance will outpace those who are not labeled as such. Part of this is how teachers treat the student, as fair as they try to be. Part of this is due to the self-fulfilling prophecy that you will live up to what you think others expect of you. It isn't that the majority of people purposely try to be biased; in fact, "we like to think we judge people as individuals, and at times we consciously try very hard to evaluate others on the basis of their unique characteristics. We often succeed. But if we don't know a person well, our minds can turn to his or her social category for the answers."[19]

These social categories can include everything from being an athlete or not, having wealth or not, being part of a racial minority group or not. Bias exists, but the vast majority of admissions officers try to raise awareness of theirs and view you as an individual. Covering up your last name to hide an identity or checking off a box to try and fit into another identity is not worth it. Admissions officers can and do sniff out a fraud.

WHAT DO NUMBERS MEAN FOR YOU?

The business of education and enrollment management is far more complex than we have room for here. The important thing to know is that there is much that is beyond your control. Enrollment managers have to pay attention to numbers. You do not.

Universities are trying to offer you an amazing educational experience. You should apply to them if you believe they can offer you that. Apply early only if you really, truly want to go there. Apply to an institution because it seems best for you, not because it's best on a rankings list which, while useful to a degree, can be manipulated. While in this modern world of enrollment management, if you have a top choice, your chances of getting into that institution are statistically higher if you apply early, but there is no guarantee.

Universities, like you, are also subject to external pressures and the numbers game.

Chapter Nine

Worrywarts and Worry-Nots

Universities are large institutions that have many competing priorities and responsibilities, and while you might be one of them, you are not the only one. Many decisions in the college admissions process have nothing to do with you. Sorry to burst your bubble. You are still a special person . . . and so is everyone else. It's not all about you.

That doesn't mean you should give up and think that there's nothing you can do about anything. It means that you can't control the entire process. For your sanity (and your family's), focus on what you *can* control, and stop fretting about that which you cannot. Understanding where and what to worry about—and releasing the rest—is a mindhack that will serve you well for life. You know people who are constant worriers. they worry about whether it will rain on their party two months from now, and they worry about what the barista thinks about their coffee order. Maybe you can relate. You also know people who seem to be completely carefree, so much so that you wonder if they are care*less*.

Good and bad things happen to all of us. But as author Maria Konnikova said, human beings "can take a minor thing, blow it up in our heads, run through it over and over, and drive ourselves crazy until we feel like that minor thing is the biggest thing that ever happened."[1] If we recognize that tough experiences can be opportunities for growth and if we focus on what we can control, we can increase our resiliency and decrease our rumination (worrying about the past). Studies show that people with an *internal locus of control*—that is, those who generally believe that they have agency or power over their own lives—tend to be more resilient. Those with an *external locus of control*—in other words, those who generally blame or attribute what happens to them to other people or situations—show less resilience. An internal locus of control and high resilience are attributed to stronger academic performance and life satisfaction.[2]

There is no one "right" way of being, but there are ways that can be healthier. Studies show that we tend to spend almost half of our waking hours ruminating on what happened in the past and worrying about the future. How many of you spend a lot of your day worrying about the comment you made in history class or the look your secret crush gave you (or didn't give you)? You might end up inventing all sorts of stories, even while the rational part of you knows that they are based on nothing but your imagination. The rest of the time, you're worried about whether you're going to get into the "right" college and make your family proud. When you spend the majority of your life ruminating about what was and worrying about what will be, you forget to live in the present. Let's take a look at what might be in your control, and what might not be.

DROP IT: *STOP WORRYING ABOUT BEING THE "PERFECT" CANDIDATE!*

There is no "perfect" candidate.

You likely have felt the pressure to do everything "right." You probably have read stories of that kid that got into all eight Ivies, and you want to know what they did to be so desirable. You also probably know that "perfect" kid who didn't get into any of their top choices, and you want to know what they did to "screw up." The truth is probably nothing.

Most admissions directors will admit: "Most of the students they turn down are such strong candidates that many are indistinguishable from those who get in."[3] With thousands of qualified and desirable candidates, the decision on your candidacy has less to do with how "perfect" you are and more to do with the sheer fact that there are not enough spots to admit everyone.

You might have 800s on your SATs or be the valedictorian, but that doesn't make you "perfect." You might have a not-so-stellar record, but that doesn't make you "imperfect." You'll never achieve perfection nor should you. Schools don't want perfection. Stop worrying about it.

KEEP IT: *ATTEND TO BEING THE BEST VERSION OF YOU*

While there is no one perfect student, you can do your best to be the best version of you. That means reflecting on why you like to learn and what makes you persist when things are tough. Yes, pay attention to your GPA and your board scores. Pay attention to being a good citizen. Pay attention to growing. These are the areas within your control. It is also within your control to know your purpose. Are you focusing on learning to get into college or are you learning to seek knowledge and to discover, regardless of the end goal? Sometimes, the learning process may be less than fun, but it might teach you persistence, delayed gratification, and lateral thinking, all skills that may also serve you in life. Reflect on what you need to positively contribute to society.

DROP IT: *DON'T WORRY THAT YOU'RE NOT GOING TO GET INTO COLLEGE ANYWHERE*

For those of you who think you will never get in, remember this: According to NACAC, colleges in the United States on average accept roughly two-thirds of their applicants.[4] That means that you have a pretty good chance of being admitted to many wonderful institutions. Before you dismiss them, remember that just because a university has an admit rate of under 8 percent does not means that it is the right place for you. It is not so much *where* you go to school, but what you *do* with your opportunities.

KEEP IT: *ATTEND TO YOUR LIST OF SCHOOLS*

What is in your control is the list of schools to which you apply. This means if you only apply to three highly selective ones, you're not giving yourself a great chance to get in. At the same time, applying to thirty schools to give yourself a "better shot" means thirty places to worry about, especially if you don't actually want to attend them.

A happy medium is within your control, ensuring that you have a few reach schools—schools that statistically will be extremely tough, no matter your GPA, 800-meter running time, or last name; a few solid schools—schools that statistically you have a shot at, even if you are not a "shoo-in"; and a few "safety" schools—schools where you have a reasonably good chance of being admitted. You should be genuinely excited at the prospect at attending each of these schools, not because someone told you to add it to your list or because you view it as a placeholder. Keep your list sane and thoughtful, considering what you hope for intellectually and academically and where you will feel at home.

DROP IT: *STOP WORRYING ABOUT THE "SECRETS" TO THE ADMISSIONS PROCESS*

You are probably convinced that admissions officers are keeping their secrets under lock and key. It is true that admissions officers can't share every single piece of data and information with you. They work with highly sensitive information and for institutions with broader priorities and directives. Yet the anxiety about the college process seems to hold admissions offices to a different standard than any other organization.

Admissions officers are not hiding any secret formulas, even though it might sometimes appear that way. While we allow social media companies to manipulate what news we receive, or cable companies to determine how much bandwidth we get without question, when it comes to getting into college, anything short of a detailed blueprint seems intentionally negligent. Are there nefarious folks out there? Yes (and they get found out eventually). But by and large, admissions officers tend to be as transparent with you as they can be.

KEEP IT: *ATTEND PROGRAM OFFERINGS BY COLLEGES AND COMMUNITY-BASED ORGANIZATIONS*

The majority of admissions officers are telling you the truth about the process. They spend months planning and sharing the "secrets" through case study workshops and sessions on how to write the college essay and how to prepare for the interview. Stanford University, for example, takes considerable time working with your guidance counselors on how they review your application—even if you don't ever apply. They don't do this because they're twiddling their thumbs and have nothing to do. They do this because helping your counselors will help them help you. Is there a side benefit of raising awareness about Stanford? Sure, but there is more. It is to dismantle preconceived notions or misperceptions about what it takes to be admitted. Admissions officers aren't in the field to make money; they are generally in it because they care about education and they want to share knowledge with you.

Pay attention to information sessions and different programming to get your questions answered. Is this the right place for you? Would you be excited to attend? These programs are not meant to get "face time" with the admissions officers. In fact, face time doesn't really mean anything to institutions that don't take demonstrated interest into account. But attend these sessions and ask the questions directly of the admissions officers. Don't assume they're lying or that only those you pay for the "truth" are actually giving it to you. Go to the source: the admissions offices. (Have you figured out by now that this book is not divulging any "secrets," but making accessible information that universities are willing to share with you if you ask?)

DROP IT: *STOP WORRYING ABOUT INSTITUTIONAL PRIORITIES AND ABOUT BEING "HOOKED"*

Universities have priorities—such as the need to raise money, or to rebuild the soccer team, or to respond to a family who helped found the institution—that are out of your control. They aren't trying to hide these things, but the directives that their presidents give the admissions office (e.g., to increase the applicant pool) don't mean that you should contort yourself to get in. The fact is that your chance of getting into one of these institutions is not high, regardless of your family name. If you start changing who you are to get in, even if you do get in, you're going to lose in the long run.

It might seem like only "hooked" kids get into top schools. Depending on the institution, having a parent who also attended the university may or may not impact your decision. The public was shocked to hear how some students applying to Harvard end up on the "Z-list"—a list of students from families of interest to the university who receive a letter of delayed admissions to allow the student a year to get their stuff together before entering the first-year class.[5] Harvard is not the only school with applicants of alumni. As we discussed, there are reasons why institutions may have to respond to differing priorities. It doesn't mean that you have no shot; it means you can't control them.

Depending on the institution and league, recruited athletes can be an institutional priority. Universities are under pressure to have high-performing teams. Still, at the selectivity level you're looking at, the majority of recruited athletes have both tremendous athletic talent and academic chops.

As longtime Harvard admissions dean Bill Fitzsimmons says, "the admissions process is eminently rational; it's just not fair."[6] You cannot control institutional priorities.

KEEP IT: *ATTEND TO WHAT MAKES YOU YOU*

Don't worry about finding a "hook." Focus on finding your story. A "hook" is an excuse for outsiders to tell you that you're not good enough. Having a "hook" isn't an automatic pass. You're good enough.

What you can control is how you tell your story. We will get into more detail later, but the important thing to remember is to spend time reflecting on what is important to you, why you want to go to university, and what you hope to gain. Your own story *is* your hook. Whether that's being an awesome knitter or a great older sibling, universities are looking for a broad array of experiences and stories to bring together to knit a canvas of interesting and promising young people. Losing sight of who you are and trying to conform to what you *think* universities want will likely backfire. You won't come across as genuine, and admissions officers will sense that. They're not looking for drama-filled stories—they just want yours.

Regardless of whether you get in, focus on knowing yourself and being able to articulate who you are. You have enough to worry about. Let the rest fall outside your circle of concern.

Chapter Ten

We're Only Human

Hopefully, this book hasn't completely scared you away by making you think that there is *nothing* in your control. Consider this: UNICEF estimates that the world literacy rate is increasing, leaving 115 million youth illiterate—"only" 115 million who can't even read what you're reading right now. If you're one of those idealistic young people who want to do something about this global illiteracy rate, remember that to truly address the world's most pressing problems with clarity and innovation, the more you're thriving and happy, the more effective you will be. You're in a privileged position simply by being literate. Remember then that while you cannot control everything, you *do* have control over who you are and who you want to become. You have control over how much you allow the myths other people create about "your chances" to shake your confidence, or how much you allow the pressures of external validation to direct your actions. In an enrollment management world with only so many available spots and many institutional priorities, you could be the bee's knees and *still* not be accepted into your dream school. That doesn't mean that enrollment managers are evil, cold, data robots nor does it mean the system is rigged against you because you are [fill-in-the-blank]. If you forget everything else you've read here, remember this: College admissions *is not a game to win.* Forget College Confidential and your friend's mom's cousin who went to Brown and told you otherwise. Listen to the folks who make the decisions about you. Listen to Bowdoin's dean Whitney Soul who has this to say about the process: "It's human. It's not a commodity—an object that is purchased and consumed."[1]

The admissions process is an unfair one. It doesn't mean that colleges and admissions officers don't work hard to make it more equitable and transparent. Most colleges try to do their best to be thoughtful in crafting communities of scholars and artists and activists and athletes and people you will call peers, but it is an imperfect system. Some of you seek a known equation that guarantees an answer: $A + B = C$, but it is a process that cannot be automated without losing a lot of what it takes to build an intentional community. While highly selective institutions have more luxury of addressing the nuances, rather than simply automate the process, some institutions employ more automation (input testing and GPA data > output of admit or deny).

Many of you want an institution that takes individualized contexts and experiences into account. After all, you're a human being who has had many different experiences, so what you've accomplished should be viewed in light of these unique factors. The highly selective institutions you're looking at tend to use more contextualized or "holistic" approaches, which allow them to consider any factor to back up a decision. Individualization also means greater subjectivity. Holistic admissions can make an unfair process both fairer and more imperfect. Reading for context means that real people are reading your file.

And so, here's the real "Big Secret" of what happens inside the Ivy Tower: *The people making decisions about your candidacy are human.* Being human means that admissions officers are as fallible, subjective, anxious, well-intentioned, thoughtful, hungry, and bright as any other human being. Just like you.

Admissions officers at highly selective colleges have the luxury of spending more time with each file, even though that time is still not as long as you might hope or think. Different readers read at different speeds, and it depends on how thorough the read is. Each office is structured differently. Some may require that every file gets read thoroughly at least once. Others twice. Or more. At one institution, your file may get a "full read" (thorough, cover-to-cover), followed by another "full read" from someone else. At another institution, your same file might get a more cursory first check to see if you meet certain metrics and a follow-up review from someone else to make sure nothing was missed. This doesn't sound like a lot of time, but there are only so many hours in the day, and some of the schools to which you are applying have 39,999 other great candidates. Admissions officers must abide by physical human limits.

There is also only so much a person's brain can hold. Admissions officers are subject to the same physiological restrictions in attentional capacity as everyone else. Decisions made on your application are subject to a whole host of factors that have nothing to do with you, regardless of a grade you received as a sophomore in the fall or the number of community service hours you've logged. The human side of the admissions process can work both for and against you.

Geek out with us for a bit as we turn to three psychological phenomena that impact our ability to make decisions and may explain why college admissions is not an impartial commentary on you: 1) hunger; 2) bias; and 3) personal experience.

PSYCHOLOGICAL PHENOMENON #1:
ADMISSIONS OFFICERS MIGHT NOT MAKE THE SAME DECISION, GIVEN THE TIME OF DAY OR HOW HUNGRY THEY ARE

The likelihood of a positive review if the admissions officer reads your file right after an oatmeal breakfast is higher than it is right before they have to leave to catch a train at the end of the day. It's biology. In 2011, a study was done on 1,100 judicial rulings by eight different parole judges. Remember that judges—unlike most admissions officers—are trained for years on how to be objective and unbiased. Yet even they are not immune to human physiology. The judges were given two different food breaks throughout their day. What the researchers found was that right after a meal break, the judges approved parole on average 65 percent of the time. As the time ticked towards the meal break or towards the end of the day, the judges' approval rate went to almost 0 percent. This means: 1) if you ever have to go up for parole, make sure you get the hearing scheduled for after a meal break; and 2) when our glucose levels drop, so does our ability for conscious decision-making. We simply don't have the energy to be as objective or thoughtful so our brains go into our default mental settings and rely on mental shortcuts.[2] When we are low on glucose, we are more likely to make decisions that rely on biases and unconscious shortcuts.

Think about when you're studying for an exam, and you "hit a wall." Your body is likely low on glucose, and your brain says, "I need to conserve energy, shut off nonessential functions—such as solving differential equations." A similar thing happens to admissions officers who, for the most part, do not have nearly the kind of training to be impartial that judges do and, therefore, are likely to be more suscepti-ble. After morning coffee, the admissions officer's brain is amped up to scrutinize your transcript and catch that dual enrollment course. But after a few hours of no food, the admissions officer's brain might miss that dual enrollment course. I once overheard someone at a conference talk about how he doesn't take a bathroom break until he reads ten files—even if his bladder is desperately shouting for attention. He laughingly said, "That last file? Good luck to ya, kid. I gotta GO." It's probably not so funny if your file is that last file. While this doesn't usually happen, admissions officers *may* make slightly different deci-sions on candidacies based on the time of day they read your file, when they've snacked, or if they've gone to the bathroom.

PSYCHOLOGICAL PHENOMENON #2: *ADMISSIONS OFFICERS HAVE BIASES THAT HAVE NOTHING TO DO WITH YOU*

We all have biases, conscious and unconscious. Unconscious biases are even more difficult to address because we are not aware of actually having them. Princeton University professor Emily Pronin and her col-leagues published the results of three studies on the *bias blind spot* to describe how the average person (including you) thinks they are less biased than others.[3] Admissions officers idealize their reading to be objective, individual, and logical. The intention is there. But biology also mixes things up.

According to scientists Michael Gazzaniga and Daniel Kahneman, humans have two types of thinking: fast and slow. Fast thinking is unconscious. It is instinctual, emotional, and often relies on stereotypes (e.g., public high school football captain means [fill-in-the-blank]). Slow thinking is conscious. It requires effort (and glucose), is logical, and considers the individual. As much as we (you, too!) think we are conscious thinkers, Gazzaniga argues that on average, 95 to 98 percent of all our thinking is unconscious.[4] Yikes.

All forms of unconscious thought show up in our daily lives, and admissions officers are not immune to them. In fact, they may play a role in deciding your fate. For decades, Harvard University's Project

Implicit researched the kinds of unconscious biases people hold about things, such as race, gender, and even political candidates, through a series of "tests," the Implicit Association Tests (IAT).[5] For example, in the IAT on race, researchers showed that while only 20 percent of test-takers *reported* having a conscious bias toward "white," the results showed that 70 percent of test-takers *actually* did on the assessment. In other words, the majority of people were convinced they did not have a racial preference, even though they did. The point here is that admissions officers, just like any other human being, are susceptible to different forms of biases that may translate into decisions if they are not mindful of them or trained on how to overcome them.

Are you less biased than the average person? If you answered yes, so do most people. It just shows how human you are, just like admissions officers.

PSYCHOLOGICAL PHENOMENON #3: *EACH ADMISSIONS OFFICER BRINGS WITH THEM THEIR OWN HISTORIES, EXPERIENCES, AND WORLDVIEWS*

Being an admissions officer does not make one immune to reacting to and viewing things from a personal perspective. Kahneman, the Nobel Prize–winning psychologist of *Thinking, Fast and Slow*, and Amos Tversky, cognitive and mathematical psychologist, studied the concept of "availability heuristic," the mental shortcut we use to make decisions with less effort. Because we're constantly bombarded with information—some of which is useful and some not—we often make decisions based on the ease of recall. Our memories are based on our experiences. The more vivid and memorable they are, the more we rely on them to inform us of what to do in the present. The dangers, of course, are that our memories can be faulty, and lead to stories that may not be useful in the current situation. Yet cognitive reality influences our decision-making process.

Each person comes in with their own experiences and perceptions about what the applicant in front of them represents, which may impact their decision on that file. For example, an admissions officer might have a certain perception of what a first-generation American college student or a fourth-generation legacy applicant is like. I once knew an officer who was extra hard on students who attended well-resourced private schools. It turned out that she herself went to a well-resourced private school, where she felt like an outsider. Based on her memories of being excluded, she extended her unresolved feelings to the applicants she reviewed who just happened to attend well-resourced private schools. Was it fair? No. Did it happen? Yes.

Admissions officers are susceptible to mental shortcuts, as well as triggers—things that bring up intense emotional responses. For example, an admissions officer might find they are more triggered by essays on religion because they grew up with a certain belief system, or they may react to a story about someone's grandmother because they recently lost their own.

Before you throw up your hands, thinking that admissions officers are mindless, biased idiots if they don't eat enough chocolate, let's take a look at three phenomena with regard to how being human actually works to your advantage, and gives your application its fair time in the sun.

HUMAN PHENOMENON #1: THE MORE EXPERIENCE AN ADMISSIONS OFFICER HAS, THE MORE THEY ARE ABLE TO CONTEXTUALIZE YOUR CANDIDACY

When human beings consider their own experiences, they can bring a broader and more nuanced understanding to the situation in front of them. The majority of admissions officers do not dismiss candidates because they remind them of their high school tormentors. The majority leverage their experiences to try and understand each applicant within their context. I worked with one colleague whose upbringing in rural North Carolina helped the team understand why a student from Appalachia had more limited extracurricular engagements, and another whose experience as a college athlete helped everyone to better evaluate the intense dedication and skill required of a lacrosse player from suburban Boston.

The more seasoned admissions officers generally have had exposure to a breadth of contexts to bring a wider lens to your file, such as why an A at your school doesn't mean the same thing at a neighboring school. (For those of you who wonder whether colleges recognize that your school grades "harder" than the neighboring school, the answer is: yes, most of the time.) The system is not perfect, but the more experience an officer has, the more they recognize nuances.

But experience is not everything. Sometimes *too* much experience can lead to more entrenched biases and assumptions. Most admissions officers spend a lot of time training—even the greenest and the most seasoned admissions officers—to build greater understanding.

Admissions officers are humans. Some, like you, are interested in learning as much as they can about how different educational systems work. Some, like your friends, are less motivated and want to just get the files read. Others, like no one you know, may be more limited in their evaluative abilities. Hopefully, the latter get weeded out of the profession quickly.

HUMAN PHENOMENON #2:
ADMISSIONS OFFICERS SEEK EXPOSURE AND COLLABORATION WITH COLLEAGUES TO WIDEN THEIR UNDERSTANDING AND TO OVERCOME BIASES

Just because the admissions officer reading your file doesn't share your experience doesn't mean they cannot understand from where you come. The majority of admissions officers spend many months of the year traveling around the world to meet you and your peers. It's not as glamorous as it sounds. It is many days driving on highways and back-roads trying to find your high school parking lot, eating terrible fast food, and bunking at the moderately priced local inn. But they do this so that they can personally speak to you and your school counselors, and even simply to have lunch at the local café to see what life is like in your community. I worked with a colleague who spent long hours driving to reach just one school on a rural reservation, where face-to-face interactions with tribal elders are a must to gain trust. Many of the more experienced officers have also gone to graduate school where they have gained a deeper understanding of the landscape of higher education, the psychology of race on standardized exams, or the geopolitical impact of educational policies. Many volunteer with community-based organizations or sit on national boards to stay aware of and updated on the most recent trends and factors that may impact you.

It might also be a surprise to some of you, but many admissions officers, even from "competing" schools, are friendly with each other. Maybe you have attended one of the multischool roadshows, where several schools travel together. Audiences are usually relieved to see that admissions officers are normal people who seem to actually like each other. This kind of professional collaboration helps them to broaden perspectives and to challenge each other's unconscious biases. Driving down I-95 in a Town & Country minivan is a perfect opportunity to ask questions like "how does your office handle undocumented students?" as well as to gain a shared understanding of a challenging, very human process. They attend professional development conferences, exchanging knowledge of what they've learned about your hometown or testing trends in your county. Imagine a ballroom of every admissions officer in the Ivy League, MIT, and Stanford. Important discussions occur, but it's not as intimidating as it sounds. It's also a ballroom of really nice and down-to-earth people taking selfies and sharing spoilers about *Game of Thrones*. They're only human.

HUMAN PHENOMENON #3:
ADMISSIONS OFFICERS ARE TRAINED TO FIND EVIDENCE TO SUPPORT THEIR DECISIONS AND TO REDUCE MENTAL SHORTCUTS

Many admissions offices train their readers to raise awareness of biases and the dangers of "fast thinking," as well as the institutional and systemic structures that may perpetuate inequities. Such training may include readings on the history and state of higher education, and tips on how to identify energy patterns for the most productive work. This is not to say that all admissions offices do this perfectly. Some institutions are extremely mindful and spend days on this topic; others have a more surface-level, one-hour show of it. Regardless, the role of bias and human subjectivity is very much on the minds of admissions officers at top-tier institutions. It is not a fair process, but it is a process taken seriously. After all, one does not go into admissions to retire early and buy a vacation home in the Maldives. Most, even those with years of experience, make less than you will your first year out of college. Most do this work because they want to give you an opportunity at higher education.

To do so, all admissions offices train their teams to review applications not just with a "gut check" but by incorporating a detailed analysis to build evidence in support of a decision. Think about your research projects where you have to find pieces of evidence that back up your hypothesis. The admissions process is similar, in what is often described as "an art and a science."

The science bit is analytical and more objective (think back to our discussion on enrollment management). While different offices use different metrics, some sort of rubric is generally used to maintain consistency among different officers and to help balance human subjectivity. For example, one school may use a four-point scale to evaluate a transcript. Students in the top 5 percent of their class might get the coveted 1. However, that doesn't mean everyone with a 1 gets accepted. Think about that senior from last year with a perfect 5.0 GPA who you *swore* would get in everywhere but didn't. You were shocked. It doesn't mean the system was rigged or that the student didn't get in because of [fill-in-the-blank]. The reality is most of these universities you're looking at have thousands who fit that profile and would earn a 1 on a transcript metric. But the reality is also that you—or your counselor, paid or not—will never know what the admissions officer is looking for at the very moment they are reading your file. That is where the "art" bit comes in. Admissions officers are looking at more than just an objective rating.

The human component means that admissions officer may find evidence in other parts of your file to build a case. For example, you might be in the top 15 percent of your class, so you might not earn that coveted 1. You might receive a 2 instead. However, that admissions officer might draw out from parts of your application how you achieved this rank with limited resources and major personal obstacles. Your 15 percent might really be a pretty darn amazing feat in light of these circumstances. That admissions officer, in their very human capacity, will find evidence to support why your 2 deserves serious consideration over a 1.

Furthermore, all offices also have some sort of check-and-balance system. While some offices might be lighter on the "check" side of things because they simply don't have the manpower or time to read every application in great detail, they create systems so that your fate doesn't lie in one person's hands. In most offices, at least two people review your file, if not more. This helps take advantage of the humanness of the process. Person A may affirm person B's evaluation that you will be a wonderful addition to the institution and help build your case for admissions. Or maybe person A thinks your essay is indecipherable, and person B thinks it's the cat's pajamas. Any such disagreements may find their way into the committee room where more admissions officers will hear your story (sorry to burst your bubble, but it's not melodramatic, like the movies).

Having multiple human beings review your file means that there are more opportunities that someone will see your application with fresh eyes. This helps to prevent bias. For example, if only one admissions officer read all the applications from Oregon, they might have a rather insular view. But if several other people—including those who've never stepped foot in Oregon—get to hear about your file, they can offer a perspective that might bypass any preconceived notions or mental shortcuts that occur when the Oregon representative gets fatigued. The bias of one person can turn into collective wisdom.

Different schools use different models. We're sure you have probably read a few books that claim to have the "secrets" as to how each institution does it, and that if you knew the secret, you could crack the code. Most institutions that practice holistic admissions will use an evaluation process by which your application gets reviewed anywhere from one to three (or more) times before a preliminary decision is made. Then your file may get moved into the final admissions decision stage where the senior leaders in the office and the dean make the final decisions, considering the composition of the class and institutional priorities. Some institutions adopt a process whereby reader 1 makes a recommendation and reader 2 makes a final decision; others have two readers make initial recommendations, and a third steps in if the first two disagree. Still others have a first reader, followed by a second reader who selects those applicants to move forward to a larger committee discussion for final decisions. Others might rely on the dean for all final decisions. Confused yet?

One newer reading model that has garnered some attention is the committee-based evaluation (CBE) model, which schools like the University of Pennsylvania, Swarthmore College, and Bucknell University have adopted. This model has two admissions officers reading your application at the same time. Each officer reads a different part of the application; one is the "driver" who looks at the quantitative metrics and academics and the other is the "passenger" who looks at the non-academic factors. They then discuss, come to a consensus, make a final recommendation, and move on. One intention of this model is to increase efficiency, requiring each team to complete a certain daily amount of material and avoid the burnout that easily occurs (admissions officers call reading season "three months of endless finals"). Another intention is to allow the territory manager to provide more context to your file. If you're from Florida, the territory manager from

Florida will be one of the two reviewing your file. It is intended to increase collaboration through peer training to minimize biases.

While this model has received some strong reviews, there are some caveats to this and all other models. The caveats are, of course, inherent in human behavior, and they can arise regardless of reading model. One caveat is social loafing, the psychological concept that we slack off if others are doing the work. You probably have a few classmates who fall into this category. Did you know that if more than three people clap, you're less likely to clap as hard as you would if you were the only person doing so? What this means is that in this paired reading model, one officer might end up carrying the conversation and dominating the conversation, potentially biasing the vote.

Another caveat is authority bias, where we place weight on the opinion of the more senior person or the one in a position of power. In the paired reading model or in a committee room, it is not out of the question that a more senior admissions officer might dominate the conversation and the junior member would be less willing to challenge.

A third caveat is status-quo bias, which occurs when we default to the familiar to reduce risks. It is not hard for two people to easily fall into a routine. If the pair gets *too* comfortable on how they decided on applicant 1 or applicant 10, by the time they get to you, they may fall back on their default decision-making habits that worked before rather than look at you with fresh eyes.

The reality is that the specific reading model of any one institution doesn't matter so much. Universities will adapt models, CBE or not, to their offices' and institutional needs. Regardless, you cannot get inside an admissions officer's human brain or know the many nuanced institutional priorities that they have taken into consideration. Remember, it's not a game. You can't "crack" the code. These models get tweaked. Perhaps a number on the rubric gets shifted, or an admissions officer gets pneumonia and has to turn their files over to a colleague who is less familiar with your territory. No amount of money can buy you a guarantee when human beings are involved.

What does this all mean for you? Let's consider three key points.

TAKEAWAY #1:
YOU HAVE LITTLE CONTROL ONCE YOU SUBMIT "SEND"

You cannot control who is reading your file, when they take coffee breaks, or which reading model an institution uses. No amount of money your mom might be willing to pay can tell you what triggers the admissions officer reading your file.

The "art and science" process is not one that you can predict. It is a human process and therefore subject to human fallibility and human brilliance. Being human means that your file isn't funneled into a machine that inputs certain data and spits you out according to some algorithm. Being human means that, in a competitive and unfair process, your file gets personalized attention from people trying to see you for you. Being human means that training, no matter how uneven, helps admissions officers to check their natural biases.

TAKEAWAY #2:
IT IS NOT YOUR JOB—OR YOUR COUNSELORS' JOB—
TO KNOW "YOUR ADMISSIONS OFFICER" SO WELL
THAT YOU CAN WRITE THE PERFECT ESSAY
AND APPLICATION

You don't know what will tickle an admissions officer's heart. You don't know who will actually read your essay (one person, two, ten?). There is little to be gained by writing what you think they want to hear, especially if what you think they want to hear doesn't really reflect who you are.

There are many websites that advise you to email "your" admissions officer, introduce yourself, and butter them up. At schools where demonstrated interest makes a difference, this might be important. But at the tier you're looking at, it typically doesn't matter if you have emailed "your" officer or not. In fact, sometimes it can backfire. Many applicants emailed me because I was "their" officer, and they wanted me to know their name so I would "advocate" for them, but with seemingly little other purpose. Sometimes, they asked questions, but these questions were so basic ("Are there research opportunities available?" I was employed at a research university. Um, yes.) that I wondered if they even bothered reading the website. If you have a legitimate question, google it first and then reach out if the answer can't be found. Multiple emails with obvious questions can frustrate admissions officers to the point where they'll remember your name, but not for good reason. After all, they're human.

TAKEAWAY #3:
ADMISSIONS OFFICERS ARE DOING THEIR BEST TO GET TO KNOW WHO YOU ARE

As unfair and confounding as the process is, there is another human being, as wonderful and as flawed as you, reviewing your hard work. Admissions officers spend more time thinking about, learning about, and reading your stories beyond your test scores and grades than you can imagine. Their personal lives often get put on hold during the evenings and weekends of the winter months spent reading files. Are they perfect? No. Are they human? Yes. Just like you.

Not being accepted is not the end of the world nor is it a reflection of you as a human being. Being accepted is also not an affirmation that you are more deserving than anyone else. On one of the most nerve-wracking days of the year for students like yourself, "Ivy decision day of 2016," Dartmouth's then–interim dean Paul Sunde penned an open letter to all of the applicants, acknowledging their already great accomplishments and celebrating their potential to make a positive impact on the world. Regardless of whether or not they got in, it was an important message and reminder of how a decision letter doesn't dictate who you are or your worth.

We're all only human.

III

Coloring Inside the Lines: What Has Been Still Is

Now that we've taken a look at the complicated and very human pro cess, let's take a look at the holistic admissions process that is currently used by many institutions. Some of you may have heard about this through the different workshops these universities run, and some of you may never have heard the term "holistic admissions" before. Regardless, you are likely curious for more.

For many institutions, individual holistic processes align with an institution's mission, taking into consideration the likelihood that you will succeed and contribute there, and the context of your experiences. The reality is that ten years from now, five years from now, things may look different in the process. For now, the holistic process can encompass many different factors.

This chapter will examine the model, what we call ATLAS 1.0, that outlines the five key dimensions often used in holistic college admissions. Every school reviews these slightly differently, which means there is not one simple equation or weighting system.

Many admissions offices take these dimensions seriously to learn about you as a whole person. This section will offer simple practices for you to navigate them with greater awareness, mindfulness, and reflection.

ATLAS 1.0

Figure 10.1.   ATLAS 1.0

Chapter Eleven

Academics

Are You Ready to Take It Up a Notch?

Do you have a 4.86 instead of a 4.93? Are you obsessed with that .07 difference? After all, someone might have told you that to get into one of the elite universities, you *must* have a perfect GPA and a .07 gap may be the difference between a happy April and a miserable one. Let's take a look at what is true and what is not about how admissions officers review "academics" and some practices to get you on track.

ACADEMICS INSIGHT #1: *ACADEMICS MATTER—A LOT*

You're probably interested in highly selective universities because of the rigor and strength of their academic programs, which help to attract some of the top professors, scholars, and thinkers. Because of this, they attract some of the top emerging minds—like yours.

This also means that at the level of selectivity you are looking at, academics really matter. A holistic process where schools "look at everything" should not be misconstrued to mean that "your academics aren't that important." If you're a really, really good tennis player, and you do really, really great community service, and you try really, really hard, those efforts won't likely overshadow a transcript of Cs. While those Cs do not reflect *who you are as a human being*, such a record will likely not instill a lot of confidence in the admissions officer who has to make fine distinctions and tough decisions regarding whether you are ready or able to succeed in a highly rigorous intellectual environment at this time.[1]

Academic performance is important. These institutions want to ensure that the students they accept and enroll are ready to take on the rigor and engage fully with their professors and peers. They have the luxury of choosing whom they would like to invite onto their campuses because of the volume of strong talent in their pool of applicants. This means that admissions officers will place primary attention on your academic performance. While this doesn't mean that you need a perfect 4.0 or 5.0 or whatever scale your school uses, it does mean that admissions officers want to see that you are performing strongly vis-à-vis your peers. Are you near or at the top of your class? If you're not, are you demonstrating academic talent and ability in other ways? Perhaps there's a notable research project that your teacher can tell us more about. Perhaps it's how you were the first person in your school to create an independent class that offered you knowledge but not bonus points for your GPA. You could have a million extracurricular activities, but if you are a B, C, or D student, there is less confidence that you are ready for the rigors of university-level academics.

The focus on academics might sound unfair, but keep in mind that institutions have a responsibility to accept students who are ready for their academic programs. Imagine if you were not ready for the challenge or pace of an institution. Instead of enjoying the process of learning and flourishing, you'd probably spend most of your time anxious and lost, which would make you even more anxious and lost, until you are in way over your head. Such a mismatch doesn't mean you're not smart or capable but that the academic fit might not be the best one at this time. No one wants you to fail.

Even if you are an A student, admissions officers are looking for more than a grade. They are considering whether you are ready to manage what will likely be an even tougher academic environment than what you've been used to. They are looking to see if you have the independence and maturity to take on rigorous academics without someone watching over your shoulder at every moment. College is a place where you might only have one midterm and a final—and no one to tell you to study every day. If you don't do the work, you're likely not going to do well. So in addition to your GPA vis-à-vis your peers, admissions officers are seeing if your academic record reflects independence and the ability to do the work on your own—and to do it well.

PRACTICE: TAKE A WALK OUTSIDE IN NATURE

During a time when things can feel terribly stressful because your academics are so important, it becomes even more important to find balance and shift. According to research, being out in nature can lead to increased enthusiasm for learning, stronger performance in core subjects such as math and science, and greater creativity, problem solving, and thinking.[2] At least once a day, take a walk outside even if it's circling your block. Bonus points if you can walk where there is grass or trees. Five minutes will boost your readiness for greater cognitive challenges. It will be worth your time.

ACADEMICS INSIGHT #2: *MINUTE DIFFERENCES IN GPA WILL NOT MAKE OR BREAK YOUR CANDIDACY*

If academic records play such a large role in how admissions officers evaluate your candidacy, does a .07 difference in GPAs make a real difference? The short answer is no.

This response may seem contrary to the messages you may have been receiving since you were a kid that every point matters in order to get into a top school. Such pressures may have taken some of the thrill and joy of discovery away. For example, biology might have been fun for you, but as soon as it seemed like getting 100 percent was more important than experimenting, biology lost some of its luster. I recall a student telling me how he and his brother had adjoining bedrooms with the doors next to each other. Both of their desks sat opposite these doors so that when they sat down, their backs were facing the entrance. Every day starting at 4:30 p.m., their mother would sit in a hard-backed chair in the hallway facing the doors so that she could watch both boys in their respective rooms doing their homework. Her job was to make sure the boys studied for the next four hours until dinner to ensure As, A+s preferred. Only one bathroom break was allowed. You can imagine how this student lost his innate joy for learning.

Before you dismiss grades as the evil, unnecessary villains, there is a reason that admissions officers look at them closely: there is a correlation between your high school GPA and how well you'll do in college. In 2014, William Hiss, the former dean of admissions at Bates College, studied twenty private colleges and universities, six public universities, five minority-serving institutions, and two art schools finding that, despite wide variations in standardized testing like SATs, high school GPAs correlated with college GPAs. Even students with poorer standardized test scores performed well in college if they also had strong high school GPAs.[3] In other words, your GPA gives some evidence as to how well you'll do in college.

PRACTICE: REFLECT ON YOUR MOTIVATION TO LEARN

It is easy to get caught up in grades as a motivator for your learning. Studies show that people perform better when they find true motivation to learn, rather than relying on someone else's directive. So put aside the focus on your GPA for a moment, get out a notebook, and write about those moments when you love learning. Think back to when you were a kid. Maybe it was making forts in the backyard or doodling. Just write. Then look back at your writing and circle those things that you notice in particular. How might you rediscover or do more of those things? How might you find new ways to express that motivation? For example, if you loved "cooking" in the kitchen, putting things together and seeing what happens, how might you bring that approach to chemistry lab?

ACADEMICS INSIGHT #3: *THERE IS NO WEIGHTING SYSTEM FOR YOUR GPA*

Unlike some misconceptions, you are not evaluated based on some made-up calculation at the majority of the institutions you are looking at. Your application doesn't go through any secret formula (e.g., 18% GPA, 22% rank, 15% personality). Rather, your GPA—if you have a GPA—is taken into consideration within a whole set of other factors.

Just because your GPA isn't particularly weighted in any specific way, it *is* "weighted" heavily. These are academic institutions first and foremost, which means that even if you are the world's best cellist, you still need the academic chops to survive the courses. The truth is that academics is of foremost importance on your application. With less than 10 percent acceptance rates, you can rightly imagine that the majority of applicants have pretty stellar records. This is not because these institutions don't care about who you are beyond your grades or recognize that you are more than a transcript, but that they are under direction from their presidents and provosts and deans of the faculty to bring to their classrooms individuals who are ready and eager to engage academically. Do they love that you've got comedic timing or can hula for an hour straight? Yes, probably. But they also want to make sure you can be an asset to their classrooms.

How heavily your grades are weighted depends on the institution and your context.

PRACTICE: BREATHE

Without any magic formula that you can turn to or rely on, there is not always a right answer or a predetermined output. You can't "chance" yourself based on some number of As or Bs. Getting yourself worked up over something you do not have control over is only going to make you anxious. To release that anxiety, breathing is a simple and powerful practice. Each time the topic of your GPA gives you heart palpitations, take three deep belly breaths. Inhale deeply to fill your belly up like a balloon, and then exhale deeply through your mouth. With each exhalation, imagine that worry being released. Then you'll be more ready to do your best.

ACADEMICS INSIGHT #4: *ACADEMIC RECORDS DO NOT NEED TO BE "PERFECT"*

There seems to be this myth that if you have anything less than straight As, you have no shot at a highly selective university. This myth is so pervasive that there are some high schools that bolster student grades instead of giving grades that are reflective of true performance; in other cases, parents fight to get that B+ off the transcript or students cheat on tests to get that A.

At one school in upstate New York, a parent bemoaned the fact the teacher yelled at *her*, the mother, for not reviewing her son's homework and making it "teacher-ready." Essentially, the teacher expected that the ten-year-old child's homework should be proofed and edited by his forty-five-year-old mother. It's no surprise that the level of student presentations at this school are at a professional level. What this teacher doesn't recognize is that she is setting her students up for failure. The children never get a chance to really learn, and when they get their first B+, they fall apart.

If all of these institutions were only looking for straight-A students, they could save themselves a lot of time and money by just tossing out any application with transcripts containing anything less than an A. Perhaps you would do anything to get that A, including getting sick or crossing ethical boundaries. It might mean that schools would give out As like Halloween candy to increase their visibility as "great" schools and to assuage angry parents.

So if it's not the perfect A, what do these schools want academically? Admissions officers know that your grades are not an accurate reflection of your intelligence or intellectual capacity. They are looking at the nuances to determine your academic readiness and potential. Academic readiness generally relates to your track record: How have you performed? Have you proven that you could handle even tougher and more complex levels of work? Academic potential generally relates to indicators that you have what it takes to thrive and grow in an even tougher academic environment. Have you challenged yourself with tougher courses or stretched yourself?

These institutions consider your context when it comes to academic readiness and potential and know that each context is different.

PRACTICE: EMBRACE IMPERFECTION

Rather than pushing yourself to perfection, remember that the most growth happens in imperfection. The Japanese philosophy called *wabi-sabi* embraces the concept of imperfection in life. If you look at wabi-sabi artwork, its exposed cracks and bumps are not seen as "mistakes" but as signs of beauty. Consider the times you have made a mistake or not gotten a perfect mark. Reframe these "bumps" as part of your perfectly imperfect journey of learning and as opportunities for exploration and expansion. Your imperfections make you human, more real, and more ready for the "real world."

ACADEMICS INSIGHT #5: *EVIDENCE AND INDICATORS OF ACADEMIC READINESS AND POTENTIAL ARE FOUND IN TRANSCRIPTS, RECOMMENDATION LETTERS, INTERVIEWS, ESSAYS, AND ACTIVITIES*

Admissions officers are trained (hopefully) to review your transcript carefully. Admissions officers pour over transcripts in great detail, looking at three primary areas: your grades and record; your rank and place in the class; and your curriculum and rigor.

Admissions officers are paying close attention to what is offered in your high school. For those who are homeschooled, transcripts are reviewed within that context (and yes, admissions officers are aware that homeschool transcripts are generally chock-full of As). For those who attend a school that doesn't give out grades, what others have to say in an interview or letter help to tease out subtle differences. For those who attend schools that dole out As, admissions officers may seek greater indicators of your academic potential through recommendation letters. This does not mean that a B or two, or even an errant C, means a death knell for your candidacy. But at highly selective institutions, a strong track record is important.

PRACTICE: OPEN AWARENESS

We can get so overly focused on one thing—whether it's your English midterm grade or that one AP chemistry paper. When we are so focused, we often forget to look at what is around us and look at the bigger picture. Opening your awareness can help you to step back and not get burdened by one small detail. Sit comfortably. You can close your eyes or lower your gaze. Bring attention to your breathing. Notice any sounds that you hear. Do not overanalyze these sounds; just notice. Notice any smells. Do not overanalyze; just notice. Notice any shadows or sights, any tastes, any touch or feeling of the air on your skin. Again, do not overanalyze any of these sensations; just notice.

ACADEMICS INSIGHT #6: *IT IS GENERALLY VIEWED FAVORABLY WHEN YOU TAKE A MORE CHALLENGING COURSE LOAD—AND EVEN MORE FAVORABLY IF YOU DO WELL WITH A MORE CHALLENGING COURSE LOAD*

There is no magic weighting system. When universities say your grades matter "a lot," this can mean many different things. "A lot" means grades matter. But by "how much" depends on your context and situation. If you struggled a bit during your first term in high school and then took off like a rocketship academically thereafter, that rise may be more compelling to an admissions officer than if you started high and your marks took a nosedive as your classes got harder. In the latter scenario, admissions officers will question your readiness for higher-level courses. What this means is that you need to rev up your engine as you get into your sophomore year, and keep your foot on the gas pedal during your junior year. Don't forget senior year—your fall term is critical to prove that you have the ability to take it up a notch as course demands get tougher.

Highly selective institutions have the benefit of top faculty, who overwhelmingly say the one thing they look for in their students is "curiosity." Your grades are demonstrative evidence of how well you've done and how you might fare when the rigor increases. While grades offer evidence as to ability and rank performance, rigor can indicate your sense of intellectual curiosity and risk-taking. Are you someone who is so driven to learn and grow that you would rather take a risk than phone it in? Are you someone who pushes themselves in uncomfortable intellectual situations to stretch your brain and broaden your knowledge? These qualities are incredibly critical at this level of selectivity, particularly as the majority of applicants will have great transcripts.

Does that mean you have to take twenty-four AP classes to show curiosity? Not every high school offers APs. If your school doesn't, then no admissions officers will expect you to take some on your own. In fact, if you take ten APs and none of them are offered at your school, they are going to wonder who you really are and why you think AP classes make good extracurricular activities.

Rigor matters, but you also are beholden to what your school offers. For example, eight elite private high schools in the Washington, D.C., area decided to drop out of the AP program in June 2018. Their rationale was that AP courses focus too much on memorization, rather than allowing for authentic and rigorous engagement with the world. These students will have no opportunity to take them. And if they decide to take twenty-four courses on their own time—in addition to their already rigorous programs—most admissions officers will likely question whether: 1) they sleep; 2) they're simply checking off the boxes; or 3) they're learning or truly engaged.

PRACTICE: GROWTH MINDSET

Remember the growth mindset, the concept that you always have the capacity to grow and learn, even if that might mean you have a few setbacks along the way. Stepping into a tougher course where you're not guaranteed an easy A may stretch you in a way that will prepare you for future challenges. Show a little bit of kindness to yourself when you don't get that A and a little bit of humility when you do. Reflect on what you can learn from each class beyond the grade. Sign up for challenging courses.

ACADEMICS INSIGHT #7: *THE SYSTEM ISN'T RIGGED, BUT SOMETIMES IT'S NOT FAIR*

Despite all this chatter about grades, you might recall examples of where peers got into universities without being academic superstars. Is the admissions system rigged for certain individuals and, if so, why bother working hard? Highly selective admissions isn't a fair process. Teachers may grade based on unconscious bias and how they feel toward a student. Students face systemic inequities from day one. Even gaps in how kindergarteners perform on cognitive (e.g., reading and writing) and noncognitive skills (e.g., self-control) have much to do with socioeconomic factors.[4] If you have poor parents, you're probably going to have unfair disadvantages before you even get to first grade. That's not fair. Admissions officers recognize this and, while they could do more, many are deeply engaged in outreach to students who previously would have been shut out of attending such institutions.

Has a student ever received an admit letter supported by strong influence from the college's fundraising office? Yes. It costs a lot to run a university and so college presidents have to consider that a large gift, say $100 million, that will support the scholarship of thousands of professors and students for years to come might be worth the acceptance of a donor's B+ student. However, these cases—as unfair as they may be—are few and far between. Rare is the case that a university accepts a student who is not capable of doing the work, no matter how many dollar signs there are.

Even in those rare cases, just because one student gets a spot does not mean they are the reason you will not. With acceptance rates dipping below 10 percent, space is limited, and no one is entitled to a spot. If you have three classmates applying to the same school, just because one gets in doesn't mean they took "your" spot. Rather than focusing on others, focus on yourself.

PRACTICE: REMEMBER THE LOCUS OF CONTROL

Take a moment to write down the things you have control over and the things that you don't. You will likely quickly realize how little you have control over—from how someone reacts to you, to what your peers are saying, to what the admissions officers are going to do. Then take a deep breath and focus on those areas that you do have control over. Stop wasting time over the things that you do not.

ACADEMICS INSIGHT #8: *ADMISSIONS OFFICERS PAY*
CLOSE ATTENTION TO CONTEXT

Admissions officers focus on your grades and track record within your context and what else is happening around you. They understand that you don't live in a bubble, and that there are many things outside your control. For example, when natural disasters strike, as they have around the globe, your grades may suffer a bit. Admissions officers recognize that a term of uncharacteristically lower grades during a time when your community had no electricity or you were evacuated due to flooding is a product of real life.

The holistic review process means admissions officers are reviewing everything in the context of your environment. Many times, I have responded to a well-intentioned parent wanting to know if we *really know* that their child's school is "so much harder" than the neighboring school and that their child's A is "so much more meaningful" than the A of their neighbor's child. In fact, admissions officers spend months and months visiting high schools around the world to learn more about the real context in which students live and learn. Driving around the school's neighborhood can offer a lot of information. Is the school situated high on a mountain in a bucolic neighborhood, requiring that its students have their own mode of transportation? Is the school situated near a busy city intersection where students must navigate commuters and the general public daily to get through the front doors? Does the school have metal detectors? Does the school have large athletic facilities? Admissions officers can't go everywhere, however. In an April 2018 *New York Times* op-ed, Ozan Jaquette and Karina Salazar studied the high school visits for 150 colleges and universities and found that admissions officers visit public schools in more affluent neighborhoods more often than in less affluent areas.[5] Increasingly, however, universities are putting greater resources for admissions officers to visit areas which previously did not "send" a lot of their students to these highly selective institutions, representing different community-based organizations or one of the schools listed by Better Make Room, an initiative started by former First Lady Michelle Obama to encourage those historically underserved to apply to four-year universities.

Some things are even more personal. Admissions officers won't know these things unless you tell them. If you get a concussion that takes you out for weeks, or you get mono, or a loved one passes away, update your file or include that in your application. This is not to say you can or should "excuse" everything (e.g., "I got a bad grade in Algebra 2 because I broke my pinky toe"—unless that pinky toe got infected and spread or something, of course), but admissions officers can better contextualize your As-turned-to-Bs.

Moreover, it is true that not all As are created equal. Students and parents anxiously want to know if admissions officers pay attention to the nuances of each high school and its programs. They do. Where you go to school does matter—but not necessarily in the way you think. You don't have to go to the fanciest school or the one listed in *U.S. News & World Report* as one of the top in the country. Rather, admissions officers pay attention to what you have done in the school that you happen to be at, whether it is a prestigious private school with a campus that rivals that of some universities or a public school ten hours away from the closest city.

An A alone is insufficient to determine academic readiness. Admissions officers recognize that As are not easy to come by at certain schools. Admissions officers spend more time than you might think pouring through your school's report. They work with counselors to ensure that the information in these reports makes sense so that they understand what a "Capstone Project" means or whether the IB diploma is an option. They review whether students performing at the highest levels in your school are dually enrolled at the local community college. They look at how many AP courses your school allows. While admissions officers may miss something (they are only human), they take great care to be thorough.

They pay attention to the curriculum and rigor offered at your high school. Most institutions will be looking to see that you have received a certain number of years of instruction in core academic areas. They want to know that you are ready and able to delve quickly into a wide range of subjects: math, English, science, social science, and a foreign language. Check each institution to see what courses and how many years of study are required; the level you achieve also matters.

If you live in suburban Denver, you may have more access to AP-level courses than if you live in rural Wyoming. They wouldn't expect an AP course from a student if none were offered. However, before you convince your parents to move you to rural Wyoming to "increase your chances" of getting in without taking any AP courses, remember that it is not that simple. Admissions officers are reviewing what you have done with the opportunities you've had and how you've taken them to the next level. Are you challenging yourself?

Different schools grade differently. They offer different courses. A 4.0 in one school may mean something entirely different at another. In some schools, a 4.0 is rare; in another, 25 percent of students receive a 4.0. In 2015, Berkeley received 37,200 applicants with a GPA of 4.0 and higher.[6] Admissions officers turn to other pieces of evidence to support the A, such as through rank and place in class. This does not mean that all valedictorians are accepted or that anyone outside the top 15 percent stands no chance. However, class rank may offer more context as to how you are performing vis-à-vis your peers. Your 4.0 might place you at the top 1 percent or the top 30 percent of the class. What admissions officers are trying to do is to really understand you as a person and your environment. Don't feel like you have to be a super-hero or a paragon of perfection. Help the admissions officers understand your situation and your story.

PRACTICE: CONSIDER YOUR NARRATIVE

Everyone has a story. Everyone also makes up stories about other people and tries to fill in the holes when they have an incomplete picture. Rather than have the admissions officers try and fill in the holes about you based on limited information, consider what your story is and what you want to share. Make sure that it is your story, one that is authentic and speaks to who you are. Provide information and details that you feel are relevant to share. Take a journal and write it down. Then go back and circle the words and themes that keep popping up so that you can start to streamline and tighten up your story.

ACADEMICS INSIGHT #9: *CLASS RANK AND PLACE IN CLASS MATTER*

As much as academic institutions like to protest magazine rankings, they are still subject to scrutiny from the public, the media, their trustees, and their alumni regarding their prestige and reputation. For example, the well-known *U.S. News & World Report Best Colleges Rankings* takes into consideration how many of the enrolled first-year class graduated in the top 10 percent of their class. That means universities need to attract and enroll students who are performing well relative to their peers. Before you get angry at these institutions for being exclusive, performance relative to peers can offer evidence as to your potential to work at the highest levels of rigor and with other top-performing peers around the world. At these institutions, you are likely not going to be the BMOC ("big man on campus") anymore. Whether you're considered the smartest kid in your school or not, one of the reasons we imagine you are applying to these highly selective institutions is so that you can be surrounded by even smarter students.

Highly selective institutions will be paying attention as to whether your rank is weighted or unweighted—meaning that, for example, an A in a higher-level class is weighted more toward your GPA than an A in a standard-level one. Because of context, admissions officers recognize your rank might have been impacted by the fact that you transferred in from a school with a different grading system or that you didn't have access to the same preparation as others.

Some schools offer clear ranks; others give estimates. Increasingly, schools do not rank as a way to reduce anxiety and competition, and some, due to parental pressure to obscure ranks so not as to give away that their child might not be performing at the top. Regardless, admissions officers—at least the well-trained, thoughtful ones—do not penalize the student for what their school policies are. Whether or why a school chooses a particular grading or ranking policy is not your decision. Admissions officers will take what they are given by secondary schools and review your rank and placement as best they can. They may look at past year performances and record to help estimate where in the class you might fit (top 25%? bottom 50%?), or they may look to other pieces of evidence, such as the recommendation letters.

Class rank helps admissions officers to understand the rigor of your curriculum. Your rank might be slightly lower because you took higher-level courses than someone else did. Class rank is not simply an indicator of performance vis-à-vis others. Remember that Stanford, with its sub-5% acceptance rate, has to reject hundreds of valedictorians each year. Playing "mean" and "edging out your competition" is not a healthy nor a kind nor a productive thing to do.

PRACTICE: TRY CONFIDENT HUMILITY

Chasing after a class rank will win you no favors or friends. Your teachers will be frustrated when they recognize that your "passion to learn" is simply motivated by the desire to beat out your classmates. Even if you are already pretty pleased with your class rank, being overly confident or arrogant about it comes through. Consider what it might feel like to practice confident humility—to be confident in your abilities and potential to do well, but not to the detriment of others. What might it be like to have the confidence to stay open to growth and learning—and to support others around you so that they also do better. Consider what it might be like to reframe a zero-sum game into one in which you can lift everyone around you—and yourself—up.

ACADEMICS INSIGHT #10: *BE GENUINELY CURIOUS*

While admissions officers are looking for whether you've challenged yourself, they are also looking for other pieces of evidence, from recommendation letters to essays to interviews, that shed more light on your attitude toward and engagement with deeper learning. It doesn't matter whether you have found the one topic you want to study forever or not. Admissions officers are trying to see if you're the one who has pushed your classmates to another level of learning, or if you've demonstrated independent thinking through a project, or if you're a committed scholar who wants to go beyond the textbook. They want to see genuine evidence that you're ready to take it up a notch. You cannot fake genuineness, no matter how much money you pay someone to help. Indicators of genuine curiosity suggest that you might be the kind of student their faculty is looking for: academically ready and intensely and unashamedly curious about themselves, other people, and the world around them.

PRACTICE: ADOPT A BEGINNER'S MIND

Recall what it was like to be a kid when school subjects were cool and new. For the next week, take one topic that you feel like you know, and look at it as if it were new to you. Imagine that you're learning about it for the first time and see what new or different things you notice. Take one or two classes that focus on things you're really interested in.

Chapter Twelve

Testing

Everyone's Favorite Saturday Pastime

Your favorite part of the college application: SATs and ACTs. For some of you, this might be the first time you're really hearing about how the SATs and ACTs are considered in the holistic review process. For others of you, your parents may have been priming you for this ever-important test since you were five. There has been much debate and discussion over its role, its importance, and its validity. The hype around these tests and how much they matter can lead to many a student passing out on top of their sharpened number 2 pencils.

Let's take a look at what is true and what is not about the "testing" component, and how admissions officers review testing and some practices to help keep you on the right track.

TESTING INSIGHT #1: *SATS AND ACTS STILL MATTER TO SOME INSTITUTIONS.*

While SAT/ACT scores are not indicators of your intelligence, they may provide additional data points. Whether colleges will eventually go "test-optional" or not remains to be seen, but studies consistently find a correlation between socioeconomic status and testing. However you might feel about them, they are still a part of the admissions process at many institutions.

The College Board advises that it is the combination of both grades and SAT/standard testing that help predict college performance. As Harvard College admissions director Marilyn McGrath noted, they "help us calibrate a student's grade."[1] A perfect SAT alone won't get you in, especially if your transcript is full of Cs. In those cases, admissions officers might wonder: 1) do you have a learning difference that might have impacted class performance; 2) are you working to your potential; or 3) are you a really good test taker, but not putting the work into class? If you score really low on the board testing but have stellar grades, admissions officers might wonder: 1) are you a bad test taker; 2) did you have an off day; or 3) does your school give out As?

For many schools, SAT/ACT scores are used as a calibration of academic record, and magazine rankings still use these scores as indicators of a university's prestige and reputation, and ultimately, their ranking. In 2016, the *U.S. News & World Report* counts SAT/ACT as 65 percent of the "student selectivity" scores.[2] By tweaking a few points, institutions can creep up the "best of" ladder list. Going test-optional might result in a higher average, since students tend to report scores only if they performed well.[3]

PRACTICE: PREPARE AND BE PATIENT

If you have to take these standardized tests, prepare for them. This is not to say that you have to spend every spare minute studying for the SAT or ACT, but being prepared can help ease some of those last-minute stressors. Find out the dates of the tests and locations—and sign up for them. Take a test prep book out of the library or watch a few Khan Academy videos. Don't expect that your scores will jump up immediately. Practice patience and know that change will happen when you put in the time and care.

TESTING INSIGHT #2: *SAT AND ACT SCORES ARE IMPACTED BY PARENTAL EDUCATION, INCOME, AND RACE/ETHNICITY, AND ADMISSIONS OFFICERS RECOGNIZE THIS*

At its inception, the SAT (Scholastic Aptitude Test) was meant as an equalizer. Instead of relying on achievement tests that could "favor rich boys whose parents could buy them top-flight high school instruction," the "father" of the SAT and former Harvard president James Bryant

Conant offered the aptitude test as a solution.[4] Of course, it's now been shown that this aptitude test itself is impacted by things such as income and race. In a 2015 study by the Center for Studies in Higher Education at Berkeley, race was found to be a key influential factor on SAT score variations.[5] Socioeconomic factors also play a large role. According to the College Board, if your family has more money and your parents have more formal education, then you're more likely to do better. The results from College Board show a clear increase in income correlated with higher test results.[6] If your family makes more than $200,000 a year, you might score almost 400 points higher than your friend whose family makes less than $20,000. If one of your parents went to graduate school, you may score 300 points higher than your friend whose parents didn't go to college. If you identify as white or Asian American, you are also likely going to do better than if you identify as Hispanic or African American.[7] It doesn't make one of you innately smarter or "better" than the other. It's just that these factors may make a difference in scores. Over the course of the last several years, the College Board has been focusing some attention to embedded and implicit biases in these exams; for example, use of the word *regatta* makes assumptions of class and access.

Given this inequity, admissions officers at highly selective institutions are, for the most part, trained to recognize these nuances. Many spend time discussing the external factors that might influence an SAT score: geographic location, parental education, access to a testing site. They try to understand the context of your application so that your SAT or ACT scores are not viewed as a singular piece of evidence. A 1450 for you, given your school, may offer different information about your readiness than 1450 for a pen pal across the country.

Just because admissions officers acknowledge that inequities exist and that some students may face additional challenges to scoring high—or even accessing—the SATs or ACTs does not mean anyone has it easier. In 2018, a former member of the Texas board of education tweeted in response to a young biracial student who announced that he was matriculating to Harvard College, "Congrats. Were you admitted on merit or quota?" While you may have dropped your jaw at the audacity of this tweet, some of you may have heard similar comments. So-and-so got in because they are X, or they have it easier because of Y. Graciously, the young man tweeted back with a response simply stating a few of his other accomplishments. It seemed the board member overlooked the fact that the student was valedictorian, student body president, and a World Champion cheerleader with strong SAT scores, because of some perception that race, gender, or income might trump merit.[8]

Misperceptions are also made when someone questions why one student, say, a white student from a less-affluent, rural community, with a 30 ACT is admitted when a white student from an affluent suburban town with a 34 ACT score is not. Perhaps the rural kid didn't have access to ACT prep courses, or maybe they had to drive 100 miles to the test center. Or perhaps there is a case where two kids from the same high school had a 200-point difference on their SATs. If the one who scored higher doesn't get in, the automatic assumption is that the other one got in because of X. What many folks might not know is that the one who got in might have scored lower but, given their particular upbringing, that score is impressive in context.

Understanding context doesn't mean a student whose standardized testing raises concern about readiness gets a "pass" because of X, Y, or Z. At these selective levels, if a student, regardless of their background, has a low enough score to suggest they would struggle in the classroom, it is unfair to place the student in such a position. Nonetheless, it does not mean if you score a 1600 on the SAT that you're going to get in, or that if you score a 1300, you're not. As Jack Kent Cooke noted, "while high test scores are indicative of advanced academic ability, somewhat lower scores do not always indicate *lack* of advanced ability."[9] After all, preparation does matter. As we will see next, performance on these tests is highly correlated with levels of income and parental education. A lower score doesn't necessarily indicate that an individual is unprepared for college; rather, lower scores are often associated with lower levels of income and/or parental education.

PRACTICE: REFRAME EXPECTATIONS

Regardless of whether your family has plentiful or limited resources, stop to consider what the statistics suggest about how you should perform. Self-confirmation bias means we're susceptible to performing only up to what others (or we ourselves) expect. Instead, breathe, pause, and release those expectations. Remember that those expectations are born out of general statistics. You are not a statistic. Reframe these external expectations and keep in mind that you are not hostage to them. Focus on what you can control and do your best.

TESTING INSIGHT #3: *PREPARING FOR THE TEST MAY INCREASE YOUR SCORES, BUT NOT AS MUCH AS YOU THINK*

As with most things, the more you practice, the better you will do. Pre-2017, the $2 billion private test prep industry made a lot of money on you and your friends with promises of secret strategies to getting those extra points. The process of elimination and shortcuts have also become strategies. College Board president David Coleman, in fact, called those who provide these services "predators who prey on the anxieties of parents and children and provide no real educational benefit."[10] The Jack Kent Cooke Foundation analyzed the Education Longitudinal Study data and found that high-achieving students from the wealthiest families were more likely to have prep courses to take the test than their less affluent peers.[11] So is it worth it to sign up for those expensive courses? It's never a bad idea to practice and familiarize yourself with the exam. However, it wouldn't be the wisest use of money or time to overdo it. Despite test prep company claims, test prep seems to produce only a marginal increase in the scores on average, although it seems to have the highest impact on low-income students.[12]

In 2017, the College Board redesigned the SAT to better align with what you're actually learning, sending a bit of nervousness across the big industry built on strategies on how to take the test. For decades, these companies built curricula and hired folks who did well themselves to serve as experts. Now the test is requiring more application of knowledge. In efforts to equalize the playing field a bit, the College Board now partners with the free online Khan Academy to offer test prep. From their research, Khan Academy reports an average gain of 115 points with their courses.[13] A free online practice or two from Khan might be what you need to get you comfortable with, rather than obsessed about, these tests. After all, at this level of competitiveness, your score is not the be-all and end-all. In fact, some schools no longer require them.

PRACTICE: LET GO OF PERFECTION

Remember that a perfect score does not guarantee you anything. Instead of shooting for perfection, prepare the best you can to do the best you can that day. Perfection is not your end goal. Reflect on what it is like to let go of the need for perfection and focus on that satisfying feeling you get when you've done the best you can, regardless of the result.

TESTING INSIGHT #4: *SOME TOP INSTITUTIONS HAVE GONE "TEST-OPTIONAL," SUGGESTING THAT TESTING ALONE CANNOT PREDICT FUTURE SUCCESS*

Over seven hundred colleges and universities are now test-optional, even though they vary in their selectivity rates. In 2018, the University of Chicago made headlines as going test-optional as a way to be fairer, particularly given the known correlation with income. Some argue that testing is unfair and that eliminating it can help diversify the pool to more underrepresented students. Others may argue that testing isn't a good indicator of performance. The more cynical may argue that going test-optional is a way to drive up applications and lower admit rates. Yet others question if going test-optional allows institutions to skew the data and helps an institution to rise in the rankings with bumped-up reported test scores.[14] According to a study by the National Association for College Admission Counseling, going test-optional led to a 29 percent increase in applications to private universities and 11 percent to public universities. It also led to an increase in the number of underrepresented applicants. Students who didn't submit scores tended to have greater financial need, were less likely to receive scholarships, and had slightly lower high school grades.[15]

The College Board, which administers the SATs, argues that as high schools are disclosing less information to colleges about student rankings and grades—partly due to parental pressure to not make their kids feel badly or seem less competitive than their peers—the SATs and ACTs provide colleges with a barometer to indicate potential. For example, their own study reported findings that: 1) SAT scores in conjunction with grades are the best predictors of college-level success; 2) over time, test-optional placement actually leads to a decrease in racial and economic diversity; and 3) four times as many students now use the free Khan Academy than all the major commercial test prep companies combined.[16]

It is notable that some top test-optional institutions have seen little difference in graduation rates or GPAs between those who submit test scores and those who do not. It is also worth noting that students who continue on to graduate schools for medicine, law, business, or to get a PhD tend to have taken and submitted SATs or ACTs for their undergraduate studies.[17] Graduate school means more standardized testing as another hurdle, so whether you like it or not, the reality is, standardized testing might pop back into your life.

PRACTICE: GO BIG PICTURE

It is easy to get caught up in the minute details of how you perform on a test on one given day. Instead of having tunnel vision, take a step back and remember that in the holistic process, your score is only but one piece. Remember that five years from now, even one year from now, no one is going to ask you what you scored—or care. Picture yourself going 30,000 feet above and seeing the bigger picture about what you hope to accomplish, where you hope to be, and what kind of difference you want to make.

TESTING INSIGHT #5: *SAT II SUBJECT TESTS, APS, IBS, AND NATIONAL AND INTERNATIONAL TESTING MATTER*

If you are looking at highly selective institutions, you're probably taking some higher-level courses, like APs or IBs or honors, if your school offers them. If so, you might be also readying to take SAT II subject tests, APs, Regents, IBs, and the like. So even if you want to throw the SATs or ACTs out the window, there are other standardized tests that matter.

Institutions use the results of these exams to get a more nuanced understanding when evaluating your candidacy. Not all schools require them, while others require specific exams. At Princeton, for example, if you're applying to the engineering school, it is "strongly recommended" that you achieve a high score on the physics or chemistry and math I or II subject tests. This is because throwing someone in there with little evidence as to a strong foundation in these areas will likely result in them failing or dropping out. No one wants that. These scores allow the admissions officer to better understand what your A means outside of your school environment. This is the same with your APs, IBs, O-Levels, and state Regents.

These exams also may benefit you in terms of the kind of credit that you might receive depending on the score. This means that you might either get real college credit or be able to bypass a certain class to take a more advanced level once you matriculate. Knowing that you don't have to repeat a course or can get credit likely makes the motivation to take these standardized tests more compelling. Demonstrating mastery of a subject that you just passed can be beneficial for you.

PRACTICE: DON'T ASSUME

Like anything, we often make assumptions about others and what is happening around us. This can lead us into a tailspin of thinking that is not useful and could even be harmful. Instead, when you are given information, pause and consider from where that information is coming and don't hesitate to dig deeper and ask, *what is really going on?* Don't make assumptions that a school only cares about X or Y because of something you read or something someone else said; ask. You might be surprised at what you find.

TESTING INSIGHT #6: *SAT/ACTS MATTER MORE THAN YOU WANT, BUT LESS THAN YOU THINK*

If you've ever been on College Confidential—and I bet more than a few of you have—you have probably seen the thread where students ask others to "chance me." Here they write down their entire lives, providing a list of their GPAs, their activities, their accolades, their testing. They wish the general public to tell them how likely they are to be admitted into said institution. These threads are terribly harmful and useless for many reasons. First, the presumption is that admissions officers review such statistics without any consideration of context. Second, any institutional priorities or areas of specialty are overlooked. Third, relying on the feedback of other students and their family members who may be hoping to rattle the nerves of others in order to increase their own or their child's chances is unwise. Fourth, the general public hasn't had experience reading files. Fifth, the "statistics" they offer perpetuate the misinformation that a school values only certain metrics, for example, test scores.

Such perceptions can make it seem as if SAT or ACT scores are the most important metrics. SAT scores do count more than you probably want; however, in reality, they aren't weighed as heavily as you might think. In fact, in the majority of institutions, there is no magic weighting system when it comes to these tests. Many schools "superscore" to put you in the best light possible and accept the highest of your test "sittings." Beyond that, many don't bother recalculating your SAT score, but still use them to calibrate the other pieces of evidence in your application. What they're trying to gauge is: Can you handle the work? As Duke admissions dean Christoph Guttentag noted, "Academic credentials become much less important once they're in the range of academic competitiveness."[18] As discussed, these tests are only one part of an overall picture. There is much more.

PRACTICE: DRINK WATER

Studies show that even your brain can get dehydrated. And if your brain is dehydrated, your cognitive performance may be compromised. Studies have shown that drinking water has a positive impact on children's cognitive performance, especially those that require speeded processing or memory.[19] In other words, stay hydrated to do better on standardized tests (and other things). Drink water (and eat breakfast) morning of your SATs or ACTs, even if you're nervous and you don't feel like it. Your brain will be more ready, and you'll be in a better mood.

TESTING INSIGHT #7: DON'T WASTE YOUR TIME ONLY STUDYING FOR OR RETAKING THE SATS/ACTS

For some students, it might seem like they have been training for this three-hour exam their entire lives. You may have heard of the kid who started taking practice exams at age five or someone else who has retaken the exam five times. Those kids are also likely really stressed out and not very happy. Not many people enjoy spending all their free time studying for standardized tests. Even though SATs/ACTs might seem like everyone's favorite Saturday pastime, trust me: they're not.

Unless you want to major in SATs/ACTs or put "SAT/ACT test taker" as your first extracurricular activity, don't overfocus on this one part of your college application. Instead, consider what other areas of study excite you, spark your curiosity, or light a fire in your belly. If you feel you had an off day, take them again . . . but not too often. After all, if you've taken the test six times, admissions officers may start to wonder why. Usually, differences in scores, if any, are so minute that it is not worth hours and hours of your time, time that you could have spent elsewhere.

As with the holistic process, because your scores are only one part, chances are if you spend your Saturdays doing something else, you might learn a new skill or refine an existing one, explore something in-depth, or help someone else. Those are the crucial, complementary pieces that help to bring your SAT/ACT scores and other standardized testing to life. And admissions officers at these institutions are looking for far more than a number.

PRACTICE: DETACH

While grit and perseverance are important, there is a fine line between sticking to something and being so stubborn that you only focus on one thing. To get your score by 10, you might think that you need to do everything to make sure you reach your goal. Being too attached to one goal or expectation can do more harm than good. Knowing that this goal of "perfection" is unnecessary, notice what it might be like to detach that expectation and pay attention to your blind spots.

Chapter Thirteen

Leadership

Queen Bees, Worker Bees, and Busy Bees

I have responded to many of you asking, "I don't particularly like MUN [or fill-in-the-blank], but my [fill-in-the-blank] said that top colleges require it. What should I do?" While MUN is a worthy and valuable activity for those who get excited about deliberating on global policy, it doesn't excite every one of you. And that's okay. What is less okay is for you to pretend that you do because someone told you that you had to list it on your application.

Let's take a look at the "leadership" component with a few insights that reveal the reality of how admissions officers review leadership, and some practice to get you on track.

LEADERSHIP INSIGHT #1: *DON'T SIGN UP FOR THINGS ONLY BECAUSE YOU THINK COLLEGES REQUIRE THEM — THEY DON'T, AND YOU'LL REGRET PRETENDING YOU CARE*

Highly selective institutions are not looking for a laundry list of "Things You Must Do." The truth is there is no "perfect" compilation of activities. In fact, trying to contort yourself into what you think the university admissions officer wants is probably one of the last things you want to do. First, overthinking what a college wants is useless. You just won't know. Colleges want different kinds of people with different kinds of interests; they are looking for a constellation of individuals who will comprise a class. With a multitude of eyes and opinions reviewing your file, no amount of money can get you inside everyone's head at the moment of decision-making. Second, contorting yourself into someone you're not is exhausting. While it might be bearable for three years, you're going to find yourself extremely tired, lost, and resentful in short order. You may lose sight of what you're really excited about and what might allow you to nurture and cultivate your natural talents. For example, if you've signed up for debate only because someone on a website said that you needed to do so in order to be a competitive applicant at University X as a prelaw major (which typically doesn't even exist at highly selective liberal arts institutions), you might ignore the inner voice that says you would rather join the math team. You might end up a decent debater, but you might also end up missing out on fulfilling your potential as a star mathlete (which, ironically, would have been more compelling for admissions officers to see your natural talent, leadership, and verve in action).

Moreover, this can have a longer-term impact on your happiness and even career choices. How many of you know an adult who "regrets" not doing things when they were younger or who is currently in a job that seems to give them more headaches than anything else? While many are in jobs out of necessity (that is an entirely different book), many are in careers because they were told they were technically good at it, even if they derived little meaning from it. This lack of engagement impacts how we show up at work. What happens is that many of us "cover," hiding a part of who we really are to contort ourselves to fit in. A 2013 study from Deloitte noted that 61 percent of adult workers "cover," or mask, at least one part of themselves: 1) appearance (e.g., "mainstream" dress); 2) affiliation (e.g., behaviors associated with stereotypes of being female; 3) advocacy (e.g., refrain from expressing concerns); and 4) association (e.g., contact with particular group members).[1] If you start covering yourself now, you are more likely to cover yourself later, potentially negatively impacting your engagement with your future work and even career choice.

However, this is not to say that you should give up the minute things seem difficult. Pretending to be someone you're not is very different than sticking through things that are challenging in the moment—even in those moments when you want to give up. Leaders demonstrate perseverance, grit, and a stick-to-itiveness. According to Angela Lee Duckworth, grit is: "Passion and perseverance for long-term goals." Those who emerge as leaders—whether out front or from the back—are those who don't give up the minute things get tough.

PRACTICE: ALIGN YOUR STRENGTHS

Positive psychology suggests that when we are doing things that work to our natural strengths, we tend to be more engaged, perform better, and experience greater well-being. Reflect on those things that seem to come easily to you, rather than dismissing them. What might seem "stupid" to you, may be someone else's Achilles' heel. For example, if you think humming a tune on key is not rocket science, for a lot of people, it might as well be. Write down those areas in which you have demonstrated a natural strength or for which you have a particular liking, and then identify different opportunities that might allow you to play out those strengths. If you love to hum a tune on key, perhaps join the choir, produce music, explore music from different countries, volunteer to play music at a senior citizens' home, or design a robotic harmonica. The point is that the possibilities are endless, and you will find greater joy and authenticity when you are doing things that allow you to play to your strengths.

LEADERSHIP INSIGHT #2: *TRUE LEADERSHIP REQUIRES GRIT AND SELF-REFLECTION*

Leaders demonstrate the willingness and ability to move forward when they are challenged, and the ability to face setbacks and willingness to fail. Admissions officers are trying to find pieces of evidence about your capacity to do so. Are you jumping from activity to activity? Or have you stuck with a few things, even when times were tough? Maybe your club lost an advisor or you faced an injury. Whether or not you had the title of president, how did you help and motivate others to get past the tough times? This quality of leadership is important not only for your college application but also to help fulfill your potential. Duckworth notes that the two ingredients necessary for success are grit and effort, without which potential never translates into a talent or strength.[2]

When looking for "leadership," admissions officers are looking for evidence that you've demonstrated a level of grit and commitment to something. They aren't looking for one thing, but are checking to see if you give up the minute things get tough or you get bored. After all, there will be many times in college—and in life—when things will be tough. Are you someone who shows independence and leadership in overcoming these setbacks, or would you call home every time there is a chance of "failure?" Title or no title, do you guide others through those challenging times?

Stick-to-itiveness is important for success and leadership. Yet there is a fine line between grit born out of purpose and stubbornness stemming from fear. Leadership is about not following the crowd telling you that you "have to." It is about discerning when it is time to move on without fearing failure. Effective leaders tend to have a practice of reflection. Why are you doing what you're doing? What is your leadership style? Do you lead from the front, middle, or back? What might it feel like to step outside your comfort zone? What might it feel like to fail?

PRACTICE: ALIGN YOUR PASSIONS

Grit is easier when you believe in what you're doing. You're more likely to remain committed and battle through those tougher times if you feel deeply about that activity or purpose. Your passion doesn't always have to align with your strengths. Passion can compensate, but not replace talent. For example, if you cannot hum a tune to save your life but have a deep passion for it, you might not get the lead role in the spring musical, but you might join the general chorus. The reward is your personal growth and joy. People—and admissions officers—value authenticity because it's a sign that you are willing to go for things for the experience rather than just the end result.

LEADERSHIP INSIGHT #3: *DROPPING AN ACTIVITY OR A POSITION DOES NOT NECESSARILY MEAN FAILURE*

Admissions officers often get worried questions from students who have discovered a new passion mid-high school, but are afraid to start something new because it means that they might have to give something else up. They fear that switching a sport or a musical instrument midstream is a sign of failure. As a result, many either keep going with the unhappy comfortable, leading to a missed opportunity and resentment, or add on the newfound passion, only to overstretch themselves with mediocre performance with both engagements.

Leadership is knowing when to give up. Before you do so, however, it is important to first reflect on why. Are you simply tired? Or it is because you recognize that your commitment to that activity has gone from a desire to learn and impact to reluctant obligation and résumé padding?

I recall a young man who was voted head of his senior class. The president of the student body is a position that many of you may dream about. This young man passed on the job. Why? He recognized the gender inequity in positions of "power" at his school and so deferred his role to the elected vice head, a female classmate. He didn't just give up; he continued to support the newly elected head, acting as *her* vice head. He did so not to "look good" but acted with authenticity and intention—he felt it was more impactful in the long run to shift the unhealthy dynamic than to have something to write on his college application.

PRACTICE: LEARN TO SAY NO

We are often taught to be obedient, and to say yes to every request made of us, even if we might absolutely hate an activity or find our health and happiness suffering. Learning to have boundaries and when to say no when you need to can be extremely empowering and lead to a healthier balance of your commitments. Saying no with thought and reflection is not the same as being a dilettante or a quitter. In fact, it often takes more courage to say no than to stay and be miserable.

LEADERSHIP INSIGHT #4: *QUEEN BEES ARE NOT JUST FAT BEES WITH FANCY TITLES; THEY WORK HARD*

At first glance, it may seem that highly selective institutions only look for "queen bees." Look at the words contained in some of their mission statements:

- Harvard: to educate the citizens and citizen-leaders for our society;
- Yale: to educate aspiring leaders worldwide who serve all sectors of society; and
- Dartmouth: to prepare the most promising students for a lifetime of learning and of responsible leadership.

You get the idea.

Does that mean only presidents of debate teams get in? Of course not. (Imagine going to a school with all presidents of debate teams—

you wouldn't get a word in!) Sure, leadership titles may reflect your ability to lead, and the trust, respect, and rapport you have with your peers, teachers, and communities. Yet admissions officers are not blinded by a shiny title, and neither should you be. Making up a club so that you can claim to be "founder and president" (when the club has three members—yourself and two besties) is not particularly notable to a trained admissions officer. Admissions officers have seen one too many websites easily designed on a free platform that make a three-person club seem like it has three hundred members.

True queen bees demonstrate leadership by their visible impact. Queen bees work hard. What does impact mean? It is evidence that the group you lead has made a difference in someone else's life. This might be something tangible (e.g., creating a community garden) or not (e.g., fostering a greater sense of community among senior citizens). It might be that you were the queen bee who challenged the status quo or reinvigorated interest in a club. It doesn't have to be the "biggest thing since sliced bread," but it does need to be genuine and authentic engagement.

Not everyone can be a queen bee, and certainly no one can be a queen bee in every hive. If you are the head of ten clubs, admissions officers will wonder if: 1) you're lying; or 2) if you could ever follow. True leadership involves leading from the front as much as leading from the back.

PRACTICE: LEAD AS YOU WOULD FOLLOW AND BUILD TRUST

Having a title isn't the be-all and end-all. Admissions officers can sense when someone focuses more on the title they hold than on what they actually do. When you get that title, consider how you would like to be led. What qualities you want to cultivate. How to motivate others, bring clarity to purpose, and offer a sense of unity. Cultivate trust with those you lead by allowing them the space to take risks, say "silly" things, and make mistakes without punishing them or calling them out unnecessarily.

LEADERSHIP INSIGHT #5: *WORKER BEES ARE JUST AS IMPORTANT IN ENGAGEMENT AND LEADERSHIP*

Author Susan Cain noted that the call for leaders from elite institutions often gets misconstrued as the requirement to be an extroverted figure of "authority and dominance . . . who 'can order other people around.'"[3] This misconception places undue pressure on you and your classmates to put on a bubbly, outgoing face to rack up the titles. While Cain suggests that admissions officers are limited in their definition of leader and "fail to define leadership as 'making advances in solving mathematical problems' or 'being the best poet of the century,'"[4] many officers travel the world trying to get out the message that they seek students who have a sense of greater purpose in service rather than simply a call to status. Yet it seems their message often gets lost in the cacophony of rumors fueled by other sources.

Leaders consider when they need to be the queen bee and when they need to be one of the worker bees. The ability to collaborate and work well in teams is a sought-after leadership skill. A 2014 Stanford study showed that people who work together in a more collaborative way express greater enjoyment, interest, perseverance, engagement, performance, and intrinsic motivation for the task.[5]

Your capacity to make a true impact might lie less in having the title of president than in being a key team player. Plays don't get produced without a tech crew. Orchestras don't make music without an ensemble. Admissions officers look at your record to see if you have the ability to play well with others, to take direction from others, and to lead from within and behind.

There is no formula to making your engagement "look good." Genuine engagement and teamwork comes through not only in what you list as your extracurricular activities but through how you speak about them, what others say about your involvement, and the evidence of your impact. Most admissions officers are trained to carefully review for quality, not quantity.

PRACTICE: LEARN TO FOLLOW AND STOP TRYING TO WIN

Some of the best leaders are also some of the best followers. They understand what it is like to follow and roll up their sleeves and do the hard work. They also know how to work in teams. Rather than trying to compete with others to become a one-person show or trying to prove you're the bee's knees, stop trying to win. Pay attention to all the moments during the day where you try to win when it's not really a competition (e.g., having the last word with your brother). Then stop trying to win. Say thank you, and let go.

LEADERSHIP INSIGHT #6: *ADMISSIONS OFFICERS DON'T JUST WANT BUSY BEES WHO NEVER SLEEP*

Students often ask, "is it better to excel in one thing or do many things?" There is no one answer. It depends on how you want to make an impact. Like many of their peers, Harvard notes,

> Some students . . . present compelling cases because they are more "well-rounded," having contributed in many different ways to their schools or communities. Still other successful applicants are "well-lop-sided" with demonstrated excellence in one particular endeavor. . . . Like many colleges, we seek to admit dynamic, talented, and diverse students who will contribute significantly to the education of their classmates.[6]

At the most highly selective institutions, the most successful candidates are engaged in more than one thing. That isn't to say if you are a Rubik's cube savant, you won't get in. But if that's *all* you do and nothing else, chances are that the admissions officers will wonder whether you are a one-note wonder. After all, these institutions are places with so many opportunities to explore. They don't want empty multimillion-dollar labs; they want students who are ready to dive in.

On the other hand, if you're piling things on and find yourself having to add ten more pages to your "résumé," you're probably over-doing it. It isn't difficult for seasoned admissions officers to see that your pages of activities are more words than genuine, deep engagement where you are making a true impact or honoring your real passions.

You might get the sense that if you are not always busy, you are being indolent, unproductive, or going to fail. You rush from activity to activity, and might even take pride in the fact that you don't start homework until 10:00 p.m., and are able to pull all-nighters or function with only 3–4 hours of sleep. The seeming importance of "busyness" is not a new phenomenon. In fact, as Danish philosopher Kierkegaard said hundreds of years ago, "Of all ridiculous things the most ridiculous seems to me, to be busy—to be a man who is brisk about his food and his work. . . . What, I wonder, do these busy folks get done?" After all, if everything is important, then is anything really important? If you simply pile on the activities, you might end up overstretched and perceived as the student who is busy for the sake of being busy.

Here's what the science tells us: The teenage brain needs 8–10 hours of sleep, yet only 15 percent of you get enough rest during school nights.[7] Sleep is not a luxury; it's essential. Studies have shown that a lack of sleep raises your risk for depression, suicide, and substance abuse. Almost 50 percent of you who sleep four hours or fewer a night express feeling sad or hopeless, as compared to the 19 percent of you who sleep more.[8] Driving with less than four hours of sleep puts you at the same risk of crashing as driving with double the legal alcohol level limit.[9] The CDC notes a lack of sleep reduces concentration by 23 percent and memory by 18.2 percent.[10]

To make sure your brain is developing properly, especially your prefrontal cortex—the area responsible for higher-executive functioning, complex thinking, decision-making, and emotional regulation—get some sleep. Your brain repairs during this time of rest. To do better in school, increase your memory and focus, and better control your emotions—sleep. Sleep every night. You cannot "make up" for it during the weekends. Your body doesn't work that way.

Not sold yet because you'd rather risk feeling sad than getting a B+ on that math exam? We recognize that the pressure to study, study, study seems omnipresent. In South Korea, for example, students are known to nod off during the day at "regular school" because they spend an additional 3–4 hours at a hagwon, an intense after-school program, before starting homework at 10:00 p.m. and getting to bed at 3:00 a.m. The rare student is the one who eschews the hagwon and engages in extracurricular activities for fun. While the short-term results may be an A, the long-term damage is more sobering. One study showed the negative impact a lack of sleep had on South Korea teenagers' academic performance, exhibiting behaviorally induced insufficient sleep syndrome (BISS), "voluntary, chronic sleep restriction,"[11] caused by long working hours and prioritizing other activities (like studying or engaging in activities). BISS unsurprisingly leads to daytime fatigue and is associated with poor academic performance.[12] Another study found that teenagers suffering from BISS reported greater suicidal ideation, depression, and insomnia.[13]

And don't think skipping meals also helps. The CDC has reported that breakfast-skipping and an inadequate intake of fruits and vegetables are associated with lower grades, decreased cognitive performance, and ability to process complex information.[14]

If you're hoping to be an effective leader inside or outside of the classroom, sleep.

PRACTICE: DISCONNECT AND SLEEP

Having technology and electronic devices in the bedroom can be devastating to your health and quality of sleep. Your brain needs that time to repair itself and to transform your short-term learning into long-term memory—like those things you likely spent all day trying to cram. The blue light radiating from your phone can impair your memory, focus, and performance when you sleep. Instead of trying to compete with your peers about who gets the least amount of sleep, ramp up the competition and see who gets the most sleep. Aim for 8–10 hours. Your brain needs it. Your test scores may improve. You may become nicer.

Chapter Fourteen

Accolades

Someone Thinks You're Special

While admissions officers operate on an honor system that what you say about your work is true, they also look for evidence about who you are beyond what you say. After all, many of you probably are tougher on yourselves than you need to be. Most highly selective admissions offices will require some sort of recommendation from at least one person who knows you well and can speak to your performance outside the classroom, your character, and your potential.

Let's take a look at a few insights that reveal the reality of how admissions officers review "accolades," and some practices to get you on track.

ACCOLADES INSIGHT #1: *RECOMMENDATION LETTERS CAN HELP ARTICULATE YOUR ACCOMPLISHMENTS IN A WAY THAT YOU CANNOT*

You can say the most wonderful things about yourself, but it is even more believable when someone else says it, too. For example, if you say you climbed mountains both ways to get to school every day, admissions officers will be looking for evidence to support this claim. They will see if anyone, particularly those who should know your situation, offers information to back up your claim. These letters also provide additional support that can help articulate your story.

These letters help admissions officers understand who you are as a person and help share what makes you unique. It might be the way you handle yourself during class discussions, or perhaps how you comport yourself in a hotly contested debate of school policy. Whether the letter is from your school counselor or teachers, as MIT says,

> A well-written letter for an outstanding applicant can highlight impressive characteristics beyond his/her own self-advocacy. We are looking for people who have and will make an impact—the difference between a letter that supports and a letter that raves about a special student. [1]

What "special" means is different for every applicant, institution, and to the human beings who happen to be reading your file. From your school counselor, admissions officers are looking for who you are in the context of your school. What kind of an impact have you made there? What do your other teachers or the staff or students think about you? Are you the one who makes others feel better when they interact with you? Are you the one who challenges school policy for improvement? Are you the one who makes things happen behind the scenes without drawing much attention to yourself or asking for praise?

Admissions officers are also looking for how you compare to others in your school academically. While most institutions will not compare you specifically with any one student (e.g., you have a 3.8765, your mate has 3.8766), they *are* comparing you in a broader sense. How are you performing relative to the top cohort of the class? What is the depth of your contribution? What is the rigor of your course load as compared to other top students in your class? These questions help admissions officers understand how you might fare in an even more elite group at the university level. While you might currently be valedictorian, chances are you're going to be surrounded by a lot of other valedictorians in college and suddenly be "middle-of-the pack." What is your record vis-à-vis your peers and how you might handle setbacks?

From teachers, admissions officers are looking more in the context of the classroom. Your academic performance is of great importance. Part of your academic performance is evidence of your academic potential. How might you fare in an even more highly rigorous environment? What is the depth of your intellectual curiosity? Since professors want students with curiosity, the letters your teachers send can be useful sources of information to help admissions officers articulate those qualities that they can then use to create a case for your candidacy. Who are you in the classroom? Are you someone who pushes others to think deeply? Are you the one who elevates class discussions? Are you the one who grapples with the difficult questions in your writing? Are you someone who has taken the initiative to pursue a subject matter on your own, going above and beyond the requirements of the class?

Teachers generally become teachers because they love sharing knowledge. They get excited when their students get excited about Milton or Rousseau. They get less excited when students panic and negotiate for that one point on an exam. They recognize when students are in it for the joy of learning—even if the subject they are teaching is not your favorite—or in it for the grade.

If you recognize yourself as someone who might get overly anxious about those extra points, reflect as to why. Is it because there was an unfair grading practice, or because you "need" that A, not an A−? The minutia of a .07 difference in GPA matters far less than what a teacher says about who you are and who you might be in a classroom of other intellectual scholars.

PRACTICE: BE YOURSELF

Don't try to be anyone else or what you *think* other people want you to be. You cannot pretend 24/7, no matter how good an actor you are. Your recommenders observe you for days and months even when you think no one is watching you. They watch how you naturally engage—how you throw away your lunch tray or handle a classmate who drops their lunch tray. All these little moments are life. And in life, you are who you are.

ACCOLADES INSIGHT #2: *LETTERS OF SUPPORT MUST BE AUTHENTIC, OR THEY WILL BE DISMISSED*

Given the importance of these letters, you might start wondering whom you should ask to write them and what they might say. There have been more than a few cases of offers being rescinded because admissions officers discover that the letters were fabricated or written by non-school officials.

Some students are advised not to waive their rights so that they can see exactly what their teachers write. This is generally not advisable because when you do not waive your rights, admissions officers may wonder if the letter is not entirely truthful. If you or your family members wanted to see a copy, admissions officers may wonder if the writer censored their letter in some way. Because you wanted control over what they were saying about you, the admissions officer will question the veracity of the letter.

Well-meaning family members often put such pressure on teachers and counselors to only report the "best" things that it backfires. A colleague shared how one teacher disclosed to the admissions officer that the family was harassing her to write a letter in a particular manner to the extent that legal action was taken. Though the young man himself was not doing the harassing, the fact that his family tried to intimidate his teacher raised enough questions to keep admissions officers from admitting him. While this was an extreme case, it is not uncommon for students not to trust what their teachers will say. If so, consider how and why your everyday behavior might raise concerns. Admissions officers want the raw you. When teachers can speak to some of your flaws, it paints a fuller picture of a real person with the potential to grow.

PRACTICE: SHOW AUTHENTICITY

Authenticity is highly valued by universities that operate on the honor system. They trust you to do your own homework, take your own tests, and abide by a code of conduct. Similarly, they are going to want to see the real, authentic you, not an overly polished version of you. Recognize there are areas to work on and that such imperfections make you who you are, a real human being with real feelings and real potential for real impact.

ACCOLADES #3: *CHOOSE YOUR RECOMMENDERS CAREFULLY, ASK NICELY, AND HELP THEM OUT*

Even though you cannot dictate what your teachers or counselors say about you, help your teachers out by sharing with them a little more about you and what is important to you. Not all of you attend schools where your counselors or teachers know you well or have the time to write. Help them help you. First, think about the teachers you like who also like you. Think about the teachers on whom you have made a real impression in your own learning and growth as a person and student. It might not be the teacher that gave you all As. Instead, reflect on those with whom you have a good rapport—those who know your name without you having to spell it for them. Maybe it's the teacher of the class where you did a terrible job on your first paper. Or it could be the one you go to for advice or the one you challenged about the theorem. If you don't know your teachers well, get to know a few of them. Really get to know them, not just to get a letter written. Find out why they're teaching this subject. Share why you're taking the course.

Know whether the institution to which you are applying requires recommendation letters from teachers in different academic disciplines. Some require a math/science teacher and an English/history teacher. Others may require a math/science teacher recommendation only if you're applying to an engineering program. Others don't care as long as it's from someone who teaches a core academic subject (math, English, science, social science, language). Most institutions prefer to get teacher recommendations from those who have taught you recently, particularly in the last two years of school. The reason is because you have changed and grown so much in the few short years of high school, and colleges are interested in your growth.

Once you've identified the teachers, ask them nicely. Give them plenty of lead time before the deadline. Ask them what would be beneficial—a résumé, a short statement of why you asked them, or a little blurb on some of your activities. Don't forget to thank them. They are writing not because they have to but because they want to. Honor that.

PRACTICE: PRACTICE KINDNESS

Don't assume that just because they are your teacher, they owe you something. Writing letters takes a long time, and many teachers spend countless hours this time of year to write on your behalf. Rather than simply shoving a deadline on them, be kind to them, and give them time and a reason why you are asking them to write.

ACCOLADES INSIGHT #4: *DON'T OVERDO IT WITH THE RECOMMENDATION LETTERS*

Some students pile on the recommendation letters. When universities say one or two, they really do mean one or two. Part of narrowing down who you want to write on your behalf is indicative of your judgment and ability to make decisions. Focusing your attention on the strongest letters is more important than the number of letters.

Some institutions will not say no to additional letters. Others will read them anyway, even if they don't like to. In some cases, an additional letter might make perfect sense. For example, if you play a significant role in a national club, and that club's advisor wants to write in support of you, that letter will likely add information about you not seen elsewhere. This is different than your congregation's pastor, whom you sort of know, whose letter is sweet but offers little more than that you're really nice. Admissions officers don't doubt you are, but that letter might not be particularly insightful or useful in the way you think it might. Others presume a fancy letterhead might do the trick, for example, from a senator or an alumnus who is a friend of your parents. Unless these folks really know you and can speak about you at a deeper level, these pro forma letters often get quickly reviewed as another attempt to bolster your application without substance.

When admissions officers say, "be judicious" about how many letters you provide beyond the required, they truly mean it. A colleague from a peer institution once revealed that they received twenty-seven letters of recommendation for one applicant. Before you scramble to see if you can even find twenty-seven people willing, note that the candidate wasn't successful. Twenty-seven was overkill.

PRACTICE: PRACTICE MODERATION

With letters, more is definitely not better. In fact, sometimes admissions officers actually get turned off if you try to submit too many letters, the majority of which don't actually offer any new or exciting information about you. Like with everything else, a little moderation can go a long way. Be judicious. Be discerning.

ACCOLADES INSIGHT #5: *INTERVIEWS ARE A CHANCE FOR YOU TO SHINE AND ASK QUESTIONS*

Interviews are another way to help admissions officers get a sense of who you are in a way that your letters cannot. Unrehearsed and conducted in different ways, by different people, and for different purposes, the interview often plays two roles: 1) to help the admissions officers get to know you from a different perspective; and 2) to sell you the institution.

First, the interview is a way for you to share things about yourself that you might not otherwise be able to do in written form. How you show up, the energy you bring when talking, or your knowledge about something might stand out. It is conversation and chance to offer stories behind your application, what really matters to you, and why you want to attend that institution.

On the other hand, the interview is also a chance for you to interview the representative to see if that institution is the right place for you. Be prepared to ask questions to better determine whether you want to call this place your alma mater. It is important, however, to remember that this one person doesn't represent every experience, and that it is up to you to do your homework.

PRACTICE: REFLECT ON FIT

Meditate on those qualities you feel best fit the institution at which you'll be interviewing. Take time to reflect on the types of environments in which you feel most at home. When asking your questions, listen for clues that suggest there might be a fit. Share how and why you see there is a fit. Tell stories. Be alive.

ACCOLADES INSIGHT #6: *INTERVIEWERS ARE OFTEN VOLUNTEERS, SO THANK THEM*

Some institutions may offer campus interviews with students who work for the institution. For others, interviews are conducted by volunteer alumni. These are alumni who have offered and dedicated their own time on behalf of their alma mater. In most cases, they do not work for the institution, are not paid by them, and do not actually make decisions on your application. Rather, their report provides additional insight to help the admissions officers know who you are and what you might be like if you get onto their beloved campus.

Because they tend to be volunteers, remember to thank them for their time. They don't have to be doing this, but they do it because they value their institution and are excited when other young people are excited about it. Also remember to keep their experiences in context. While the interview is a chance for you to ask about the institution to see if it is a place you want to attend, remember that some volunteers may have graduated decades ago and, thus, their experience is different from the one that you might have. Whether all positive or terribly negative, do your homework and ask around before deciding on an institution based on one person's experiences. Regardless, being prepared for the interview is important.

PRACTICE: PRACTICE GRATITUDE

Studies show that when we practice gratitude, we not only can improve our relationships with others, we also experience greater well-being. After every interview—or letter written—make sure to take a moment to thank that person. It doesn't have to be overly sugary or lengthy, but a simple "thank you" can speak volumes.

ACCOLADES INSIGHT #7: *BE PREPARED, BUT NOT TOO PREPARED*

For some of you, the idea of an interview might make you immediately freeze up. It is important to prepare, but not to overprepare. In preparation, know why you're applying to that institution. Don't go into an interview for an institution whose name you cannot pronounce or by declaring you have zero interest in living on the West Coast when said institution is on the West Coast. Know why you're applying and reflect on your intellectual pursuits and extracurricular engagements. Speak honestly about the things and people that matter to you.

Be careful of overpreparing. There is no need to internet-stalk your interviewer. There is no need to go prepared with a thirty-page dossier. Most interviewers will have no information about you beyond your name, high school, and basic contact information. The rest is up to the interviewer to ask and you to fill in. The interview is not the place to be talking about your SAT scores or your GPA. The admissions officers already have that information. Your interviewer might ask you, to give themselves some context, but otherwise they would rather know: What interests you? What would your friends say about you? What do you want to learn? Why do you want to go there?

Overpreparing can also make you sound too canned. Sometimes, if you practice too much about what the answer "should be," you are no longer listening to the question or truly engaging with your interviewer. Moreover, by being canned, your answers will sound so rehearsed that the interviewer might question the authenticity of the entire interview.

Interviews don't mean that you have to be super extroverted, but this is not the time to retreat. After all, you're your best cheerleader.

Stay true to your own style, but don't be shy about talking about yourself. This is your chance to share who you are beyond a piece of paper.

PRACTICE: LET STRESS WORK FOR YOU

Science shows that we need the right level of stress to motivate us. Too much stress can lead to burnout or being overwhelmed. Too little stress may lead to apathy. The right level of stress will motivate you to prepare for the interview with a reflection about your achievements and ready questions about fit. Reflect on the level of stress you have, and whether you need to find ways to lessen it or dial it up as needed. Get that stress to work for you so that you can work in peak performance.

Chapter Fifteen

Spirit

Showcase You, Don't Tell

Coming alive from a flat piece of paper is challenging. It's probably caused you many sleepless nights and heart palpitations. You may have heard admissions officers from these selective institutions say, "we want to get to know you beyond your grades and test scores." What they actually mean is that they want to get a better sense of what you might bring to the table beyond your GPA. They want to know who you are and what matters to you: your spirit.

Let's take a look at how and why admissions officers look at your "spirit," and some practices to get you on track.

SPIRIT INSIGHT #1: *LET ADMISSIONS OFFICERS MEET A COHERENT YOU, NOT A BUNCH OF NUMBERS OR WORDS*

At the top schools you are exploring, the majority of applicants will be, at least on paper, academically prepared. Your board scores and grades likely demonstrate capability and potential for growth. Your extracurricular activities and recommendation letters are positive. So how do admissions officers make the finer distinctions? They are looking at what matters to you, what your values are, what kind of a spirit you are. Are you someone who loves to help others? Are you a problem solver? Are you a rebel with a heart of gold?

It's not so much that you have to fit into one mold but that you have a personality beyond your grades. If you have dedicated your past seventeen years to crafting the "perfect" college application, that likely will come through. As human beings, admissions officers prefer to know that there is a human being behind the numbers rather than a robot checking off the boxes. They look for evidence of who you might be in a larger community, whether as a soccer-playing flutist or a mathematically inclined poetess. They want to see that you have been a presence of some sort at your school because such evidence suggests you might also contribute to the university. They honestly want to "meet" you, even if they cannot do so in person. One way that they do this is the one part of the application over which you have control: your essay.

You have probably been agonizing over your college essay. And while this isn't the only thing that will get you in—or out, it *is* an important part of this process. Your essays may be one of the first ways admissions officers will be "introduced" to you. When there are thousands of highly quantifiably qualified applicants, your story *can* help you stand out. The essays that stand out aren't necessarily the ones that are the most well-written or composed with the eye of a parent and the editing pen of a consultant. Rather, they are those that genuinely give a sense of your spirit and how you hope to contribute to the world, offering a coherency to you as a whole person.

Imagine when you meet someone new. You might get a sense of who they are through your conversation, but you get a fuller picture of their personality by how they interact with others, their actions, or what others have to say about them. Similarly, admissions officers are looking at every piece of your application and, hopefully, there will be some consistency and agreement as to who you are. Every now and then, admissions officers get applications where the student comes across as one way in their activities, and then some evidence that is inconsistent with who they first appeared to be pops up—what was "passion" is now "obsessive," "motivated" is now "hypercompetitive," and "leader" is now "domineering." When there is such a dissonance, the admissions officer's radar will go off: Who is the real person?

That said, most trained admissions officers recognize they cannot simply rely on words alone. After all, there have been cases where someone attempts to sabotage someone else with a terrible letter or accusation of some sort. Before you become paranoid about this, know that this is extremely rare. Moreover, admissions officers tend to have their radar up and so when something seems suspicious, they often will follow up on it—even if you don't know about it. They don't take anonymous letters at face value. They might call your counselor, for example, to check the veracity of any statement. The point is that even though you cannot control how others view or write about you, one thing won't "make or break" your candidacy. The important thing to remember is that admissions officers seek coherency, not a mismatch of character traits that says little about who you are or why they should care about you or want to get to know you more.

PRACTICE: LIVE OUT YOUR CORE VALUES

Don't be such a chameleon that you forget who you really are. Recall your core values and consider how you live them and how they show up in your life. For example, if you value hard work and grit, how does hard work and grit show up in your life? If it's courage, how does courage show up in the activities in which you choose to engage?

SPIRIT INSIGHT #2: *DON'T PRETEND*

Unless you're an axe murderer, admissions officers never deny a student because of who they are. While not being admitted may feel like a judgment of you as a person, it really isn't. Too often, angry parents call and spend fruitless minutes asking, "what is it about my child that you did not like?" It isn't that admissions officers don't like you—in fact, many of them try to plead with their deans for a candidate's reconsideration—it's that there is not enough room to say yes.

While a candidate's spirit might nudge an admissions officer toward a "yes," rarely is the opposite true. While you cannot control how an admissions officer responds to your application, take time to reflect on who you are and who you want to be. Regardless of their decision about your candidacy, admissions officers want to know that a real person exists behind the numbers.

No matter how much you try, even if you pay someone, to craft an image of the "perfect" applicant, it can't be done. And admissions officers do not want a curated version of you. The more seasoned the officer, the more they can sniff out a pretender. After reading thousands of files, it becomes possible for an officer to pick up on things that don't quite seem "right." Even if an applicant who invented a story about who they are and where they come from gets admitted, they generally get found out eventually. Having an offer rescinded is not something you want to risk. It jeopardizes your chances of attending any institution, let alone the one you were hoping for, not to mention your integrity and sense of self-worth.

In 2017, one case made the news when an incoming freshman at the University of Rochester was told to leave the day after she arrived for orientation because she had lied about being homeschooled when she had actually attended a private high school.[1] A young man was expelled from Bowdoin College in 2010 for plagiarism. That didn't stop him, and he fabricated another application that earned him a place at Harvard. At Harvard, he crafted an entire suite of accomplishments that earned him $14,000 in grant money. It wasn't until he sought out both a Rhodes and a Fulbright scholarship that he was discovered.[2] Known as the "Ivy League Imposter," he was found guilty of twenty criminal charges, ordered to repay close to $46,000 to Harvard, and sentenced to jail time. While these cases are clearly at the extremes, even fudging a little bit can get you in a whole lot of hot water.

Stay true to who you are and not to what you think admissions officers want to hear. As mentioned earlier, there are detrimental effects that come from "covering" or hiding an aspect of who you are; pretending to be someone else hurts you. If you aren't able to show up as who you in the application, you're certainly not going to show up as yourself in college. Imagine living the rest of your life pretending. In time, it will break you.

If you try to write an essay based on what you heard helped someone else get it in, you're probably not telling your story in an authentic way. One popular piece of advice that admissions officers share is this: "If your name wasn't on top of your essay but it was thrown on the ground with 100 others, your best friend or your mother could pick yours out." Only you can write about you. Don't try to be someone else. If you're funny, don't be afraid to be funny. If you're on the more serious side, this is not the time to start trying out for *Saturday Night Live*.

Think about this: Are you more drawn to the person who gives off a genuine sense of personality or the person who rattles off their résumé? Similarly, you want to show your true self, not just a litany of your accomplishments that might "look" good but devoid of your spirit.

PRACTICE: REVEAL, DON'T SHIELD

Rather than try to cover who you are because you're afraid that someone won't like it, remember that you are the only person in the world who can be you. And universities value that uniqueness. Explore what it is that makes you you, rather than hide aspects of yourself that you might to "fit in" at school and with your classmates. The things you think make you "odd" might be the very things that a university seeks.

SPIRIT INSIGHT #3: *PAINT A PORTRAIT FOR ADMISSIONS OFFICERS AND HELP THEM HELP YOU*

Help admissions officers really get to know who you are by painting a picture of yourself—not a literal portrait, but one in which the pieces of your application are like a painting where different colors come together in harmony. After reading your file, your readers should be able to talk about you in a brief statement or two. Admissions officers will be distilling you down to a few lines to encapsulate you spirit so that they can bring your case up for further review.

As human beings, admissions officers are not immune to the psychological phenomenon of categorization, the process whereby we sort and classify things, including people. Because of our cognitive limitations, our brains make shortcuts, what psychologists Amos Tversky and Daniel Kahneman call *availability heuristic*. We use these mental shortcuts to help us assess what is specifically in front of us by drawing upon what we might know or that with which we are familiar. When admissions officers are reading your file, they need to make sense of your spirit as a cohesive portrait, not as random splotches on a canvas that doesn't make sense.

Cognitive disfluency occurs when people have a hard time mentally classifying things. When that happens, there tends to be a negative effect toward that thing. In other words, "when we struggle to categorize something, we like it less."[3] If you haven't coherently painted a portrait of who you are, whether it looks like a Picasso or a Monet, it becomes challenging for the admissions officer to get a sense of who you are, and why they should move your candidacy forward. Help them by simply being yourself and presenting yourself in as honest a way as possible. That way, you're helping admissions officers "categorize" you in a positive, cohesive way rather than as a stereotype. Perhaps you are the dancing chemist from Lubbock or the data-driven writer who two-steps on the weekends. Given the volume of applications at these institutions, it is impossible for your full file to be read by every admissions officer on the team, so help them with a cohesive to present your case. If they can't figure you out, they won't be as inclined to make a case for you.

PRACTICE: SIMPLIFY

It might be tempting to add bells and whistles to your application, maybe a pretty package or something you create to send to the school to demonstrate how much you adore them. All those shiny things don't matter (sometimes, too much flash suggests not enough substance). Simplify your story and your delivery of that story so it is clear, concise, and consistent.

SPIRIT INSIGHT #4: *FIT MATTERS,*
AND YOU CAN'T SHOEHORN YOUR WAY IN

For many students, one big mistake they make is that they try to contort themselves into a version of who they think admissions officers want. Students often ask, "what are you looking for?" and they seem rather disappointed—thinking that admissions officers are lying when the response is generically "intellectual curiosity, passion, and kindness." Yet all of these are desired characteristics (can you imagine a university looking for an "intellectually lazy, complacent, and mean" applicant?)—and the truth is that each university has a different flavor and culture, and you can't fit into all them. To make things even more complicated, most universities are actively looking for diversity in the most pluralistic of meanings and want students who might challenge their institutions. Many times, applicants think there is one stereotypical student that universities are looking for. This is untrue. After all, can you imagine attending an institution that has five thousand clones? Pretty boring. What universities are looking for is a wide variety of students who might align with the spirit of the place and who might be able, despite being out of their comfort zones, to thrive there. With these seemingly different wants, how are you supposed to know what to say to prove that you belong?

It's not your job to "prove" that you belong. Your job is simply to present who you are and, hopefully, you've also done some of your own research into the institutions to which you are applying in an attempt to determine whether you think they'd be a good "fit" for you, rather than relying on what your parents or friends told you or on a magazine ranking list. The notion of "fit" is a nebulous one, but one that many institutions use to narrow down the thousands of otherwise qualified applicants. According to research presented at the American Educational Research Association, of sixty-three highly competitive institutions, 21 percent measure "institution fit"—that is, they question whether you might thrive at or contribute to their institution in some way.[4] Basically, the concept of "fit" refers to the general alignment between you and the institution, predicting that the school will meet your preferred intellectual, social, geographic, emotional, and personal interests. This isn't to say that you will find a 100 percent match but that there will be a sense of welcoming when you get there.

The rationale is, if the fit is there, you're going to feel more at home there. If you feel more at home there, you're likely to be happier there. If you're happier there, you're more likely to do well there. If you do well there, you're more likely to be a happy alumnus and spread the word. The list goes on. But the fit question isn't just about you; there is a more selfish aspect to it on the part of institution as well.

Universities get that if there is a fit, there is a greater chance that: 1) you will attend; and 2) you will graduate. These two metrics, yield and retention/graduation rates, play heavily into many calculations of "best of" lists. If your entire application talks about how you want to stay on the West Coast forever, chances are East Coast schools will wonder why you are even applying. Not only does it seem that you're unlikely to attend, even if someone forced you, you probably would be pretty miserable, pining away for the Pacific Ocean. Some schools take demonstrated interest into consideration; some don't. Some schools will note how many times you visit or attend a college program as a signal of your interest in that school, indicating that you would likely attend if admitted. But even those schools will still consider whether you have demonstrated that you would be happy and thrive there. It also helps with yield; the higher the yield, the more it helps to boost university ranking ratings because it suggests to others that it is a "desirable" school, and that more people say yes than no to its offers of admission. It's similar to how you might decide on a restaurant or movie. If a lot of people give it one star, you're less likely to go, but if even more people give it five stars, you're more likely to go, presuming that the "product" is a desirable one.

Second, if you "fit," you're more likely to graduate. Yes, this abso-lutely helps institutions rise in many of those calculated ranks. Yet even more broadly, top institutions aren't looking to accept people who won't ever finish or who will transfer out. Fit isn't the same as being complacent. Rather, they're looking to invest in students who have that commitment, interest, and desire to graduate and, hopefully, to become alumni who will continue to raise the profile and reputation of the institution. Plus, it serves the higher educational intention of preparing you for the world.

Trying to understand whether or not you fit requires more than just a perusal of *U.S. News & World Report.* While it requires a bit more digging, it is not too difficult to get a sense of the atmosphere, culture, and sense of place of an institution. Whether via a personal campus visit or a virtual one online, do your due diligence. Due diligence is not entrusting your future to trolls on College Confidential or to one ill-informed neighbor who attended the institution forty years ago. It means asking around, reading, reflecting, and seeing which colleges make sense for how you want to learn, where you want to be, and from whom and with whom you want to learn. It is also a family decision that doesn't include your friends or your parents' friends.

Once you have a better sense of where you might "fit," it is no longer a matter of trying to shoehorn your way in. If you're a circle, cramming yourself into a square might work temporarily, but it's going to be painful. But when you find that sense of home, you will be able to navigate challenges and step outside comfort zones. But you cannot change who you are.

PRACTICE: RELINQUISH CONTROL

Once you have thought carefully about what you want in an institution and how there is a fit and alignment, then all you can do is share your story and why. Then let go of control. You can't control the admissions officers' minds. Just like you cannot control everything in life that you want, relinquishing control is an important step toward accepting that there are things in life that you cannot dictate. Your job is simply to present as fully as you can who you are and why you want to contribute to and fit within that institution.

SPIRIT INSIGHT #5: *DIVERSITY MATTERS, BUT NOT IN THE WAY YOU MIGHT THINK*

Without getting into the historical and contextual institutional and societal influences on affirmative action and diversity efforts—as these topics would require complete volumes of their own—no institution at the level you are looking will deny that diversity is important to them. Why not? Because it is important to them. Diversity is important for a robust intellectual community to facilitate learning, and it is important for future global leaders to engage in a community of individuals from different backgrounds. These institutions are not looking for students from the same backgrounds with the same experiences. In fact, you probably wouldn't attend an institution where you had five thousand peers who all had the same background, experiences, interests, or physical appearance as you.

When it comes to the word "diversity," many people jump to the conclusion that it only means race, or that certain groups are held to a different standard. The truth is, at this level of selectivity, every candidate is held to a pretty tough standard, and it is a long shot for anyone to get in, regardless of what box they check on a governmental demographic data form.

I have handled more than one angry parent telling me that they wish their child had more "disadvantages" so that they could have an easier chance of being admitted (these parents often inform me that their child's spot was "taken away," as if their child was entitled to a place in the class). Let's look at the facts behind the perception that disadvantaged students have an advantage. According to the Jack Kent Cooke Foundation, "being admitted to a selective institution is actually *harder* for the high-achieving, low-income student than for others."[5] The foundation's research showed that students from the top economic quartile represent 72 percent of enrollment in the most competitive schools in the United States, whereas those from the bottom economic quartile make up only 3 percent. Before you jump to the erroneous conclusion that most students from poorer backgrounds must not be "as smart," COFHE (Consortium on Financing Higher Education) research estimates that "highly selective schools could increase the representation of low-income students by *30 percent* without compromising SAT or ACT standards and with increased social diversity."[6] Even for those who score in the top 10 percent nationwide on the SAT or ACT, they are three times less likely to enroll in a highly selective college. The point here is that admissions to these institutions are tough for any candidate, and much of the anxiety about not getting in unfairly gets blamed on "diversity" writ large.

Whether you come from affluence or a lack thereof, universities are looking for diversity in infinite ways. Maybe you're a conservative in an uber-liberal community or vice versa. Maybe you're the only female on an all-male basketball team. Maybe you're the only transgender male on an all-female rowing team. Maybe you're a suburbanite who doesn't have much life experience but a deep desire to make the world a better place. Regardless, it's not about "gaming the system." You might try to convince your parents to move to North Dakota to show geographic diversity and to have a "better shot" than if you lived in Connecticut, but is that genuinely reflecting who you are or who you want to be?

Not only are these "shortcuts" or games people play silly, they don't work. Admissions officers are not blinded by a box checked simply to stuff people into categories. If they were, they wouldn't spend countless hours reading or discussing your files. They would just enter you into an algorithm, and poof, out comes your decision. You can't change who you are, just as you can't change who your parents are.

PRACTICE: EMBRACE DIFFERENCES
IN ALL THE WAYS THEY EXIST

Diversity means demonstrating your unique voice, being genuinely yourself, and recognizing that your perspective, no matter how "mainstream" you think it is or is not, is one that no one else but you has. Embrace that and how that might add a different lens to all that you say and do to promote greater understanding and progress with others.

SPIRIT INSIGHT #6: *SAY LESS, SHOW MORE*

At the outset of this chapter, we talked about how admissions officer are looking for evidence to support and craft a portrait of who are you and what your spirit is. Similarly, they are looking for evidence that you might be a "fit." Some students learn to parrot the website or an admissions officer in terms of how they come across to try and match up with what they think the university is looking for. Admissions officers can see through this pretty easily (especially if the words are more or less lifted from the website). What they are looking for is not so much the words that you say but how you express yourself—in your activities and in how you show up—so that they can communicate with others about you.

It is therefore more important to demonstrate that you're independent-minded and a good fit for an institution that celebrates its own sense of independence; don't just keep saying you're independent. Help the admissions officer understand how your independence has played out in your class, how it has impacted the way you engage in your activities, and how it has shown up in your relationships with others. By showing, not telling, you're helping the admissions officer to get a more genuine feel for the real you rather than a shiny "respond to prompt" version of you. This aspect of the holistic admissions process is one of the toughest because if you are not admitted, it can often feel like a rejection of you and your spirit, as if you are not good enough. That is not true.

PRACTICE: SPEND MORE TIME DOING THAN SAYING WHAT YOU HOPE TO DO

Instead of spending months writing and rewriting all those things you want to do or hope to accomplish in an effort to prove to universities that you are a productive citizen, do those things. Try them. Don't just settle for the planning of life. Live it. Universities are eager for people who engage in life, not just in the theory of it.

IV

Charting a New Course: Whole-Being Well-Being

The current model of competitive college admissions, ATLAS 1.0, may help you to stay focused and thinking about what you need to do to put your best foot forward in the admissions process. But following it alone may only be a short-term path. Your life doesn't end the moment you get a college acceptance; it is but one of many milestones of your life. If you're still thinking you have to curate the perfect profile, keep reading, as you've missed the point. ATLAS 1.0 is an insufficient way to live with fulfillment, joy, and meaning.

Some institutions are on the forefront, using rubrics to draw out noncognitive skills. For example, Bucknell looks at grit, self-regulation, and creativity; the University of Denver at resilience and motivation; Wesleyan University at persistence; and MIT at adaptability. [1]

Your future success won't depend on how well you color in the lines, or your test scores, or some other prescribed notion of success, but on your capacity for creativity, innovation, and empathic thinking to live and embrace the ongoing challenges, and to weather the ebbs and flows in life. ATLAS 2.0 is a framework to help you thrive during the college admissions process and beyond.

ATLAS 2.0

Figure 15.1.   ATLAS 2.0

Chapter Sixteen

Awareness

What You Feel Is Not Who You Are

Have you ever met anyone who just doesn't seem at all aware about what they say or how their actions impact others? They might seem like they have it all together, but if you asked them, "what do you care about?" they can't answer you. What these folks are lacking is self-awareness. Instead of just focusing on your academics as a way to reach your full potential, knowing yourself may be even more important.

Self-awareness may help you to maximize your academic potential, and to go way, way beyond it. What is self-awareness? Self-awareness is your ability to know yourself and to understand your emotions.[1] Self-awareness is necessary to build your emotional intelligence (EI).

Let's take a look at how self-awareness impacts your growth as a full human being, your candidacy as an applicant, and some practices to get you on track.

TUNE INTO, WITHOUT BECOMING, YOUR EMOTIONS

There is little doubt that you're feeling all sorts of stress. Whether it's getting yourself to school or meeting someone else's (or your own) expectations, it might seem like you're living in a pressure cooker, and you're going to explode in a bad way if something doesn't let up.

Breathe. You're not alone. You're experiencing pretty intense feelings and emotions. And because your brain is not yet fully developed to be most able to handle them, these feelings might get the better of you sometimes. What might start as a little nervousness about an exam can quickly turn into a full-blown panic attack. This is where self-awareness becomes so critical. When you begin to turn inward, you're more adept at figuring out when your lid is about to blow.

Dan Siegel uses the term "mindsight" to describe the focused attention to what's going on *inside* our brains. When we pay attention, we increase our self-awareness and wake up the parts of our brain—especially the area behind our forehead—that help us to "make maps of mental life."[2] We then can have greater "presence of mind to be flexible in how [we] respond, centered in knowing how body informs . . . judgment."[3] There are networks of neurons that, if turned on, can raise our capacity to process information with greater wisdom and speed. Imagine self-awareness as the key to attending to these processes. It isn't about being selfish or simply feeling good. By "turning our attention to our inner world of thoughts and feelings,"[4] we become more attuned to our emotions and better able to understand and handle them, "even when rocked by disturbing feelings . . . these are life skills that keep us all on track throughout the years, and help children be better learners."[5]

Remember that your brain takes internal and external stimuli and tries to make sense about it based on previous experiences and memories. As Northeastern professor Lisa Feldman Barrett says, emotions "are how you make sense of what's going on inside your body in relation to the world."[6] Since it is the brain's job to regulate your body, it's constantly trying to understand all these experiences. For example, when we feel depressed, it might be because we've overspent our brain's and body's resources and "your brain believes that you need more glucose [for energy] than you actually do. So it's flushing your system with cortisol so you can get glucose into your system as fast as possible."[7] Your brain is filling your body with a stress hormone as a physiological response to something.

It is therefore critical for you to better recognize what's going on inside so that you avoid being held hostage by your emotions and in order to better recognize what truly gets you excited and motivated to learn and grow. Awareness of your feelings and the emotions you ascribe to them is critical to managing yourself and your dealings with others. The earlier you start attuning to your emotions, the more adept your brain will be to handle stresses later on (sorry, folks, but life will likely get even more stressful).

Self-awareness also prepares you with essential life skills to help you thrive. In 2018, McKinsey & Company partnered with Microsoft to conduct a survey of over four thousand teachers and students across Canada, Singapore, the United Kingdom, and the United States, finding that both students and teachers ranked social and emotional skills as one of the top five key skills to be successful in the ever-changing technological world.[8] Many of the jobs that your parents have now might not exist by the time you graduate from college. Things are changing and evolving, and if you're not aware of what's happening inside, you're not going to be aware of what's happening outside. And if that happens, you'll be left behind, no matter what fancy diploma sits on your wall.

PRACTICE: NAME YOUR EMOTIONS

When something triggers you, name and label what you are experiencing. Doing so will give you a moment to distance yourself and enable you to recognize what is happening, rather than avoiding or suppressing your feelings. You will then better know how to make sense of it before reacting. Instead, take a moment to name it—"I am experiencing anger; I am experiencing anxiety."

YOUR BODY HOLDS THE EVIDENCE

Your body holds much information as to what is really going on for you. Raising your body awareness can help you raise your level of self-awareness. In a Finnish study known as the Nummenmaa study, seven hundred participants across different cultures were shown two body silhouettes. They were asked to color into the bodies what they were feeling when they looked at a series of pictures and movies. What the study showed was that human beings, regardless of culture, experience similar physiological reactions depending on the triggered sensation, even if we may ascribe different meanings.[9] For example, when we sense a faster heartbeat, we may interpret it as either joy—like a bursting feeling from inside your core—or anger—like an intense feeling of rising heat. When we feel a heaviness to the outer limbs—like a sinking feeling—we often interpret that as depression.

When you become more aware of what your body is telling you, you'll be able to more quickly tap into your emotional state: "Your body definitely is a source of wisdom because it contains information that your brain can learn so that it can construct better. So it can construct your perceptions in a more functional way. It can tailor your actions in a way that's more precise to the situation, as opposed to using a stereotype."[10] Before you make assumptions or react in a way that might get you into trouble, tuning in to your body may give you a hint to what you're feeling and enable you to navigate that situation with greater effectiveness.

PRACTICE: PAY ATTENTION TO YOUR BODY

Pay attention to your body because it tells you a lot. Over the next day, notice what your body is experiencing. Maybe when someone cuts you off on the road, you notice that your heart beats faster. Maybe when your teacher tells you a quiz is coming, your eyebrows furrow. Instead of letting yourself just jump to panic mode, consider what the physical sensation is telling you.

AVOID SPINNING OUT OF CONTROL

Your brain is in a rapidly growing phase. Its ability to say no to your impulses is not yet fully developed. When you get triggered or feel anger or anxiety, unlike an adult whose more-developed prefrontal cortex might help them to self-regulate, your anger or anxiety is more likely to explode.

The good news is that if you start practicing self-awareness now, you can train your brain to check in whenever you're upset so your heightened sensitivity and emotional reactions don't take over and lead you down a rabbit hole. This is why Goleman argues that SEL is critical during these years and, in fact, for doing well in school: "The brain's centers for learning operate at their peak when we are focused and calm. As we become upset, these centers work less well. In the grip of extreme agitation, we can only focus on what's upsetting us—and learning shuts down. For these reasons, students learn best when they're calm and concentrated."[11]

It's not just simple attention that is critical to your regulating your emotions. Rather, specifically, it is about *cognitive control*. The prefrontal cortex (PFC) plays a big role here, as it "allows us to resist distraction, inhibit harmful impulses, delay gratification in pursuit of our goals, be ready to learn, and stay focused on our goals."[12] The more cognitive control we have, the more able we are to manage any destructive emotions. The moment we feel anxious about something, instead of letting that anxiety take over, we can be more aware, recognize it, and then manage it.

In a longitudinal study with 140 eighth graders and a replication study with 164, Angela Lee Duckworth and Martin Seligman noted that, even more than IQ, "self-control is a more reliable predictor of academic success."[13] In other words, it's not just about how much you know but how well you control your attention and your emotions. This, along with your levels of perseverance, love, gratitude, hope, and perspective, help to predict stronger GPAs, more than IQs or where a person goes to school.[14] With self-awareness comes a stronger capacity to recognize those moments that might sidetrack you, thus, potentially helping you to avoid pitfalls which could have a negative impact on your academic career.

PRACTICE: PAY ATTENTION TO YOUR ENVIRONMENT

Jot down what environmental factors help you remain calm and focused. Do you find that you are calmer working by yourself away from others? Do you find that stillness working quietly, but surrounded by other individuals? Also pay attention to those moments where you feel triggered to react. What happens when you take ten seconds to breathe? How might that enable you to take back control of your emotions and your wandering mind?

AT THE VERY BEGINNING

You don't always have to have all the answers. In fact, those who truly love to learn never stop learning and questioning. These institutions recognize that the majority of their applicants will be academically ready. What they're seeking are those who demonstrate intellectual curiosity. Intellectual curiosity isn't something that you can manufacture, no matter how hard you try and how much that consultant is charging your family. But it can be developed and strengthened. The most intellectually curious leaders and changemakers are the ones who are willing to approach things with a beginner's mind. They have the self-awareness to recognize what they know—and don't know—and they have the confidence to approach situations as if they're just starting out. By being genuinely curious, they ask questions that inspire learning, reflection, and deeper understanding. They push thinking beyond the boundaries.

Taking a beginner's mind approach actually helps you to look at situations and problems with a new pair of eyes, including your AP calculus problem set. Doing so may position you to be that invaluable person on the team who comes up with status-quo-breaking ideas and thoughts. Many colleges want this kind of innovative thinking, which can be nurtured and honed with greater self-awareness and the willingness to fail, to be incorrect, and maybe, to look a little silly.

PRACTICE: START ANEW

Think about a problem that you or your team have faced. Instead of trying to be the "expert," pretend you are totally new to the situation. What are the factors influencing the situation? How might the problem be addressed? Look at the situation as if you had no vested interest in one approach or outcome.

While academics is clearly an important component of your application, self-awareness enables you to go deeper and consider your values, intrinsic motivators, attitude, and emotions. All of these have been shown to be critical—even more so than IQ—to your future success. Self-awareness gives you the confidence and willingness to look at things from different perspectives, to be vulnerable, and to be more open to learning. These are things admissions officers are looking for that you cannot manufacture. What you can do is to train your brain to have greater awareness of yourself, of others, and of your impact in the world around you.

Chapter Seventeen

Thinking

Like a Jedi, Be

Awareness of others is critical to helping you establish the foundation for understanding your feelings and emotions so you don't become hostage to them. This awareness is vital to how you actually perform in and out of the classroom, not only making you a better candidate for college but setting you up to thrive in life. Awareness also helps you get into the right mindset.

For those of you who have seen *Star Wars*, you were probably quite taken with Yoda, the wisdom-dispensing green Jedi, who understood the importance of helping his young charges to develop the right mindset before they set off to save the galaxy. This mindset requires focused attention, perseverance, resilience, and curiosity as well as the ability to reframe challenges and difficulties as positive opportunities. It is critical as you seek admissions—and beyond. Let's take a look at how "thinking" and the right mindset is critical at this stage, and some practices to get you on track.

FOCUS TO GROW

Your teachers, families, and coaches have likely asked you: "Are you paying attention?" Sometimes you are, but many times, you are off in daydream land. It's normal to have your mind wandering. Our minds are wandering 47 percent of the time.[1] We're not as happy when our minds are wandering. Think about the last time you were happy doing something. It might have been working on your Eagle Scout project or taking your little brother to school. You were likely so present and focused on the moment that you weren't daydreaming about what else you could or should be doing. As the adage goes, "a focused mind is a happy mind."[2]

Not only does mind-wandering lead to your greater unhappiness, it probably at some point cost you an A. Psychologist Ellen Langer spent forty years researching how we can "reduce stress, unlock creativity, and boost performance"[3] by simply paying attention to what's happening around us. When we are actively paying attention, we are more able to connect and see things from multiple perspectives and, therefore, we are better able to respond to the situation with greater wisdom and discernment, prioritize what is important, and relate to others. And as Langer notes, "it's energy-begetting, not energy-consuming."[4]

Staying focused and paying attention to the present isn't a fad. The more attention and focus we place, the more our brains will accommodate wiser decision-making and complex thinking (needed not only for calculus but for life) which allows us to see more opportunities for growth. Brain science suggests how interventions, such as mindfulness, can impact the brain's capacity to focus. A meta-study by the University of British Columbia and Chemnitz University of Technology found that meditators had greater activation in the *anterior cingulate cortex* (ACC) (self-regulation) and the *hippocampus* (the gray matter), resulting in more complex thinking, protection from toxic stress, and more effective decision-making.[5]

Emerging studies also suggest that interventions targeting the mindset and attitudes toward learning and belief in ability can have a positive impact in academic outcomes.[6] How one thinks about academics is highly correlated with how one engages and ultimately performs. Stanford professor Carol Dweck argues that a growth mindset offers the notion that intelligence and academic ability are not fixed but can be changed and improved with effort. In her research on classrooms in three different communities, children performed better in classrooms where the teacher brought the growth mindset. For example, in the South Bronx, New York, a class of fourth graders rose from one of the bottom-ranked to the number one class in state math tests in just one year. On one Native American reservation, students went from the bottom of the district to the top in eighteen months, beating out even the far more affluent sections of Seattle where the test-prepped kids of Microsoft employees lived.[7]

A fixed mindset, however, can exacerbate the stress of academics. In a 2018 Texas study, scientists found a connection between cortisol levels and a growth or fixed mindset. The students whose cortisol levels peaked and dropped (some stress is necessary to boost motivation and decision-making) were more likely to report a growth mindset. Those who had consistently high levels of cortisol were more likely to report a fixed mindset.[8] An unhealthy chronic level of cortisol means chronic stress, which can cause long-term damage with impaired brain functioning and immune system suppression.

The environment in which you learn also has an important influence. In 2003, a random group of seventh graders had a mentor who taught them about how intelligence is not fixed. Another group met with mentors who focused on why drugs are bad. Those in the former group ended up with significantly higher state assessments on reading and math.[9] In a diverse urban school district in Clark County, Nevada, a large study of over 120,000 students and 6,500 teachers found that while the majority of students believed in a growth mindset, Black and Hispanic students, English Language Learning (ELL) students, and students from schools with more economically disadvantaged classmates exhibited less of this mindset.[10] Other interventions showed that when students, including African American and low-achieving students, are encouraged to view intelligence as malleable, their GPAs and test scores rise,[11] suggesting mindset impacts outcomes.

Growth mindsets also help students to develop resilience—the ability to cope, maintain, and recover during and after adverse moments. Five Chinese primary and middle schools were the subject of a study on positive education—"education for both traditional skills and for happiness."[12] In addition to academic performance, the skills emphasized included resilience, optimism, character strength, and other ways for flourishing. The study showed that education that positively promotes a growth mindset, well-being, *and* academic achievement is positively correlated with resilience, psychological well-being, and school engagement.[13]

When students view intelligence and learning as malleable, they are more apt to interpret tough academic challenges and failures as part of the learning process and do not get mired in failure. According to the Psychological Well-Being Scale (PWB) that addresses "all important components of well-being such as meaning and purpose, engagement and interest; supportive and rewarding relationships; contributing to the well-being of others, competency, self-acceptance, optimism, and being respected," growth mindset is critical.[14]

PRACTICE: GROWING PAINS

Think about something you want to improve. What is it about this activity that leads you to have a growth mindset about it? Now think about something that you believe you have no chance of ever getting "good at." Consider how you might take some of your beliefs about yourself in the first example and apply them to this one. What support do you need to help you move further along?

IT'S ALL ABOUT ATTITUDE

Even if you've got a pretty good handle on your emotions, have spectacular focus, and know your values and motivation, if you have a sour mental attitude toward learning, you're always going to sell yourself short. Remember the kid who sat behind you who was a straight-B student but *loved* to learn and was never afraid to make mistakes? Even if you were the A student, you might end up working for that kid.

That's because attitude definitely matters.

One of Yale University's most popular classes is "Psyc 157: Psychology and the Good Life," reflecting a need for stressed-out students to reframe their attitude towards learning. Many students clamored for the A to get in, but their anxiety didn't end until they started to challenge their *thinking* about what will bring them happiness.

Psychologist Sonja Lyubomirsky suggests that 50 percent of our happiness is not even within our control. Ten percent is made up of thoughts, actions, and attitudes. Forty percent *is* within your control because it's what you think and how you act. It's your attitude.[15] She and other psychologists observe that those who are happy demonstrate greater devotion to family and friends, practice gratitude, are physically active, and work on their optimistic outlook. It's not money that determines happiness. *Stumbling on Happiness* author Dan Gilbert notes that lottery winners are only slightly happier than those who don't win, and those who suffered from permanent paralysis are only slightly less happy. Within three months of either winning the lottery or losing physical movement, the majority of those Gilbert studied went back to their baseline of happiness.[16]

Boston College researcher Karen Arnold looked at high school valedictorians and salutatorians over the course of fourteen years and found the majority of them achieved a degree of success. They did well in college on average, many went on to graduate school, and about 50 percent landed a top-tier professional job.[17] Not bad, right? While these top students end up doing pretty well, they tend not to be the change-makers of the world. In fact, seven hundred millionaires had an average high school GPA of 2.9.[18] Why is that? Arnold found that those truly engaged in learning and exploring often struggle in high school because of its "stifling" nature. That desire to explore will serve them well later in life. On the other hand, "valedictorians often go on to be the people who support the system—they become a part of the system—but they don't change the system or overthrow the system."[19] Author Malcolm Gladwell studies Ivy League graduates and why some of them didn't turn out to be the superstar leaders their SATs may have suggested.[20] In other words, if you only care about the A to get into your dream college, you'll do fine, yes. But if you really want to change the world and make a positive impact as many of you say you do, consider your true motivation and attitude toward learning.

Your attitude has more to do with your performance than you think. A University of Kansas professor compared the academic achievement of freshmen and found that the differentiating piece is that of hope: "Hope was a better predictor of their first-semester grades than were their scores on the SATs . . . given roughly the same range of intellectual abilities, emotional aptitude makes the critical difference."[21] It's not that you simply wish for the best and don't bother studying. You have to both study *and* have a positive outlook. After all, you can be the happiest, most hopeful person in the world, but if you ignore your studies or lack the perseverance to study, you're just going to joyfully receive a zero on that test.

On the other hand, "anxiety undermines the intellect."[22] But it depends on what kind of anxiety as, in and of itself, anxiety is not always a negative thing. Richard Alpert and Ralph Haber note there are two different types of anxious students. The first includes the kind of anxiety where a student doesn't have the ability to harness their emotions, which ends essentially with a self-fulfilling prophecy; the more they worry about doing poorly, the more likely they are to do poorly on exams. It is a negative cycle. The second includes the kind of anxiety where a student leverages those nerves to "motivate themselves to prepare well for it, thereby doing well,"[23] which becomes the adrenaline push to try even harder. It is a virtuous cycle. How one approaches anxiety makes a difference in performance. In other words, it's not about getting rid of those butterflies in your stomach; it's about how to get those butterflies in formation.

With heightened self-awareness, you can build your EI, which means that you're less willing to give into overwhelming anxiety or setbacks. Like optimism, you gain a perspective that "things will turn out all right in life . . . an attitude that buffers people against falling into apathy, hopelessness, or depression in the face of tough going."[24] This is useful not only for you now during application season but well beyond.

A study of five hundred University of Pennsylvania first-year students in 1984 showed that a test on optimism better predicted their first-term grades than SAT scores or high school grades.[25] The good news is that, as the father of positive psychology Martin Seligman notes, optimism and hope can be learned. While we all have different baselines, we can all train our brains to see things with a more positive outlook. In fact, as Intentional Change Theory (ICT) professor Richard Boyatzis observes, people with a more positive outlook tend to demonstrate greater persistence through challenges, see failures as opportunities, and expect the best out of others.[26] You can cultivate more of this outlook and when you do, those around you will not only feel better, they are likely to perform better as well. As you're thinking about how you want to learn to lead, modeling a positive environment is important. And the most impactful leaders spend time on being aware of their own attitudes and outlook so that they can role model for others.

PRACTICE: TURN THAT FROWN UPSIDE DOWN

Think of a disappointing moment, setback, or failure. Label your emotions around this disappointment. Take three deep breaths and with each exhale, and release that moment. Now take a look at the situation and consider how a friend might view this situation as a potential opportunity for growth and learning. Write down a few ways to reframe the situation and how you might take that situation and build something more positive.

ATTENTION! CONTROLLING COGNITIVE CAPACITY

It turns out that cognitive control can help us regulate emotions and contribute to how successful we can be in the classroom and elsewhere. Your brain can only hold so much information. As smart as you might be, you've got limits. Ever have those multi-quiz days where you're feeling great about the morning algebra test but, by last period, you can't make heads nor tails out of that English quiz? When you have to process something quickly, say, some vocabulary for a quiz, the resources your brain uses to learn the first word means that it takes a little processing time before you're ready to learn the second word. This phenomenon is what researchers call the *attentional-blink deficit*.

The good news is that you can train your brain to expand that capacity. Researchers flashed a series of letters with two numbers embedded. They took a group of people with a three-month Vipassana meditation experience, a type of mindfulness meditation, and a group with no mindfulness practice. They found that those with meditation experience were more likely to catch both embedded numbers, whereas the nonmeditators missed the second number more often.[27] Their brains could only pay attention to one, not both. Yet meditation allows our brains to better absorb, process, and retain information. The more you train your brain to focus attention, the larger your attentional capacity becomes, allowing you to be more able to control your cognitive limitations. Imagine what that might do for your third pop quiz of the day?

PRACTICE: THREE-COUNT BREATH

Take a comfortable seat—but not so comfortable you're falling asleep. Place your feet on the ground, hands in your lap. Close your eyes gently. Notice your breathing. On the inhale, breathe deep in your belly so it expands like a balloon and bring that air into your chest. On the exhale, release that air from your chest and from your belly as it deflates. Count to three as you slowly belly breathe in and out for a minute. If you lose focus and your mind wanders, that's okay. Just bring it back to your three-count breath.

STICKY FINGERS

Cognitive control also helps us to be more able to stick to things, even when things are tough. You may have heard of the famous Stanford "marshmallow test" by Walter Mischel whereby four-year-old children were put in a room with a delicious, plump marshmallow in front of them, tempting them. They were told that if they could wait a few minutes by themselves and without adult supervision—*and* not eat the enticing marshmallow!—the "teacher" would come back and give them two marshmallows as a reward. It turns out that fourteen years later, those kids who could wait out the painful minutes for a second marshmallow outscored those who couldn't resist on the SATs by 210 points. This gap was even larger for those whose parents didn't have advanced degrees. [28] This study has been replicated in New Zealand where about one thousand children born in Dunedin were tested starting in 1972–1973. As of 2012, 95 percent of these individuals were still being followed up. [29] By the time these children reached their mid-thirties, researchers found that those who waited for the second marshmallow were in better financial and physical health than those who couldn't wait. [30] In other words, "this ability turned out to be remarkably powerful as a predictor of life success—stronger than childhood IQ or the social and economic status of the child's family." [31] Young children with the capacity to slow their overactive brains enough to delay instant pleasure were more able to control their emotions and behaviors throughout the rest of their lives, especially through challenging times.

Think about those times you wish you could just go out and play but you have to study. As our brains mature, we strengthen our capacity to persevere and delay playtime until after study time.

Duckworth suggests that grit helps us to identify a goal and keep going, particularly when we encounter difficulties. She defines grit as passion and sustained persistence applied to a longer-term achievement, even if there isn't a particular end goal or a reward. Even though self-control and grit are both determinants as to why some people are more successful than others, it is important to understand that self-control and grit are not the same thing. Self-control is staying focused and composed even when tempted, like with a marshmallow, and requires willpower. Grit, continuing despite setbacks, is the stick-to-itiveness that allows one student to make it through a first term at the grueling West Point Academy versus another who drops out. [32]

One study showed that individuals with "exceptional" talent weren't so much simply "born with it" but had actually spent a minimum of ten years involved in intense practice. [33] While certainly there is some influence of genetic factors causing some of you to be more prone to excel in one area than another (Michael Phelps is built like a dolphin), genetics isn't everything. You're not going to get really good at something until you put the time in. So next time someone nags at you to sit at the piano, the more grit and perseverance you show, the better you're likely to go to be; and the better you are, the more pleasure and joy you're likely to derive from it; and the more pleasure and joy you have, the more likely you're going to want to share with others; and the more you want to share, the greater your impact will be on others; and the . . . it's a virtuous cycle. It's also important to recognize that it's also about improvement. Otherwise, you're just spinning wheels. For example, if you're learning to tread water and you don't have the proper form, you can spend 10,000 hours in that pool and end up only with pruney fingers. Greater attention to what is happening inside your head can help you to make discerning choices, stick with things through tough times, or delay instant pleasure, as well as recognize when you need to tweak and refine things so that you continue to grow.

Admissions officers know that things can and will get tough in college, no matter how brilliant or prepared you think you are. When students demonstrate grit during their high school years, admissions officers are more assured that they will be able to face challenges, from angry roommates to their first bad grade to being homesick, without giving up or falling apart.

PRACTICE: RETHINK YOUR LIMITATIONS

Consider something you are trying to get better at. Reflect on your current approach. What is the self-limiting belief you might have about your ability to get better at it? How might you reframe your narrative around your "limitations"? How might you tweak or refine the way you practice that could boost your ability?

I AM RUBBER, YOU ARE GLUE!

Not falling apart requires a high degree of resilience—the ability to "bounce back" from difficult situations and setbacks. Even if you're under a heck of a lot of pressure, it's unhealthy and unhelpful to wallow in self-pity. As psychologist Richard Weissbourd notes, one of the key factors of your anxiety is "achievement pressure—the pressure to excel across academic subjects and a wide range of extracurriculars, culminating in the stress of putting together an impeccable college admissions package."[34] You might be doing well in one area, but the moment you fail in another, it's like a delicate house of cards flattening out in five seconds. Your ego becomes fragile. Your well-meaning family may have tried to prevent anything "bad" for you, so you never learned failure. You don't ever get a chance to truly confront the bad and build your resilience. One setback sends everything else tumbling.

Life happens. And life isn't always easy. You get cut from a school play. Your ride to school breaks down. Your friend is mean to you. The key is how you react to and bounce back from setbacks. Recall our earlier discussion about an *internal locus of control* and resilience. There are three major characteristics of resilient people: 1) staunch acceptance of reality; 2) belief that life is meaningful; and 3) flexibility and ability to improvise.[35] It is not about pretending bad things don't exist but learning to accept them and still see the positive. Just as your immune system has to be exposed to viruses for it to get stronger, exposing your brain to embrace moments of failure is critical. As *The Talent Code*'s Daniel Coyle notes, "experiences where you're forced to slow down, make errors, and correct them . . . are the ones that lead to genuine learning and success."[36]

The good news is that resilience is trainable. According to Daniel Goleman, the secret is in how quickly we can recover from a "hijacked state."[37] When your brain gets triggered, it often wants to jump into protective mode by freezing, fleeing, or fighting—even before your brain has made sense of what the trigger actually is. Goleman found that after eight weeks of 30-minute mindfulness practice, participants showed greater leaning toward the left side of the brain, associated with resilience. Building resilience isn't about forcing you to study until one o'clock in the morning, however. It is about knowing when to stop, rest, and let things go.

Some schools are implementing programs to build resiliency. For example, the Resilience Builder Program, a 12-week intensive training course, teaches children stress management, emotional problem-solving, and stronger communication. Initial findings indicate that this program to build resilience, rather than simple "happiness," has had a greater impact, especially since happiness is a fleeting emotion.[38] Admissions officers are keen to know if you're someone who gives up easily the moment you get a less-than-perfect A or if you recover from setbacks because you are willing to face them.

PRACTICE: ONE-MINUTE DELAY

Next time you have an urge to say something, buy something, or do something, pause. Just stop for one minute. Sixty seconds might seem excruciating, but that minute might make a whole world of difference in how you respond and act.

CURIOUSER AND CURIOUSER

You might be dreaming of being the next Elon Musk or Steve Jobs, inventing the hottest new revolutionary "thing." Well, you can't do that if you're not training your mind to be at an optimal level for creativity. Your mindset is critical to your capacity for innovative thinking.

When you are able to build your self-awareness and attention, you no longer are trying to run away from the recesses of your own mind but willing to approach what is there with a sense of kindness and curiosity. You're judging yourself less for your thoughts and you're more curious about them. Why are you thinking this? What makes you feel that? This curiosity allows you to explore your experiences, both good and bad. Author Scott Barry Kaufman defines curiosity as "the recognition, pursuit, and intense desire to explore novel, challenging, and uncertain events."[39] As it turns out, admissions officers are also looking for this ingredient that separates smart students from those they want on their campuses. If you talk to admissions officers, they will all likely say that the one thing they are looking for and that defines their student body is intellectual curiosity. They will never say "a 4.0 GPA."

Some of you may have been identified as "gifted" at some point. You might remember taking the SAT when you were in fifth grade and doing shockingly well. While that may have measured one aspect of giftedness, the majority of "gifted programs" focus on such standardized tests rather than on your sense of curiosity or motivation to learn. In fact, only three states consider motivation as a metric for their gifted-and-talented programs.[40] Certainly, your IQ has some bearing. Researchers with the Fullerton Longitudinal Study, which has examined giftedness for more than thirty years, have found that while cognitive giftedness matters, it is not the only thing that does. High school GPAs correlate with IQ scores *and* intrinsic motivation. Usually, students with high IQs also demonstrate greater curiosity, but this isn't always the case. What is true is that those with gifted curiosity outperform those who don't, in SAT scores and in college attainment.[41]

Curiosity has been correlated with a greater sense of well-being, creativity, and improved relationships, and academic achievement. Moreover, teachers notice the more genuinely curious students easier because they tend to ask more questions. They enjoy teaching them more and students enjoy learning more. As it turns out, when your curiosity gets piqued, your *hippocampus*—the part of your brain associated with memory-making and reward and pleasure—lights up.

When your curiosity is deep and genuine, your teachers and peers notice. They will write about this in their recommendation letters. Admissions officers will see this. You might have a better chance to get into a school when your excitement has less to do with getting in than with the opportunity to pique your curiosity over and over again. To cultivate your curiosity is to train your brain to be open to what is happening around you without getting caught up in it. Rather, "it's about seeing those distractions as precisely what they are and choosing which ones deserve your attention."[42]

PRACTICE: CHILD'S EYES

Think of something that you use every day. It might be something that you take for granted. Now imagine that you are a newborn baby (with the capacity for language and higher-order thinking) or you are an alien from another planet. Observe the object from that perspective—as if every little thing is novel. Try to remove your assumptions or preconceptions of what it is used for. Imagine if you were a baby or an alien, what else might this object be used for? Who might use it?

Chapter Eighteen

Listening

Teamwork Makes the Dream Work

Are you listening? Sometimes you are, sometimes you aren't. Most people think that they are better listeners than the average person. The reality is that most of us aren't terribly good listeners.

In the admissions process, you're evaluated on how you engage in class and the school community, and how you lead and interact in teams and extracurricular activities. But other than trying to get the title of "founder" or "president," have you really thought about how well you pay attention to others to help make these teams function more than in name only? Let's look at how we "listen," despite our mental shortcuts and biases, as well as at the various levels of listening, empathy, and gratitude and some practices to get you on track.

SHORTCUTS AND FILTERS

Our brains have limited capacity to pay attention, so we make mental shortcuts when interacting with people. Are you ever talking to someone, and it's clear that they are waiting for you to finish so that they can talk? Guess what: They're not really listening.

Most of us rely on our mental shortcuts to help us process the overabundance of information in front of us. We rely on these "availability heuristics" to help us navigate the world more efficiently.[1] We depend on previous experiences to help us make decisions more quickly. This unconscious processing is useful in many ways (hot stove? You're not going to touch it again). However, sometimes, shortcuts can limit our ability to make better decisions. Instead of really listening to the other person, we just want them to hurry up and finish so we can make our decisions based on our own shortcuts. We listen through our filters of experience. That means whatever someone may be telling you, you're listening to them through your own existing notions and you may not really be open to what they're saying.

All of this can have a negative impact on your potential contribution on teams or as a leader, inside or outside of the classroom. For example, imagine that you are put in charge of the soccer team's bake sale. One teammate included on the list of bakers is someone you had heard was not a great team player. So you start filtering everything. Every suggestion that teammate offers, your brain filters out. You only half-listen to their ideas because your brain is more ready to reject their input. By relying on such mental shortcuts without really exploring what is out there, you might miss out on a great opportunity—perhaps this teammate has the most brilliant idea ever.

PRACTICE: FILTERING OUT

Next time you are working on a team project, consider one person on the team whom you tend to make mental shortcuts about based on previous experiences or perhaps what someone has told you. Instead of filtering out what that person has to say, don't make any assumptions. Listen for three minutes without saying anything. You can nod or affirm through body language that you're listening, but don't try to resolve the problem or jump in with your story. Give that person your full attention by listening for at least three minutes.

HIDDEN BRAINS AND THE LADDER OF LISTENING

According to Leonard Mlodinow, 95 percent of what happens in our brains is unconscious.[2] In other words, we're only aware of 5 percent of what we think or act or feel. It therefore shouldn't be surprising that listening bias occurs—a lot. And many of us tend to default to these unconscious biases to help us navigate the vast amount of information out there.

Similarity bias occurs when we unconsciously favor those who are similar to us. This affects how we listen and to whom we listen. In one study, researchers found that people are 260 percent more likely to donate to hurricane relief efforts if the hurricane's name begins with the same letter as their name.[3] What this means for you is that you have to increase your level of awareness to examine how your unconscious biases might be impacting they way you listen to others. If you're prone to listening favorably to those like yourself and less favorably to those unlike yourself, you might not be receiving all the information you need to make the wisest decisions for you and the team. You might end up with project ideas that are not creative or innovative because you're simply listening to friends who are most like you. Because they're most like you, you probably have similar ideas.

People also fall into the easy trap of confirmation bias, which happens when we really only listen for what we want to hear. When someone speaks, we're only listening to affirm what we're already thinking, ignoring or minimizing that which doesn't fit into our narrative. In so doing, we might be shutting out a lot of useful information that can help us not only perform better but also forge a deeper, more authentic relationship with the other person.

The good news is that if we raise our awareness of how we listen, we are more apt to engage with a broader spectrum of individuals and not just with those who are most like us. There are six levels of listening, according to Jonathan Passmore, which are:

1. Ignoring
2. Waiting to talk
3. Listening for words
4. Listening for words and body language
5. Empathetic listening
6. Active constructive listening[4]

Ignoring and waiting to talk are fairly self-explanatory and probably quite familiar in your experience. When we listen for words, we are doing exactly that, trying to find the key phrases that we know we want to hear or are expecting to hear. In so doing, we leave out a lot of information that the other person is telling us (or not telling us) that can help us be more effective team players or leaders. When we listen for words and also pay attention to body language, we're engaging in behaviors that help us become more effective communicators, build stronger relationships, and impact teams. You probably know by now how large a role body language plays when it comes to communicating.

The same is true with listening. The more attuned you are to someone else's body language, the more able you are to really listen to what they have to say, which helps to minimize misunderstandings and strengthen relationships—all qualities that are noticed by your peers and teachers, and subsequently, by admissions officers. In fact, in one study of sixty kindergarteners, the more popular children—those whom the other kids wanted to play with or sit with—were those who were more adept at reading other people's body language. These children were more able to form social structures and navigate them well because of their ability to understand and "listen for" body language. [5]

The more we're able to move beyond just waiting for someone to finish or simply listening for the words we want to hear, the more we're able to challenge our own biases and raise our awareness. Doing so will likely help you to connect with people, both those who are similar and dissimilar to you, on a genuine level. When we pay more attention to the present without relying on our shortcuts or filters, we also become less susceptible to bias and avoid simply placing people into "buckets" based on assumptions. We become more able to appreciate what they do, even if we don't completely understand or agree with their reasons.

This capacity and ability to bridge differences in productive and constructive ways is what admissions officers are looking for in students. As Zenger and Folkman articulated, "the best listeners make the conversation a positive experience for the other party." [6]

PRACTICE: STEPPING UP

With your next few conversations with a classmate, play around with the different levels of listening and notice how the quality of the relationship might shift. Notice how, as you listen with greater depth, you're better able to bring attention to unconscious biases.

I FEEL YOU

With empathetic listening, the person is wholly listening and trying to feel what the other person is feeling. With active constructive listening, the person listening will also try to respond constructively, thinking positively of the other person. We can always work toward listening at these levels. One way to do so is to cultivate empathy.

What is empathy? As important as self-awareness, empathy is having an awareness of others' emotions and concerns. To do so, we must choose to listen and find points of similarity even when they don't seem to exist, feel with the person, and offer kindness.[7]

Having empathy for others doesn't mean you're a pushover. In fact, it's quite the contrary. Evidence indicates that more effective leaders are those who show more empathy, partly because they are perceived to be better at building stronger relationships.[8] The strongest leaders and team players demonstrate empathy because if others believe that you truly care about them, they're more likely to trust you. When they trust you, they're more likely to follow you.

Think about those teams you've been on where you and the team leader are totally in sync. There's total trust. The likelihood is that the team also did some pretty great things. Now think of those teams you've been on where it was a struggle every time you met—with lots of catty chatter going on. The likelihood is that the team didn't do as well as they could have. Rather than think about these experiences as simply fodder for your admissions essay, consider the level of empathy that was demonstrated—or not—by the leader and by the team members.

Empathy seems to be hardwired into our brains. The neural circuitry used to process our own emotions is the same one that is used for you to understand what other people are feeling. For example, a baby cries when it hears another baby cry. A similar modality of mimicry has been demonstrated in charismatic leaders. Two studies were done in 2006 to look at how individuals—from college students to both Presidents Clinton and Bush—who smiled more and held longer and more frequent eye contact with audiences were able to spread their upbeat energy, leading to more positive affect toward them.[9] In other words, empathy helps us to understand others' emotions and it helps us to better spread our emotions to others. So if you want to radiate positive leadership, you need empathy.

Yet fewer students exhibit empathy now. A University of Michigan study showed that from 2000 to 2010, college students were 40 percent less empathetic than their predecessors. Fifteen percent fewer freshmen say it's important to have a "meaningful philosophy of life" than in the 1980s.[10] That means fewer college students may be ready for meaningful leadership. These trends counter the science suggesting that empathy leads to better performance. Want to be a great doctor one day? Be empathetic. A study of Korean doctors found that patients reported greater satisfaction with their doctors and listened more to their advice when the doctors were more empathetic.[11] Want to be a successful entrepreneur one day? Be empathetic. Design thinking, a hallmark of entrepreneurs, cannot happen without understanding customer needs. Want to be a great boss? A study of over 6,500 managers from thirty-eight countries showed that managers with greater empathy were better performers.[12] Or maybe you just want to be a good friend. In studies of Blue Zones, the areas in the world where people live a long, long time (over 100 years), one of the key factors that contributes to longevity is that people in these areas have strong social networks. They demonstrate and practice empathy. They listen to each other. And the health benefits are evident, for the "quality of relationships as well as their sheer number seems key to buffering stress."[13] These young-at-heart old people are better at managing stress.

Of course, it is far easier to demonstrate empathy for those who are like us. But if we only practice empathy and listen to those similar to us, we limit our opportunities for creativity and innovation, and we might also compromise our health. For example, college roommates who dislike each other actually are more susceptible to colds and flu. And you do not want to go through your first term with the flu. By practicing empathy, you might be amazed at how much more willing you are to find what's similar, and how much more open you are to listening to what others have to say.

PRACTICE: WE ARE ALL THE SAME

Sit in a comfortable position. Place your feet on the ground and your hands in your lap. Close your eyes. Bring to mind someone you are having a challenging time with or who is dissimilar to you. Consider these thoughts as you think about this person. This person is a fellow human being—just like me. This person has a body and mind—just like me. This person has feelings and emotions—just like me. This person has been hurt, been sad or angry—just like me. This person has experienced joy and happiness—just like me. This person wants to be healthy and loved—just like me. This person wants to be happy—just like me. Send a positive intention for that person to be happy. Open your eyes.

THANK YOU, THANK YOU

We take a lot for granted. People help us out all day long, and no matter what you think, you did not accomplish everything by yourself. You had people who have supported you—perhaps they are your parents, perhaps they aren't. Regardless, when we don't take time to listen, we don't take time to truly appreciate what others have done for us.

Listening helps us to be more aware of the things that we can be grateful for, and to be more ready to acknowledge these things, rather than barreling on without a moment of reflection. Demonstrating gratitude not only is a lovely thing for the recipient, but it can also help you to be a stronger team player and leader. Professor Sonja Lyubomirsky found a list of factors that increase well-being. None of the top factors had to do with income or SAT scores; number one is expressing gratitude.[14] In fact, what she and her team have found is that gratitude is an energizing force that allows you to better pursue your goals and be more engaged.

There is also evidence of gratitude positively impacting health and performance. In one study, participants who counted their blessings exercised an extra 1.5 hours more than those who didn't, and they had fewer illnesses.[15] In another study of over one thousand high school students, those who demonstrated more gratitude had higher GPAs, were more engaged in extracurricular activities, and reported a stronger desire to contribute to society on a broader scale. They also reported more social engagement, lower envy of others, and greater life satisfaction.[16] Pay attention to this if you're trying to get into colleges that evaluate you on your GPA, extracurricular activities, and desire to impact the world. True gratitude matters.

True gratitude increases the closeness of relationships. In one study of ninth and tenth graders, students who took the time to express gratitude for their parents, teachers, and coaches felt more connected to them, thereby increasing their motivation to improve themselves and their confidence to do so.[17] Their stronger social networks cultivated a sense of wanting to do better and believing they could do better. Expressing gratitude also helps you to recognize there is much more beyond yourself. One study showed that doing so can cultivate humility, not in a passive way but in a way that actually encourages people to pay it forward. In this study, one group wrote a letter of gratitude and then imagined a response to an angry person, whereas another group just did the latter. Those who wrote the gratitude letter were more apt to consider the other person's point of view.[18] Gratitude can help you to recognize another person's point of view better, listen more, and then be more motivated to try and help others. Three years after the first *Turning the Tide* paper, Making Caring Common published its second to recommend more tangible actions that parents and schools can take to reduce college admissions anxiety and cultivate ethical character. One key action it recommends is to practice gratitude for these very reasons.[19]

One way to cultivate gratitude is by keeping a journal or simply by writing down one thing to be grateful for every day. Studies repeatedly show this has positive effects. For example, one study asked one group to write about what they were grateful for in a week, a second group what they were irritated by, and a third what they had experienced. After ten weeks, the first group demonstrated greater well-being and optimism—and fewer stress-related health issues.[20]

There is, of course, brain science behind this. Gratitude actually stimulates the *hypothalamus*, the part of your brain associated with stress management, and the *ventral tegmental area*, the part of your brain associated with the pleasure of reward.[21] Cultivating a practice of gratitude not only gives you a natural high because it feels good to say thank you, it also makes the other person feel good. All of this requires a level of empathetic listening and pausing to listen, which may positively impact how you engage with or lead a team.

PRACTICE: THREE GOOD THINGS

Before bed, write down three things you are grateful for every evening. The next day, verbalize one of these things, if possible.

Chapter Nineteen

Alignment

Peak Performance at the Optimal Time

You may have heard the well-intentioned advice to "follow your passion" and you're panicking because you don't know what your passion is. Don't worry; ask the adults in your life —they probably don't know either. Stanford design school (d.school) professors Bill Burnett and Dave Evans argue that this belief that everything will "magically fall into place" once we find our passion is terrible advice because "less than 20 percent of people actually know their passion."[1] If four in five adults have no idea what their passions are, you're okay if you don't know yours. Those aged 12–26 years naturally have greater confusion about who they are or want to become, according to William Damon, the director of the Stanford Center on Adolescence. After all, you're just getting started.

If you have no clue what you *really* want to study or do or be, you're not alone. There are ways to bring more clarity, however. Let's look at how "alignment" of our values and intrinsic motivations is important to finding flow and making an impact, and some practices to get you on track.

TRUE VALUES

When your emotional intelligence heightens, you will begin to pay closer attention to what matters to you and the values you hold dear, and then you can identify the people and places that will help you live accordingly. Raising awareness about your values helps you to understand the kind of person you want to be, the kind of life you want to lead, the kind of learning environment in which you'll thrive, the types of careers you'll choose, and the people with whom you'll surround yourself. Doing so will translate into how you act in the classroom, the school, and the community. When you have consistency in what you value and how you live, others will take note of this. The consistency of your behavior speaks to your character and to your past and potential impact in a broader community. When you have greater awareness about what your values are, you're more likely to live them out, and when you do, it is easier for others to speak about them on your behalf. Admissions officers are more likely to understand who you are and see how you may (or may not) fit at their college campuses. If you're confused about who you are and what matters to you, so are your behaviors and actions, and then so are your teachers and the admissions officers.

This is not to say that awareness of your values is only important for gaining college acceptance—far from it. Since the majority of our values are formed in our late adolescence and remain fairly consistent for the rest of our lives (barring any dramatic or life-changing events), the more aware you become of them now, the more able you will be to live accordingly and to find greater well-being and satisfaction. It is important, however, to remember that we often say we have values, but we don't actually live by them. Values are just ideals until they are tested. For example, you might say you value honesty. That's great. But let's say you get into a situation where you have to be honest about a transgression and face potentially negative consequences (e.g., divulging the fact that you took an extra two minutes over the allotted test time, which may mean you'll receive a bad grade). Would you try to make an excuse to avoid discomfort, saying something like: "It wasn't really my fault," "I didn't see the time," or "What's two minutes anyway?" What would you do? We all like to think we'd be honest, but how many of us really would put that ideal into practice? We may idealize honesty, but we may not live it; that's the difference between an ideal and a genuine value.

PRACTICE: NOTE YOUR VALUES

Think about three people you admire. They can be famous or not, real or imagined. Then write down the values they embody. Perhaps it's Michael Jordan, who embodies values of persistence, patience, and boldness. Perhaps it's your neighbor, who embodies values of kindness, empathy, and selflessness. Circle those values that resonate with you. Consider how these values show up in your life. Are they values you abide by?

LIVING IN VALUES

Just as you consider your personal values, you might want to consider doing the same for where you want to go to college. Do more than look at a magazine ranking. Get a sense for what the institution idealizes. This requires a bit more digging, as the majority of universities seem to value similar things: kindness, community, curiosity. If you've attended more than one information session or college tour, you might have gotten some of them confused with each other. All their brochures boast: "Undergraduate teaching! Study abroad! A fun community that loves to learn!" Institutions advertise in this manner because they recognize that these are aspects of the educational experience that help to develop human beings into curious scholars wanting to make the world a better place.

When you look deeper, you will find that even these seemingly similar institutions hold different values. It's not in what they say, but what they do and how they do it. If you value close connections with your professors, investigate what the school actually offers and what current students and recent alumni say. Sure, there may be Nobel Peace Prize–winning professors there, but do any of them actually teach? And if they teach, what is the quality and depth of that teaching? Do they lecture to three hundred people or conduct a weekly seminar with fifteen students? What do you value? Perhaps you value their personal presence and being in a large classroom is perfectly fine with you. Perhaps you value more individual interaction, so being in a class of ten is more your speed. There is no right or wrong, better or worse—it's just what's right for you.

PRACTICE: NOTE INSTITUTIONAL VALUES

Think about what is important to you in your next learning environment. Ignore what you "should" care about. Truly look inward at your values, your preferences, and what makes you feel like you will be authentically yourself. This is not the same thing as playing it safe, however. Think about what environments might push you to a level of discomfort that will encourage you to grow and become a better version of yourself. Take a look at some of the institutions on your list and start investigating whether their values align with yours. Review their website, their student blogs. Review the official channels and the unofficial ones—what are current students saying? Recent alumni? Is there someone who recently graduated from your high school who is there whom you can ask? Consult multiple sources, as it is important to gain different perspectives beyond one experience.

FIND YOUR MOTIVATION

You're likely caught up day-in and day-out with a long list of things you *have* to do. You go to Kumon because your mom makes you; you run three miles a day because your coach makes you; you volunteer on Saturdays because your guidance counselor says you should. You probably have this inner nagging feeling of wanting to push back and say, "ENOUGH. What about what *I* want to do?"

That's your inner self trying to get your attention.

When we're driven by external motivations, we may get things done, but we are less invested, and when we are less invested, we aren't giving it our all or our best performance. Once we complete a task, we check off the box and move on. If you continue on this path, you might do fine—at least externally. You might even end up at your top-choice school, graduate with top honors, get the top job, marry the top person, have the top children, and die the top way. But for many people, even those who seem to "have it all," if they never find their true, inner motivation, all of those trappings are just that—"trappings." Many adults find themselves in "golden handcuffs," where they have the resources and things symbolizing that they have "made it" in modern society, but they are deeply unhappy. This leads to over 70 percent of American adults being disengaged at work, and 50 percent of them with wandering minds, daydreaming about "what ifs."

That doesn't sound like a great way to live, does it?

This is not an invitation to ignore the advice of everyone around you who cares about you, and just say, "I'll do my own thing." Life *is* about learning and being part of a greater community. There are times when your parents making you get up every morning to go to practice *is* valuable; it helps you to learn about persistence, grit, and delayed gratification. Just because something is unpleasant in the moment doesn't mean it's not worth experiencing. You can shift these experiences; instead of resisting and hating every minute it, try paying attention to what you might learn and gain from it— even if you're not loving every second of a piano lesson.

Starting with understanding what really matters to you and what engages you might give you a great advantage in truly finding your intrinsic motivation. Maybe you want to be a doctor—not because someone says you should but because there is something about the field that truly excites and engages you. As Goleman notes, when a student just follows "the teacher's goals for what she *should* learn . . , not thinking much about her own goals, she can develop an attitude that school is all about other people's agendas—and fail to tap her inner reservoir of motivation and engagement."[2] If you never tap into that inner reservoir, you're going to be at a great loss later on. Daniel Pink, author of *Drive*,[3] notes that the strongest performers (and those with greater satisfaction) find three things in what they do: a sense of mastery—they know what they're doing (more or less); a sense of autonomy—they have some degree of latitude and freedom to do things as they desire; and a sense of purpose—they find greater meaning beyond a paycheck or prestige in what they do. When you can tap into these factors, you can not only find this greater sense of purpose but also the courage and grit to stay on course even when things get tough.

PRACTICE: DISCOVER YOUR PURPOSE

Keep a journal and write down things that bring you a sense of satisfaction, joy, and meaning. It might be something as simple as, "I picked up some litter today, and it made me feel good." Return to this journal weekly and circle those things that keep popping up. You might find some patterns about the things that you find gratitude for, experiences that you value, and actions from which you draw fulfillment.

LET IT FLOW

It might seem like highly selective institutions are only looking for Olympic-level runners or Academy-Award-winning-level thespians. And you're just you, trying to figure it all out.

The reality is colleges aren't only looking for Olympic fencers (though they may be intrigued if one happens to apply). They are looking for students who have made some sort of contribution, bring positivity to others, demonstrate a level of creativity and initiative, and take a level of risk to stretch themselves. Maybe you're the student who *has* discovered that one or two things that make you super engaged and happy. Maybe you're the one who has a million-and-one things in mind, and you can't seem to choose one over the other. It's okay. The key is to be aware of what brings you energy and joy—and the knowledge that these things will likely evolve and change over time. It might not be until you reach college, or when you're sixty, that you discover a passion for kayaking, and that's OK too.

You don't have to have it figured out (a secret many adults don't realize is that you don't *ever* have to have it really figured out).

Colleges are looking for students who have the desire to stay curious and keep learning—throughout their lives. And you can take steps to help you identify your interests. In Burnett and Evans's popular course using design thinking and applying it to personal lives, they push the notion of "whyfinding" for finding coherency, whereby one lives "in such a way that you can clearly connect the dots between three things: who you are, what you believe, what you are doing."[4] In order to do so, it is important to have awareness of what is around you, what you find yourself fully engaged in, what energizes you, and what leads you to be fully immersed in the experience. Everything we've been building on so far—enhancing self-awareness, shifting into a more positive mindset, and practicing mindful listening—can support you in finding greater alignment with what energizes and engages you.

According to psychologist Mihaly Csikszentmihalyi (it's pronounced "me-HIGH chick-sent-me-HIGH-ee"—you'll impress a lot of people at parties for saying it correctly), finding *flow* is a critical component of finding this type of engagement. Flow is a term often used in the world of athletics. It is that moment where you're so totally and completely engaged in whatever you're doing, time flies. Top athletes operate at peak performance when their level of skill is being appropriately challenged—they're neither overwhelmed nor overqualified.

Have you ever been on a road bike or making a five-course meal, and you're so immersed in what you're doing that you lose track of time (not like the loss of time spent playing Xbox for seven hours)? There's a sense of ecstasy and clarity, as if time is standing still, when your strengths and abilities are being utilized, and you are challenged enough but not too much. You feel completely involved in what you're doing—there is a feeling of elation which is simultaneously serene, a sense of inner clarity as though you're where you should be, you know you can do it, you want to do it (even though no one is telling you to), and time just passes.[5]

That feeling of ecstasy and clarity isn't just your imagination. Your brain is actually producing chemicals that give you a natural high. What professor Richard Davidson has observed in studies is that, with more practice where the brain can focus on the present moment, your brain actually releases a neurotransmitter chemical called *acetylcholine*. This chemical is what gives you a sense of calmness and focus so that you can more easily slip into the "zone."[6]

When we do that *and* we have trained ourselves to be more aware of our values and motivations, we're more likely to know what gets us excited, keeps us engaged, and brings us joy. Maybe it's watercolor painting; maybe it's hiking in the woods; maybe it's an algorithm to solve. Whatever it is, when you're more attuned and view things with a positive attitude, you're more likely to find yourself in a state of flow. You know those moments where you're doing something and you totally lose track of time? Not because you're zoning out and watching a movie but because you're so engrossed. And it doesn't necessarily mean things are easy. Maybe you're in the zone when you're in mile 22 of your first marathon or on hour 5 of a day-long "Chemistry Olympiad." You feel it. All your senses are engaged; your brain is fully present and focused on what you're doing, and you might be so caught up that you forget to eat. You get a sense of thrill and satisfaction. Flow allows us to operate in peak performance. When we are in flow, we are being challenged adequately while maintaining skill and mastery, so we don't feel like things are too easy, and we don't feel totally overwhelmed.

It's also important to note that, according to scientists, it's not about having a million moments where you feel sort of "fine" but about having those "high" moments. Psychologist Ed Diener noted that the intensity of positive emotions, not how often you have semi-positive experiences, is a better predictor of your happiness.[7] In other words, fewer "oh, wow!" moments can help boost your sustained happiness more than many "meh, cool" ones. Flow can give you more of those intense "wow" moments.

Whatever you are doing may or may not be your passion. Goleman argues that it doesn't matter if the passion isn't set in stone, but that "initial passion can be the seed for high levels of attainments, as the child comes to realize that pursuing the field . . . is a source of the joy of flow. And since it takes pushing the limits of one's ability to sustain flow, that becomes a prime motivator for getting better and better; it makes the child happy."[8] When you find yourself in flow, you're likely going to take on extracurricular activities from which you draw meaning and joy. And when you do, you're more likely to do better and others will recognize that. You might end up leading these efforts— whether in a formal or informal position. And if you do, your teachers and counselors can speak more about your impact to admissions officers, and your application becomes even stronger, NOT because it is well crafted but because it is genuine. Admissions officers can be skeptical about long lists of extracurriculars, particularly those that seem a bit too curated. But when they're genuine, it becomes pretty evident because that thread of authenticity flows throughout.

PRACTICE: FINDING FLOW

Over the next week, jot down the times when you lose track of time because you're completely immersed, and your skills and senses are fully engaged and being utilized; make notes about these specific activities in a journal. Reflect on those moments to see if there are any areas of similarity or difference. Consider how you might find more moments that allow you to utilize those skills and face challenges for even greater flow.

CHASING HAPPINESS

It might seem like all the adults in your life are always pushing— pushing to get ahead and to help you get ahead—as a way to achieve happiness. Even the most well-meaning of us can misconstrue material things and wealth as the providers of joy. Yet you probably see the level of stress people are under, trying to chase dreams that will somehow ultimately bring them happiness. But they don't seem very happy.

Author Shawn Achor rightfully said that "we're not happy when we're chasing happiness. We're happiest . . . when we're enjoying the present moment because we're lost in a meaningful project, working towards a higher goal, or helping someone who needs it."[9] Paying more attention to your brain, to awareness, and to a purpose beyond yourself are key to happiness. In addition to sharpening mental agility, when you observe more and have greater awareness of these higher goals, you not only find greater relief from undue stress but you also can channel your energy into more positive things that bring a greater sense of well-being.

Positive psychologist Martin Seligman identifies five components that support well-being, none of which includes money, getting an admissions letter, or a fancy car. These five components he names PERMA: 1) Positive emotion, such as hope; 2) Engagement, such as flow; 3) Relationships, such as meaningful connections; 4) Meaning, such as service; and 5) Accomplishments/achievement, such as life satisfaction. As you can see, much of this has do with finding meaning—meaning in relationships, in actions, and in emotions.

Having a greater sense of meaning can also give you the space to be more creative and open. No longer are you just doing things because you "should" or struggling with things that deenergize you, you're doing things that bring a smile to your face. Some of you might be keen to become the next great entrepreneur. However, you cannot if you're stuck and mired in the "should" rather than the "what could be." That's where innovation comes in. As Dan Siegel notes, bringing personal joy and values leads to playfulness, which permits creativity and innovation.[10]

Even if you have figured out some of your core values and purpose for doing what you do, it's another thing to do something about it. Colleges are not just looking for what you *say* you care about; they are also looking for what you've actually *done* to get a sense for what you *might do* on their campuses and, subsequently, in the world. Impact, as admissions officers say. They want to know what kind of an impact you have had in school and your community.

Putting your values into action is a part of understanding the "how" and the "why" of what will prepare you for a life of contribution and impact. With the privilege of higher education comes a level of responsibility for you to pay it forward. Research suggests that if you pursue status for status sake, you might be doing your health and well-being a disservice.[11] The pursuit of higher education is not just about you. It's about how you can make a positive impact in the world. By setting a purpose statement, you're then able to articulate smaller goals to get there. For example, if your purpose statement is to help bring joy to others, maybe your immediate short-term goal is to join the Kindness Club at school. Your next three-month goal may be to initiate a letter-writing campaign to peers in need, and so on and so forth.

Moreover, you need to ensure that you have a support network. You cannot do it yourself, even if you think you can. For each goal, it's wise to hold yourself accountable to others so that you actually follow through with it, and also so you can find the necessary support to help get you there. Putting into action that which gives you meaning and purpose is essential for a life of well-being and impact. And doing so with others offers greater satisfaction and likelihood of success.

PRACTICE: PURPOSE TO IMPACT

Reviewing your values and motivations, consider what your purpose is and remember that it will evolve over time. Your purpose shouldn't be "get into college"—that is but a milestone that serves a deeper and broader purpose. Then identify three to four other milestones to help you reach your purpose statement. Identify at least two individuals, such as a teacher or a friend, to help you get there and to hold you accountable.

Chapter Twenty

Self-Compassion

You're Pretty Darn Awesome

The college admissions process can be a brutal one. High school is not always easy. Adulting is not always easy. Nothing really is. Even those people who always seem like they have it all figured out often feel the way you do. Yet while we are so encouraging of others, we tend to be super hard on ourselves, which messes with our confidence and our ability to truly thrive. Those things affect your performance and how you show up. Keep in mind that colleges aren't looking for "finished products" and it's important to not beat yourself up over imperfection. In fact, it's important to celebrate it.

Let's take a look at how "self-compassion" and compassion for others is key to thriving, and some practices to get you on track.

DON'T BE AN "A**HOLE"

It might seem on most television shows that to get ahead, you have to take everyone else down. After all, only *one* kid from your school is going to get into Princeton, right? And that person better be you. So if that means bulldozing your way through, you're gonna do it.

Is that the kind of person you want to be?

You have heard repeatedly that going to college is not just about you but what you're going to do to help make the world a better place. Colleges love to boast that they have the happiest campus or about the warmth of their communities. After all, who wants to be known as the college that breeds selfish jerks—who would want to go there? You probably wouldn't. Jerks aren't fun to be around and they don't make the most positive impact in the world. And no college wants to have a highlight reel of "jacka**" alumni.

Rather, colleges are looking for students who will be alumni they can be proud of. This is partly why the most selective institutions aren't going to just ask for your grades but for evidence as to who you are as a person as well. Are you someone who would make a great classmate or roommate? Are you someone who shows a level of self- and other-awareness and who extends kindness and generosity to the people around you? Are you someone who sees beyond themselves? Want to be known and respected as a leader? Be selfless, not self-promoting. Psychologist Robb Willer studied how generosity increases reputation, status, and ability to influence others.[1]

If you want positive recommendation letters or positions of influence in clubs or recognized honors from your school, you actually have to be nice, kind, thoughtful. When you are, people around you will respond more positively, which enables you to be more effective and impactful. Your teachers will notice. Your classmates will notice. Then the admissions officers will notice. Your kindness and character may be the reason why you are admitted despite having a lower GPA than the valedictorian who seems cold and mean. That same kindness also prepares you for a lifetime of contribution and positivity, and a greater sense of well-being.

Many colleges and universities are open about how they consider your level of "a**holeness." Pay attention to how a college writes its essay questions. As the *New York Times* noted, "even subtle differences in criteria may reveal something about a college's values, or at least those of its admissions dean. Maria Laskaris, the [former] admissions dean at Dartmouth College . . . said she directed her staff to consider 'empathy' rather than 'kindness.' 'It's a broader term,' she said. 'And it speaks to what you want students to learn from each other.'"[2] Other institutions have similar practices, placing some level of value on how you engage with others and how you behave with others. This concept is not exclusive to undergraduate students. In fact, Dartmouth's business school, Tuck, made headlines for being open about including "kindness" as part of their evaluation process. While how you measure kindness is a trickier metric, the fact that a leading MBA program explicitly articulates that kindness belongs in the traditionally cutthroat environment of a business school speaks volumes about why it's important not to be a complete jerk.

PRACTICE: ATTEND TO KINDNESS

Pay attention to the essays a college asks you to write. Pay attention to their communications and brochures, and how they describe the community. Don't just take their word for it. Pay attention to what alumni and students say about the community. Consider how and why this matters to you. What is the role of empathy and kindness at the institution? How might you bring greater awareness and kindness to the community?

CONNECTION TO OTHERS

Not being a jerk to others is only part of the equation. To be less of a jerk, we have to understand how other people feel because, when we do, we're putting ourselves in their shoes and recognizing that they, like us, are just human beings trying to figure it all out. We can better place ourselves in other people's shoes by practicing empathy and compassion. It's not simply sympathizing with others but truly feeling (emotionally) as they do. Let's take the analogy of being in an airplane where the cabin pressure has dropped, and so have those oxygen masks the flight attendants demonstrate how to use before takeoff but to which you pay no mind. With sympathy, you're putting on your mask and you look over to the other person, truly feeling sorry for them but not so much that you do anything. As you put on your mask, you look on with pity as they pass out. With empathy, you're feeling the other person's pain so much that you first fumble to put on their oxygen mask. As you fumble with it, feeling their pain, you forget that you haven't taken care of your own mask and you pass out. With compassion, you're feeling the pain of the other person—but you know that, to be of service, you have to first put on your own oxygen mask. *Then* you're in a place where you can help the other person with their mask. And you both survive.

Empathy allows us to feel what others do. Empathetic concern helps us resonate with others. Empathetic distress gets us to take on the pain of others. Compassion goes beyond caring about or feeling for someone else; it's like empathy and then some because it adds the motivation to help the other person.

These feelings aren't just feelings—there are physiological responses that actually occur in your brain. The *insula* is the part of our brain where we feel pain when we perceive pain in someone else. Our insula gets triggered when we practice empathy and share the other person's emotion. If you get stabbed in the hand with a pencil (ouch, did you flinch?), my brain might trigger that same area of pain "feeling" for you. I'm feeling your distress, but not so much that I'm still motivated to actually help you.

Goleman articulates three kinds of empathy that activate different parts of our brains:

1. Cognitive empathy: Understanding how others see and think about the situation
2. Emotional empathy: Sensing another's emotions with an inner sense or "chemical connection"
3. Empathic concern: Being motivated by basic human desire to care and act with empathy[3]

He argues that classrooms that support empathy actually give students' brains the space to achieve a more optimal state of cognitive efficiency and empathy. Think about the classrooms and teachers with whom you felt super safe, sensing that they genuinely cared about you. You didn't feel like you had to always prove yourself or walk on eggshells. Rather, you felt secure. And when you felt secure, your brain was so much more ready to learn, to take risks, to be creative, and importantly, to care about your classmates.

PRACTICE: OTHER AWARE

Next time a friend or someone else is sharing something of importance to them, instead of trying to "solve" their issue or share your opinions, simply be present. Observe their body language, their tone, their word choice. Imagine what it feels like to experience what they are experiencing. Put yourself in the other person's shoes.

BE YOUR OWN FRIEND

It's easy to think that your admittance to college dictates your worth. As Frank Bruni notes, "A yes or no from [an elite college or university] is seen as the conclusive measure of a younger person's worth, an uncontestable harbinger of the accomplishments or disappointments to come. Winner or loser: this is when the judgment is made."[4] Even if you get in, you will likely continue to judge yourself. No matter what someone else says to comfort you, you are constantly nagged by this sense that you're a loser or something else that is not so nice.

How many times harder are you on yourself than on your friends? Do you say things about yourself you would never dare to say to another person, particularly a person about whom you care deeply? When you experience a setback or failure, do you say things like, "You're such a moron! You're never going to get in anywhere. You're a loser. Give up!"? Many of us would never say this to our best friend but we do to ourselves.

Some of us also experience the imposter syndrome, the inner critic that makes us live in fear that someone will find out we don't know what we're doing. For example, you got into the AP class but now you're worried that others will discover you don't "belong." Did you get into college and wonder if the admissions officers made a "mistake" and will kick you out? These feelings of inadequacy can be pervasive in life if you do not pay attention to how they show up.

One of the most difficult yet most important things to do is to be your own friend. Know that you are enough. You are worthy. You deserve happiness. Self-awareness and mindfulness is critical to building self-compassion. When we face any kind of setback, we often turn criticism inward. But when we turn kindness inward instead, we "reduce over-identification with the difficult experience, making it easier to remain mindfully aware of it."[5] With self-kindness, we aren't dwelling on or presuming that a particular setback defines us forever and ever but, rather, that it was a temporary experience. Beyond mindfulness and self-kindness is self-compassion, which empowers us to act and to help ourselves and others.

Compassion researcher Kristin Neff's studies show that self-compassion can reduce rumination and depressive symptoms and increase positive affect and life satisfaction. Turning compassion inward has other added benefits, particularly for people your age, by actively disengaging your habit of ruminating (what you shoulda/woulda/coulda done) and releasing judgment. As we now know, your sympathetic nervous system is particularly sensitive to stimuli, so you may be super reactive to anything that anyone says. Someone likes your shoes—you're on cloud nine. Someone makes a comment about how your hair looks like a hornet's nest—you're down in the pits of despair. At this age, you are particularly vulnerable to psychological distress and sensitive to self-criticism, judgment, and feelings of shame.[6] If you live in this space for too long, you may elevate the risk for the development of mental health problems and a lifetime of anxiety.

Think about those times you get down on yourself for a grade or a performance and start going down a rabbit hole, certain that you're never going to get in anywhere, or that you'll be the laughingstock of your school, or that you'll be written out of your parents' will for not getting into *their* dream college. It's not enough to just "pick yourself up." For a long time, self-esteem served a panacea for all your woes. You may have even received instruction on building your self-esteem.

Telling yourself that "You're awesome! You're the best!" doesn't seem to work, or at least not in a sustainable way. You might feel initially better, but the minute you face another setback, you're back down that hole. Neff's research suggests that self-esteem tends to be more an evaluation of your self-worth ("are you a good or bad person?"). On the other hand, self-compassion is a different path to building your confidence. It is about relating to yourself with greater kindness, recognizing that you're not alone and that others are likely feeling the same. It allows you to see what is happening within a larger context and to be more present and aware. Self-compassion may help with depression and anxiety, and can give you greater life satisfaction and connection with others.[7] It can offer a more stable sense of self so that when your self-esteem takes a tumble, your self-compassion steps in to pick you up and keep you afloat.

Psychologist Tania Singer's research shows that while empathy allows us to resonate with the pain of others, if we're not careful, we may respond with empathetic distress and burnout. Compassion, on the other hand, allows us to feel concern without feeling snowed under. Compassion engages a different circuitry of the brain. Instead of the area associated with pain, it is associated with the area related to warmth, love, and concern. As Neff articulates, self-compassion allows us to hold pain—ours or someone else's—and try to amend the situation.[8]

There are also physiological changes that occur with more practice of self-compassion. It can reduce your stress hormones, including *cortisol*, and release *oxytocin*, the happy one, that makes you feel safe and secure.[9] This primes you to thrive and stay motivated, so that when life gives you lemons, you're not sour forever.

In her fifteen years of research, Neff saw that self-compassion increases longer-term well-being, decreasing your chances of anxiety and depression, and building your life satisfaction and even your immune function. While some people think that being "compassionate" means being soft and easy on yourself, she found the opposite. Self-compassion increases motivation because it allows us to face our fear of failure, which is often our biggest block. It also makes us take more responsibility for our mistakes so we own up to them and can improve.[10]

Dr. Richard Davidson studied two hundred monks to better understand the nature of compassion, and discovered that there are physical changes to those with a deep practice. Another study involved laymen who had a two-week compassion intervention for thirty minutes a day and compared them with a group taught cognitive reappraisal techniques—in other words, to reframe things—and found that the former demonstrated more prosocial skills, reacted less, and recovered more quickly from being negatively triggered than the latter group.[11]

PRACTICE: SHOW A LITTLE COMPASSION

Think about a recent setback or failure. Let yourself feel the disappointment, sadness, anxiety. Now imagine that you step outside of yourself, and you see yourself experiencing these feelings of disappointment and sadness. Imagine that you are a friend to yourself, watching and experiencing these not-so-great feelings. What would you say to yourself as a friend? What are the positive and supportive words that you say?

IT'S NOT ALL ABOUT YOU

Emotional awareness and intelligence are critical foundations for generating more compassion for yourself. While a few critics might think that focusing on yourself is selfish, the opposite happens when you enhance your levels of EI. If you're practicing self-compassion because you think it will give you an advantage to get into your dream school, keep practicing.

Doing so builds your capacity to understand how others are feeling and what they are thinking. When we build our capacity for empathy, we are better attuned to another person. When they feel pain, we feel their pain. When they feel joy, we feel their joy. When we pay more attention to these interactions, we can build our sense of compassion and caring for others.

Self-compassion helps us to be kinder to ourselves and empowers us with the capacity for truly helping others. Dr. Antoine Lutz studied how compassion training actually impacts our brain in a different way and allows us to act, rather than just sitting and thinking "aw, that's too bad!" In a study of monks with over 10,000 hours of meditation, he found that compassion training triggered a different neural pathway where they could share emotions but not feel distress. Instead, it activates the brain regions associated with affiliation and positive affect.[12] If I train in compassion, I can not only feel and empathize with your hand hurting, but I'm actually motivated to do something to help you.

As His Holiness the Dalai Lama notes, "compassion is the wish for another being to be free from suffering; love is wanting them to have happiness . . . genuine compassion is based not on our own projects and expectations, but rather on the needs of the other."[13] While anger can take over our rational brains, remaining humble and sincere is critical to maintaining a more compassionate approach to everyone and everything. The Dalai Lama also states that it isn't simply up to some big government bureaucracy to impose a kinder, more service-related populace. Rather, he notes, "a genuine change must first come from within the individual, then he or she can attempt to make significant contributions to humanity."[14]

You may recognize this call to contribute to humanity from institutions of higher education. Universities often have a mission to prepare leaders and individuals who want to move society forward. It's not just about your grades and your SATs; it is also about how you find and bring meaning and purpose to all that you do. Compassion allows you to attend to the greater good in the world and look beyond yourself.

Even if you aren't quite at the stage of "saving the world," studies show that compassion practices build a more generous and kind world. Little children who learn compassion are more willing to share. By protecting oneself *and* extending that caring to other people, you can be in a better position to be of service to others in a meaningful way. For example, some of you might want to check off community service as a "must have," but it has to come from an authentic space. Admissions officers can often sniff out when you're doing something because someone told you to or if your heart really isn't in it.

Although many colleges will say they don't care what you do, a NYU study showed that it *does* matter what kind of extracurricular activities you choose to an extent. The study showed that especially for low-to-middle-income students, what they decided to do outside of class impacted their academic achievement. Over a three-year study of 625 low-income NYU students, those who were involved in community service and sports teams did better academically. School-based clubs, however, "have zero impact on students' grades."[15] In short, you could be in a million clubs—the Knitting Club, the Finance Club—but it is the involvement in a service-oriented team trying to achieve a greater goal that "makes student[s] feel more connected to a cause bigger than themselves and to others."[16] Helping others is critical not just for others but for your own development. Service-learning (SL) has become a popular way of teaching, which is a way to integrate community service with academics. A meta-analysis of almost 12,000 students showed that SL programs have five key positive outcomes, including improvement in: 1) attitudes toward self; 2) attitudes toward school and learning; 3) civic engagement; 4) social skills; and 5) academic performance.[17] All of these outcomes are beneficial for you as you navigate high school and beyond.

PRACTICE: AT YOUR SERVICE

Consider someone else in need. It can be someone you know well or not at all. Imagine this person in front of you. Imagine what it is like to extend them kindness and warmth. Imagine what it is like to extend them a spirit of generosity and compassion. Imagine what it is like to support their happiness. Consider what steps you can take to help them. Now turn those same feelings of kindness, generosity, and compassion in on yourself.

IT TAKES COURAGE

Some people criticize kindness, empathy, and compassion as being passive and soft. It is quite the opposite. Compassion is not about running away from the problem, but it "begins with accepting what's happening without turning away."[18] Facing reality is no easy feat. You're not avoiding what isn't working nor are you overlooking a transgression. Compassion is not about excusing bad behavior. Rather, it is about facing bad behavior, extending kindness, and doing something about it. Compassion also allows us to really see each other.

Juliana Breines and Serena Chen explore how self-compassion "motivates people to improve personal weakness, moral transgression, and test performance."[19] Self-compassion allows us to treat ourselves how we would treat a friend—with greater warmth and kindness, yet at the same time being more willing to have a realistic appraisal of what is happening. Breines and Chen found that "self-compassionate individuals have also been found to hold greater mastery as opposed to performance goals, a relationship mediated by self-compassionate participants lowers fear of failure and [increases] perceived competence."[20] In other words, those who practice self-compassion aren't just focused on the A but demonstrate mastery over something, have lower feelings of the imposter syndrome, and have greater beliefs in their own abilities. All of these aspects are things that speak well to your record and to your potential. Even if you aren't an Olympic fencer (yet), you may have faced the fact that you are not a natural runner, and because of that, you have committed extra time and dedication to improving your time. That boosts your confidence about your abilities and lessens your feeling of "being found out," since you have already acknowledged your shortcomings.

For adolescents, research suggests that self-compassion is even more paramount to well-being. Remember that up to 20 percent of youth exhibit mental health problems. These mental health challenges stem from stress, anxiety, and depression. Especially since "adolescence is a time of significant biophysical change, as such adolescents' sympathetic nervous system[s] are highly 'primed' for activation, thus elevating risk for development of psychopathology. Adolescents have a magnified need to exist positive[ly] in others' regard. This need may be a source of increased self-criticism, self-judgment, and shame."[21] The good news is that a meta-analysis showed that mindfulness and self-compassion can predict lower levels in all these areas of potential risk. A small study at the University of Wisconsin's Center for Healthy Minds showed that even two weeks of compassion meditation helped to build participants' resilience so that they could empathize with others' suffering without becoming so upset that they became paralyzed.[22]

His Holiness the Dalai Lama dismantles the myth that compassion is entirely other-serving to the sacrifice of oneself, or that it means acceptance of injustices. In fact, he argues that "the first beneficiary of compassion is always oneself. . . . Compassion reduces our fear, boosts our confidence, and brings us a sense of connection."[23] Compassion results in caring about the welfare of others, which brings up our sense of ethics and, therefore, makes us more willing to help others and bring about action that adheres to our ethics—in other words, we are more willing to fight for justice and for what we believe to be right. And, he adds, "the more one gives, the more one enjoys giving."[24] Serving ourselves allows us to serve others, which again allows us to serve ourselves.

Such service can have big impact. Major General Walter Piatt shared a story in which a practice of mindful compassion shifted the entire relationship between the U.S. armed forces and an Afghani tribe. After a medical demonstration in a village, a grenade was thrown at U.S. armed vehicles. Instead of immediately retaliating and shooting the grenade thrower and potentially harming children milling about, the U.S. gunner paused. He noticed that the grenade thrower was a child himself. The Major General then went door to door to find the person responsible, and two weeks later, the elders of the village brought a man whose son was the culprit. They begged the Major General to arrest the father in place of the son. However, Piatt decided to extend compassion and instead introduced the boy to the military unit. Both sides saw a common humanity. From that day on, the community provided information to the soldiers and refused to allow the Taliban into the village. In other words, "by not acting, [they] acted decisively."[25] This "inaction" took tremendous courage and resulted in a battle-free cooperation with the village: "We built more relationships with that tribe that day through compassion."[26]

Self-compassion takes courage, and courage enhances your capacity to grow and to make a genuine and broad impact on the world around you. It is not only what colleges are looking for but also a noble purpose for your life.

PRACTICE: FACE THE MONSTERS

Bring to mind a setback or failure. Rather than dwell on what you don't do well, extend compassion toward yourself. Extend a sense of kindness while acknowledging what didn't work well. With the same feeling of kindness, consider reframing the situation and see what positive learning you can draw from it. What do you need to make improvements for the next time? What does it feel like to permit yourself imperfection in the pursuit of growth?

V

Go For It:
Embracing Peaks and Valleys

As we have seen so far, emotional intelligence competencies can enable us to recognize what we can and cannot control, manage our internal anxieties, and navigate relationships with others such that we can move through the college admissions process with greater centeredness. They can support our capacity to manage the ebbs and flows in life, to celebrate but not be swept away by fortune, and to accept but not be buried by failure.

Yet getting into college, wherever you may land, is only one milestone. Thriving in college can compound existing anxieties and add new ones. Emotional intelligence may offer critical tools that can help you thrive, not just while you are trying to get into college but as you embrace the ups and downs during college—and well beyond.

Chapter Twenty-One

College 101

What Your Prereqs Won't Teach You

So you got into college! Congratulations!

Now what?

You're likely relieved, scared, anxious, excited, in disbelief (someone made a mistake, right?). You're worried about fitting in, about graduating, about getting a job. You're worried about making friends, the grades, and the tuition.

You're also at risk of burnout. Some of you may be so exhausted that you feel like you don't have the bandwidth to handle any more pressure. But you know college is about to start. Here's the thing about college admissions—after that intensely stressful process, you might end up *attending*. And attending and graduating means a whole host of new stressors and challenges and opportunities. While you may have stretched yourself thin to "get in," hopefully, you will have started employing some of these tactics so you have navigated the process with a bit more ease and grace, now less at risk of burnout, and more primed to embrace new challenges.

How do you take advantage of these new challenges and not burn out? We've already talked about how there has been a dramatic rise in the need for mental health services among college students. While there are many reasons for this increase, the rise can be partly attributed to the fact that the same anxiety-ridden stressors and lack of tools to handle them in high school are following students straight into their first-year dorms.

Like these students, you likely have a number of different advisors—a faculty member, a dean, an upperclassman. They are all there to help you transition from clueless high school student to clueless college freshman. They will show you how to register for classes, the difference between APA- and Chicago-style citations, and the hidden messages of the *Iliad*. They will point you in the right direction to apply for a Rhodes scholarship or help you make sure you have compelling action verbs on your résumé. But a lot of what you need to thrive—not just survive—in college isn't going to be found in Biology 101.

Let's take a look at some of the tips to help make your transition a healthier, happier, and more hopeful one.

BEFRIEND THE IMPOSTER

Remember the imposter syndrome? You know, that inner voice that keeps saying to you, "Hey you! You got in? It was a mistake! Someone is going to find out and then you're going to get kicked out of school."

Here's a little secret: Pretty much everyone around you is feeling the same thing, even those who seem super confident and flawless. They, too, harbor a little voice telling them to doubt themselves.

Remember this: You got in. You belong. Admissions officers take so much time doing this work, they don't often make mistakes. As a human being, you're always going to have various thoughts going through your head. Sometimes, the voice that tells you to be cautious is there to protect you. Sometimes, the voice that tells you you're no good is simply your own self-doubt. Rather than trying to push these thoughts away or pretend they don't exist, befriend the monster.

How?

- *Practice mindfulness.* Come back into your practice and bring awareness to what you're feeling and where in your body you are feeling it. Do you feel tension in your chest or a heaviness? Bringing awareness to what and where you are feeling these things is the first step in acknowledging rather than avoiding.
- *Avoid judgment.* Witness these thoughts of inadequacy or doubt without judgment. They are just thoughts—not good or bad, but simply thoughts.

- *Be curious.* Consider viewing these thoughts with a sense of curiosity. From where might this doubt be coming? For what purpose?
- *Be gracious.* Thank the imposter for trying to protect you, and let the imposter out the door of your mind. It was visiting, and now your house is too full for it to stay.

From time to time, the imposter might knock on your door. It will happen a lot, in college and afterwards. Instead of trying to run from it—the more you do, the more it will chase you—open the door and acknowledge its presence, thank it for trying to protect you, and let it retreat back to the wild.

EMBRACE DISCOMFORT

No one really likes to be uncomfortable, or at least, not for too long. No matter how much we like to say we love change, human beings are creatures of habit (just think how often you switch toothpaste brands or what you have for breakfast). But you're quite on your way to one of the most unsettling of times—you're a first-year student in a sea of strangers, without the comforts of the familiar. Even the food is different, maybe the weather is, too, and so are your friends.

College is meant to put you in new situations. You already made a huge leap that pretty much proves that you are willing to step outside your comfort zone. If you didn't, you wouldn't bother going to college. However many years you decide to take to finish college, and whatever comes thereafter, never let yourself become too complacent. When you become too content and secure, you are less likely to strive to do your best. Maybe you'll still graduate from college, but you will be doing so likely missing out on all the amazing things that are there. You might even get a job—but remember, there are many, many other people who would also love your job. Being complacent means you might not be aware of the trends and opportunities out there—maybe it's a study abroad or internship opportunity. If you're too satisfied with what you have, it's like you're putting blinders on to new experiences. Being complacent means you might not be maintaining or building your network—and this network is going to be important during and after college. Being complacent for fear of disrupting the status quo means you're not being totally honest with others or yourself.

College is a time for you to try things you might never, ever do again in your life (healthy things, that is). For example, if you've never joined a singing group before, why not give it a go? You might be horrible at it, but what's the harm? It might be an experience you'll never forget. Who knows, you might end up uncovering a hidden talent.

College is a time to learn new things. Did you enter college knowing you want to be an economics major? Why not take an art history class? You never know whether art history might become useful in your study of economics—or even your career.

College is a time to make friends and connections with people you never thought you would. That kid with the blue hair or the popped collar that you would *never* say hello to in high school? What's the harm in sitting next to them in the cafeteria? It might be a short interaction that lasts two minutes or it might turn into a lifelong friendship.

Trying new things and being in new spaces can be unsettling and uncomfortable. But it may significantly improve your college experience and prepare you for a lifetime of courage.

How?

- *Start small.* Perhaps signing up for a musical is too big a risk, but maybe attending a chorus meeting for an evening or two might just be the dose of discomfort necessary for you to feel what it's like to make a bigger leap.
- *Sit in awareness.* Instead of avoiding your emotions, settle into discomfort and bring awareness to your thoughts and where in your body you are feeling sensations. Don't suppress them; let them be, label them, and release.
- *Try something new.* Every day, try something new or different that you haven't done before. Maybe it is something as small as switching your morning apple with morning oatmeal. The more micro-changes you experience, the more comfortable you will become with the bigger changes.
- *Sit in the discomfort.* Remember that when you're feeling uncomfortable with new things, you're likely growing. You probably don't remember it but when your teeth were growing in, your body hurt. A bit of pain and discomfort is necessary for you to grow.

LEARN. FAIL. LEARN.

School for you might have lost its luster because you were so focused on the SAT or the Regents. Many of you bemoan the loss of intellectual curiosity and freedom. Guess what? This is your chance to reclaim it.

College is not just about parties or sitting in a huge lecture hall bored to death. It is an endlessly full candy store for the curious. If you don't see that, then you might want to rethink why you're in college in the first place. If you think going to class is a chore, then you might want to reconsider that this might not be the best place or the best time for you to be in college. And if you do, be kind to yourself; it is not good nor bad but just where you are right now. If you miss learning, this is your chance.

You also probably went through high school and most of your life *never* failing. Failing meant a rejection letter—or worse. We run from failure. Yet the reality is that failure is actually vital to progress and growth. Author Kathryn Schulz argues that "far from being a sign of intellectual inferiority, the capacity to err is crucial to human cognition."[1] In fact, if you look at the most successful people, these are the people who also failed the most. Even though it might seem that successful people became successful overnight, those instances are rare. In his famous response to what it was like to fail 1,000 times before the light bulb worked, Thomas Edison said that it was simply an invention that required 1,000 steps. As a baby, you likely took way more than 1,000 falls before you actually learned to wobble, let alone walk or run.

College is the time for you to intellectually experiment. Sure, you might not get the 4.0 every quarter, but you might end up with a device that can save the lives of millions. Sure, you might not invent a device that can save the lives of millions, but you might end up with the resiliency that will enable you to navigate the vicissitudes of life with greater ease and grace.

If you fear failure, you fear learning. And the reality is that your family and you are investing a lot—in money and time and energy—for you to learn. So embrace the opportunity to learn. Step into the subjects you never heard of before or that sound "not like you." Ever say, "I'm not an English person; I'm not a math person"? The magical thing about college is that an English class can take so many different shapes, as can math classes. So try them out. You never know how those experiences might expand your thinking—or even take you in a totally different direction, one that will bring you incredible joy.

How?

- *Embrace the growth mindset.* Recall Dweck's work and shift your mindset from one that is fixed. Recognize that your current skillset or understanding is expandable, and that you can train your brain to learn new things.
- *Get to know your professors.* According to Frank Bruni's research, most students miss out on one of the most important relationships to invest in in college: that with faculty members.[2] These aren't just talking heads; these are potentially your mentors for life. They may help you break through and reach your intellectual potential. They may end up supporting you for graduate school now or ten years from now. They may end up becoming important life coaches.
- *Go to class.* Don't just show up and sit in back of the lecture hall. Speak up. Debate your professors. Create study groups. Soak it all in. Rare is the time in your life where you will have another opportunity to simply engage.
- *Be vulnerable.* Recognize what didn't work. Own up to the part you might have played when you fail in some way—maybe you didn't study enough, maybe you procrastinated, maybe your body just isn't designed optimally to be a basketball player. Be honest and open with yourself, even if the truth is uncomfortable.
- *Be kind.* Show yourself some kindness. There is no need to judge or criticize—just recognize the effort.
- *Reframe the experience.* Rather than ruminate and dwell on what didn't work, consider the situation and reframe it so you might learn or gain from it.
- *Add necessary support.* Consider what you need or who you might need to talk to in order to make the next attempt more successful. If you repeat the same action with the same mistakes, you can't really expect a different result, so adjust as necessary.
- *Try again.* Get out there and try again. You'll likely have to make a few adjustments, but then give it a go. You might fail again, and have the opportunity to learn again.

BUILD RESILIENCY

Failures and setbacks *will happen.* They will happen for the rest of your life. A fancy college admit letter doesn't inoculate you against life's ills. The key is not to pretend or avoid these setbacks, but to build your resiliency so that you bounce back from them more quickly.

Emerging science shows that those who have a steady mindfulness practice, for example, meditating, can build their resiliency so that they are not as anxiety-ridden in anticipation of stresses, and they also recover more quickly when things don't go well.

You're going to have times when you get a bad grade, or your lab experiment is messed up, or you don't get the lead role, or you don't get that internship. Your roommate gets mad at you. Your crush doesn't return your feelings. Your parents get mad at you. Instead of ruminating and dwelling on these setbacks, building your resilience means building your capacity to bounce back and recover—not by avoiding but by facing setbacks and emerging even stronger.

How?

- *Journal.* Studies show those who keep a journal are more likely to achieve their goals and gain a better sense of well-being than those who do not. It also allows you to take note of your emotions and thoughts as they evolve, and gives you a space to express. Writing things down can help raise your awareness of what is happening around you without necessarily ruminating about it in your mind. In one study, participants who practiced "expressive writing," that is, free writing for 20 minutes, had greater optimism and engagement with life.[3]
- *Practice self-compassion.* As we saw previously, extending the same kind of warmth and kindness to yourself as you do to your friends will help you to face what didn't work with a gentle honesty and the courage to do something about it and improve upon it.
- *Be present.* Our resilience falters when we're stuck in the past or not trying to live in the present. By bringing more awareness to what is happening in front of us with a sense of curiosity and nonjudgment, you start to build your ability to face what is in front of you without running away from it or pushing it away.

MAKE FRIENDS AND BE NICE

It's important not to be a jerk. This is important not just for getting into college but for how you do in college and after. If you're attending a selective institution, you probably have thought about the network into which you have now entered. While every institution has a few jerks, the hope is that the majority of people you meet are well-meaning and kind. Even those jerks are generally well-meaning people who have a few things to work on.

Much of your learning in college isn't going to happen in the class-room. Much of it is going to happen in your dorm hallway at one o'clock in the morning or in the dining hall eating fried pizza. It doesn't matter if you're a natural extrovert or introvert. Make friends. Make friends outside your usual circle. This isn't high school where you have to have one "clique." In fact, one of the most amazing things about college is that you'll learn that people move in multiple, overlapping circles. You want to surround yourself with people like and unlike you—people who will challenge you and, importantly, support you. These are the folks who make up this community you worked so hard to enter.

To really make the most of this network of which you are now part, play nice. It isn't about just asking alumni for a job or befriending someone because you think they'll help you get something you want. Being a nice, kind person can take you far. For one thing, it feels better to be nice. Second, being nice is not about being passive or soft. In fact, try being nice to the person that everyone else can't stand. It's one of the hardest things to do but, possibly, one of the most rewarding as well.

Your college years are only four years or so, but you're likely going to be part of an alumni network for many years to come. It seems silly to dismiss your alumni network—after all, you worked hard to be part of this, so be part of it. It isn't just about you, however. It is also about how you're going to help others in the network, younger students who will seek you out. These relationships will evolve over the years, but playing the mentor and the mentee can bring you great joy and satisfaction, not to mention that it might help you get that cool job fifteen years later. It is therefore important to cultivate authentic, real relationships that aren't just based on what you can get out of them. After all, no one likes a user.

How?

- *Say hello.* Say hi to folks who look familiar and those who don't. Don't be afraid to be that person who sits down next to a stranger at a meal. Your interaction might not last more than dessert, but it might last a lifetime.

- *Be genuine.* There is no need to pretend or cover who you are. If you do so now, imagine what you'll have to do to maintain that relationship? It would be exhausting. Just be you—maybe not everyone you meet will become your bestie. And that's okay.
- *Make connections.* Help make connections with your connections. Met someone who loves to play squash, and your hallmate plays squash? Offer to make an introduction. You might not gain anything from it other than that beautiful feeling of connecting human beings with human beings. And that's enough.
- *Be nice.* Avoid the gossip. Avoid bad-mouthing people. Avoid posting things on social media. You've probably heard horror stories of people who've lost jobs, internships, and even college admissions acceptances for posting things on social media that raised questions about their good judgment. Don't be that person. You also never know who someone you bad-mouth might end up being.

BUILD EMOTIONAL INTELLIGENCE AND A HUNGRY MIND

You want to get a job or get into medical school? Sure, your GPA matters. But it's not the only thing. In fact, most HR hiring directors argue that they are not the most concerned about your GPA. One head of research at a global executive search firm says that "CEOs are hired for their intellect and business expertise—and fired for a lack of emotional intelligence."[4]

The World Economic Forum lists emotional intelligence as one of the top ten skills critical to succeed in the twenty-first-century workforce. In a recent Bloomberg Next study, 40 percent of companies and 50 percent of academic institutions believe that folks like you—those with the shiny college degrees—actually lack the skills to be successful. Graduates might have the technical "how-to" and they may have memorized the steps needed to navigate an Excel sheet, but those essential business/life skills—previously dismissed as "soft skills" and almost unnecessary, including emotional intelligence, negotiation, and complex reasoning—are missing.[5] A survey of senior-level leaders speak honestly that they are not just looking for your GPA. Even if they require your transcript, they are also looking for what you do outside of class to get a better sense of your track record of impact, contribution, and engagement. Your ability to have impact and contribute is also attributed to your ability to be aware of your emotions, to regulate them, and to engage healthily with others. These are not skills that come automatically with a 4.0.

There is often the misperception that you have to learn everything before you get the job. The reality is that what you actually need to know at work, you're going to learn *at* work. [6] You want to be a lawyer? You're not going to learn it in a "prelaw" class. You're going to learn how to practice and be a great lawyer once you're at work. What these law firms and other organizations will want from someone new is one who has the emotional intelligence to engage professionally, productively, and positively with others. Over half of 2,000 employers surveyed in 2018 listed the most valuable skills in an employee as: problem-solving, collaboration, customer service, and communication. Hiring managers look for adaptability, cultural fit, and growth potential. They look at your "learnability," how curious you are, and how hungry your mind is as a signal of your potential for success.[7] Emotional intelligence can build your hungry mind.

How?

- *Build self-awareness and emotional balance.* Bring awareness to your emotions and how to regulate them. Recognize how your behaviors are impacted by your emotions.
- *Reframe to the positive.* Consider setbacks and failures as opportunities for growth and learning.
- *Practice empathy and compassion.* Extend kindness to others and to yourself. Put yourself in someone else's shoes without losing yourself, and consider how you might be of service.
- *Be a team player.* It's not just about you. Being a leader means actually having followers. People will follow when they believe in you and what you stand for. People will follow you when they believe you are a team player and that you are not just concerned with yourself.
- *Show gratitude.* Take time every day to write down three things for which you are grateful.

Chapter Twenty-Two

A Preference for Manual Driving

Even if you've made it through college (congratulations!), life doesn't just become easy. How you navigate life will determine your overall satisfaction and well-being. You might have a mansion with five Teslas, but if you don't have a good sense of well-being, it might be an empty life.

Let's take a look at some lessons drawn from leading experts and executive coaches with years of experience. Consider it a mini–boot camp that top CEOs and leaders pay a lot of money to attend.

THE EMPTY, AUTOBOT LIFE

There are plenty of adults who live empty lives. According to the United Nations World Happiness Report (yes, there is one), America's happiness went from #3 in 2007 to #18 in 2018.[1] Part of this has to do with fewer community relationships and less trust among neighbors, economic stressors, and widening gaps in wealth distribution. Stress levels rise, and many, even those with rising incomes, find themselves in golden handcuffs, hostage to their fancy cars and houses, staying in soul-crushing jobs just to keep the paychecks coming. You probably see on a daily basis adults who look dejected and miserable, or who lose their tempers because they are simply unhappy. Many of these adults have the select college degrees you're seeking, and many have the zeros in their bank accounts.

There are a few consistent, general themes of "highly successful" individuals in today's modern world:

- Everyone feels like an imposter—at some point
- Everyone gets overwhelmed
- Everyone wonders "what if?"
- Everyone feels like they don't have enough time
- Everyone wishes they could be more present
- Everyone wishes they had stronger, healthier relationships
- Everyone wishes they took better care of their bodies
- Everyone wishes they didn't simply react to things and thoughts
- Everyone has great moments
- Everyone has disappointing, even debilitating moments
- Everyone wishes they could navigate life with more grace and joy

Particularly for overachieving adults (think you in twenty years), the drive to win and achieve and get the "prize" started when they were young. They did what they were told they should do to get into the "right" school, marry the "right" person, live in the "right" neighborhood, and get the "right" job. No matter how much they try to convince themselves that they are doing it "to better themselves and their children," there often is a nagging feeling that they simply aren't enough. They worry that their neighbors are judging them and that their boss is going to fire them. Many move through the world on autopilot, going through the motions. Some adults reach the point where they have everything they dreamed of—great car and house and career and family—but they find themselves locked in "golden handcuffs," remaining in jobs that bring them misery or deenergize them but which pay the salaries that enable them to keep the fine trappings.

Consider this: Erase what you think is the "right" school/job/career.

STOP TRYING TO WIN

A renowned author, and one of the top executive coaches in the world, Dr. Marshall Goldsmith contends that what separates good from great are not the technical skills you learn in class but behavioral skills learned by engaging with the world. These behaviors, such as expressing gratitude, active listening, pausing and allowing for silence, and acknowledging mistakes, are what make that distinction. As overachievers, we like to win. Who doesn't? From Monopoly, to the spelling bee, to being valedictorian, you know that feeling of working hard, accomplishing a goal, and being recognized for it. That need to win can be so consuming that sometimes we lose sight of what is really important.

Think about your daily interactions. It might be something as seemingly simple as trying to outwalk the person next to you. Why? Just because. Or perhaps it's making a comment in class just to prove that you know more than the other kid. Why? Just because.

We like to win.

As much as you want to go to a highly selective institution for the "academics" and "intellectual life," are you *sure* that rankings, prestige, and branding had nothing to do with it?

We like to win.

Goldsmith gives this simple yet tremendously difficult-to-do piece of advice to the CEOs with whom he works: Stop trying to win. When someone triggers you or even when someone is telling you something you already know—and you're dying to tell them that, just say, "thank you." Resist the urge to prove you're right.

Doing so doesn't make you less competitive or achievement-oriented. It does, however, make you less of a jerk and more open to seeing potential opportunity everywhere instead of being yanked around by your ego. Professor Vijay Govindarajan of the Tuck School of Business, who has advised top CEOs and companies, recognizes that competing against others is futile in the long run. He asserts that "the only competition that matters is true potential."[2] In fact, top companies aren't just looking to compete against their peers; if they were, Microsoft wouldn't exist—nor would Google, Apple, Tesla, or Starbucks.

Consider this: Stop trying to win and just say "thank you."

STAY IN THE GRAY

Nothing is black or white. You're going to discover this more and more, whether in a classroom debate or trying to figure out your roommate. As you continue into your college career, things will get muddier and muddier. Decisions will get tougher to make. While your exams generally test what is "correct" and "incorrect," life doesn't quite happen that way. In fact, it's usually the opposite. Yet ambiguity doesn't mean you have to wallow in it or to ruminate about what you coulda-shoulda-woulda. Our brains tend to dwell in the past or fast-forward into the future—as if we're trying to avoid the discomfort of the unknown of the present. When we begin to be more comfortable sitting in the gray, we begin to see more possibilities.

You'll start to notice that the most highly successful and creative people dwell not in certainty but in the cloudy. Instead of letting that cloud confuse them, they use it to recognize what's working and what's not working and, in fact, they expand their awareness to recognize what might be possible. It's not easy, but the more you sit in the gray, the more resilience you build. You'll never be 100 percent comfortable in it—if you are, then something's off. You *should* feel a bit off-balance, for that is what enables you to build your resources to navigate the unforeseen circumstances that will always be thrown at you, whether in college or career or life.

Consider this: Try sitting in the discomfort of uncertainty.

RECOGNIZE THINKING TRAPS

It is easy to get into our thinking traps, such as negativity bias, where our brains grasp onto the one negative thing and ignore all the positives, or the imposter syndrome, where a little critic inside tells us it's only a matter of time before someone will discover we're a fraud.

Your college classes are going to prepare you to become amazing (hopefully) writers and thinkers who consider everything, analyze everything, critically examine everything. All of these are incredibly important skills to build and cultivate, yet they can also trip you up if you overthink and overanalyze all the time.

When we're able to bring greater self-awareness and awareness of what our bodies are trying to tell us into focus, we're more attuned to those unconscious thinking processes that can trip us up. When we're more aware, we can be more deliberate about the stories we spin about ourselves and about other people. These stories can do more damage than we're aware, particularly if they perpetuate a myth or belief that we're not good or worthy enough, or that another person isn't worth our time and attention and forgiveness.

Consider this: Notice what your body is trying to tell you.

TRUST AND BE KIND

When you get to college, you're probably going to be blown away at what community can mean. It can be a spectacularly beautiful thing, but it can also be tremendously isolating and lonely. Depending on you, your college, and your community, there will likely be times when you will feel out of place and isolated and or that you don't belong.

It. Is. Normal.

You're not alone. There will always be times where you feel out of sorts and out of sync with others. The great news is that others are likely feeling that way too and crave connection. However, university courses don't usually teach you how to build connections.

Kindness goes a long way—it doesn't make you softer or weaker; in fact, kindness makes you stronger, more discerning, and more courageous. It makes you less tolerant of behaviors that are hurtful. It makes you strengthen your network and power of influence. It makes you more able to collaborate, innovate, and create.

When you read or hear about people's end-of-life stories, you probably notice that even the richest, most successful CEOs never talk about their IPOs or stock prices. They will speak about their relationships—good or bad. So begin now.

Start by trusting others and building trust. It isn't easy, but when you're willing to be open and authentic and honest, you begin to spread that sensibility to others. It's called emotional contagion. Leaders who are particularly self-aware understand that their feelings have tremendous impact on what others are feeling. If they're happy, others around them are. If they're angry, others around them are, too. By extending trust to others and being willing to be vulnerable, yes, you are opening yourself up to get hurt and dinged a few times. But the benefits outweigh those moments. When you live authentically and give authentically, you receive authentically.

Doing so allows you to share with kindness who you are and what matters to you. When you give out kindness, it will be reflected back onto you. Help others whenever you get the chance, even if it doesn't "get" you anything. That is one subtle difference between leaders who lead with fear and leaders who lead with trust and inspiration.

Consider this: Share a vulnerable part of your story with someone else.

LEAD WITH INTENTION AND INTEGRITY

It is so easy to get caught up in your college search and thereafter, once you get into college, with the search for the right job and partner and peers. We spend so much of our lives trying to prove that we have what it takes. Yet we also know leaders who are externally driven who lose sight of who they really are.

Think about your role models and your values. Think about those crucible moments in your life—those that shape your most deeply held values and beliefs. Doing so gives you that awareness and space to know where to come back to when things are confusing or challenging.

I trust that you're not pursuing college just for the sake of it, nor, after you've worked so hard, that you want to attend college just to get a piece of paper to prove you did it. Likely, you are seeking ways that you can learn so that you can make a positive contribution to the world, whether by being a teacher or an entrepreneur or an activist. It matters less what you're doing than why you're doing it.

When you bring awareness to your values, you can become more deliberate in the classes you choose, the clubs you join, and ultimately the careers you enter. When we're not motivated by some sort of external validation, we can live with greater intentionality so we're not swept up in pursuit of shiny baubles or empty promises. We are able to stay the course when we are challenged, which we undoubtedly will be. Awareness allows us to stay true to our code of ethics.

As Goldsmith quotes business author Peter Drucker: "Our mission is to make a positive difference, not to prove that we're smart or right."

Consider this: Reflect on how your values show up in your everyday engagements.

MINDFULNESS, CHANGE, AND IMPERMANENCE

Recognizing and accepting that we don't have control over most things is challenging but powerful. The reality is that we actually can't control most things—not the weather or other people's reactions. We don't have control over how quickly and mercurially things change. If we don't build our resilience, we won't be able to navigate those ups and downs.

When you get to college, there are going to be some great "up" moments and plenty of "down" moments. Whether it's your first bad grade or a breakup or not being elected as a club officer, your classes are likely not going to teach you how to recover with grace and learn from the situation. Science shows us that when we're upset, our ability to focus and make good decisions is compromised. Without the right tools, we are susceptible to feelings of inadequacy, sadness, and anger. Mindfulness acts like your inner rudder and helps to keep you focused and present when your mind has wandered off—which it will do. Mindfulness makes you less apt to be yanked around by the vicissitudes of life and directed instead by your own inner compass. Being motivated and driven by your moral code takes tremendous courage. Being guided by your own North Star allows you to stay flexible without being lost.

This awareness shines light on three truths about life: 1) we are all the same and no one is above or below experiencing joy AND sorrow; 2) what happens to us has happened to at least one other person in the history of mankind; and 3) everything is fleeting and temporal. Mindfulness helps cultivate that capacity for us to hold this awareness. Being focused on the present facilitates this ability to navigate change. As Goldsmith says, "don't get so busy chasing what you don't have, you don't see what you have."[3]

Consider this: Identify one mindfulness practice to commit and integrate daily.

GO FOR IT!

Marshall Goldsmith has strong advice for everyone—from the highest-earning CEO to the newly minted intern. "If you have a dream, go for it."[4] He asks everyone to imagine themselves at ninety-five years of age and consider: "What is the one thing you wish you could tell your younger self?" For most people, he notes, it's not about making more money or buying a new house; it's regret over things they wished they'd done—they'd tell themselves to go for it.

University courses will teach you how to read, crunch numbers, clean a pipette. What they won't always teach you is to live. Experience life. Take risks.

Consider this: Go for it! And have fun.

Notes

INTRODUCTION

1. Valerie Strauss, "Kindergarten Show Canceled So Kids Can Keep Studying to Become 'College and Career Ready.' Really," *Washington Post*, April 26, 2014.

2. "NYU Study Examines Top High School Students' Stress and Coping Mechanisms," New York University, last modified August 11, 2015, http://www.nyu.edu/about/news-publications/news/2015/august/nyu-study-examines-top-high-school-stude nts-stress-and-coping-mechanisms.html.

3. Editorial Board, "A Few Telling Freshmen Trends," *New York Times*, August 4, 2017, https://www.nytimes.com/2017/08/04/education/edlife/a-few-telling-freshman-trends.html.

4. William Deresiewicz, *Excellent Sheep: The Miseducation of the American Elite and the Way to a Meaningful Life* (New York: Free Press, 2014).

5. William Deresiewicz, "Don't Send Your Kids to the Ivy League," *New Republic*, July 24, 2014, accessed July 16, 2018, https://newrepublic.com/article/118747/ivy-league-schools-are-overrated-send-your-kids-elsewhere.

6. Amy Adkins, "Employee Engagement Stagnant in U.S. in 2015," Gallup, last modified January 31, 2016, http://news.gallup.com/poll/188144/employee-engagement-stagnant-2015.aspx.

7. Admissions officers are constantly reviewing their processes to ensure that they are thorough, consistent, and responsive. ATLAS 1.0 is a general collective overview of many current practices.

8. I have read for organizations such as Dartmouth College, Barnard College, the Kenan-Flagler Business School at the University of North Carolina–Chapel Hill, and the Fletcher School of Law and Diplomacy at Tufts University. I have also served as a reviewer and evaluator for scholarships and opportunities with organizations such as the Jack Kent Cooke Foundation, the Mandela Washington Fellowship for Young African Leaders, National Honor Society, Management Leadership for Tomorrow, and the Goldman Sachs Foundation Prizes for youth.

FROM ANXIETY TO AWARENESS:
THE CASE FOR EMOTIONAL INTELLIGENCE

1. Frank Bruni, *Where You Go Is Not Who You'll Be: An Antidote to the College Admissions Mania* (New York: Grand Central Publishing, 2015).
2. Richard Weissbourd, "Turning the Tide: Inspiring Concern for Others and the Common Good through College Admissions," January 2016, retrieved from https://mcc.gse.harvard.edu/reports/turning-the-tide-college-admissions.

1. WILL MEDITATING HELP ME LEVITATE?

1. Jo Confino, "Thich Nhat Hanh: Is Mindfulness Being Corrupted by Business and Finance?," *Guardian*, March 28, 2014, https://www.theguardian.com/sustainable-busi ness/thich-nhat-hanh-mindfulness-google-tech.
2. A note to long-term mindfulness practitioners: I recognize a concern about "using mindfulness for the wrong intentions," or commercialization of a deep and revered set of practices. I suggest that many of us find mindfulness as practice in search of something. Most of us didn't come into mindfulness because we felt a calling to bring joy into the world. In listening to the numerous podcasts and reading the many books and articles out there, it seems that many of us, particularly in the West, have come upon mindfulness as a way to address a concern, such as an addiction to technology/drugs/bad relationships, or as a means for dealing with anxiety/depression, or to help boost something, like an increase in productivity or a reduction in stress. Mindfulness can often be more easily understood and practiced when we make it relevant and real in our everyday lives. It shouldn't be a surprise that most young people are not going to be drawn to mindfulness for the sake of being present. But building such habits at a younger age and meeting people where they are helps the journey become the practice and, from there, possibilities become infinite.
3. Jonathan Kabat-Zinn, *Mindfulness for Beginners: Reclaiming the Present Moment and Your Life* (Boulder, CO: Sounds True, 2012), 2.
4. Howard E. Gardner, *Multiple Intelligences: New Horizons in Theory and Practice* (New York: Basic Books, 2006).
5. Matthew Lippincott, "A Study of the Perception of the Impact of Mindfulness on Leadership Effectiveness" (unpublished doctoral dissertation, University of Pennsylvania, Philadelphia, PA, 2016), 29.
6. Marc Brackett, Susan Rivers, and Peter Salovey, "Emotional Intelligence: Implications for Personal, Social, Academic, and Workplace Success," *Social and Personality Psychology Compass* 5, no. 1 (2011): 88–103.
7. Daniel Goleman, *Emotional Intelligence: Why It Can Matter More Than IQ*, tenth anniversary edition (New York: Bantam, 2006), 36.
8. Pamela Morris, et al., "Impact Findings from the Head Start CARES Demonstration: National Evaluation of Three Approaches to Improving Preschoolers' Social and Emotional Competence," *OPRE Report*, June 2014.
9. Cary Cherniss, "The Business Case for Emotional Intelligence," prepared for the Consortium for Research on Emotional Intelligence in Organizations, 1999.
10. Farah Ahmed, et al., "The Effect of Emotional Intelligence on Academic Performance of Medical Undergraduates," *International Journal of Educational & Psychological Researches* 3, no. 2 (2018): 83–86.

11. Boon How Chew, Azhar Md Zain, and Faezah Hassan, "Emotional Intelligence and Academic Performance in First and Final Year Medical Students: A Cross-Sectional Study," *BMC Medical Education* 13, no. 44 (2013).

12. Lippincott, "A Study of the Perception," 36–37.

13. Jessica Morey, "How Self-Compassion Can Help Teens De-stress," Engaged Mindfulness Institute, August 26, 2016, https://engagedmindfulness.org/how-self-com passion-can-help-teens-de-stress/.

14. Sunnie Giles, "The Most Important Leadership Competencies, According to Leaders Around the World," *Harvard Business Review*, March 15, 2016.

15. Stella Mavroveli, K. V. Petrides, Carolien Rieffe, and Femke Bakker, "Trait Emotional Intelligence, Psychological Well-Being and Peer-Related Social Competence in Adolescence," *British Journal of Developmental Psychology* 25, no. 2 (2010).

16. Leonard Mlodinow, *Subliminal: How Your Unconscious Mind Rules Your Behavior* (New York: Vintage, 2013).

17. Tim Ryan, *A Mindful Nation* (Carlsbad, CA: Hay House, 2012), 85.

18. Daniel Goleman and Peter Senge, eds., *The Triple Focus: A New Approach to Education* (Florence, MA: More Than Sound, 2014).

19. Goleman, *Emotional Intelligence*.

20. Ryan M. Niemiec, "VIA Character Strengths—Research and Practice: The First 10 Years," in *Well-Being and Cultures: Perspectives on Positive Psychology*, ed. H. H. Knoop and A. Delle Fave (New York: Springer, 2013).

21. Katherine Pendergast, "The Role of Resilience, Emotion Regulation, and Perceived Stress on College Academic Performance" (unpublished doctoral dissertation, University of Tennessee at Chattanooga, Chattanooga, TN, 2017), 7.

22. Moira Alexander, "Why Emotional Intelligence Is Key for Project Success," *TechRepublic*, May 5, 2017.

23. Darren Good, et al., "Contemplating Mindfulness at Work: An Integrative Review," *Journal of Management* 42, no. 1 (2015): 114–42.

24. Lippincott, "A Study of the Perception," 36–37. See also, Peter R. Drucker, "Managing Oneself," *Harvard Business Review* 83, no. 1 (2005): 100–109; David Rosete and Joseph Ciarrochi, "Emotional Intelligence and Its Relationship to Workplace Performance Outcomes of Leadership Effectiveness," *Leadership & Organization Development Journal* 26, no. 5 (2005): 388–99; Peter Jordan and Ashlee Troth, "Managing Emotions During Team Problem Solving: Emotional Intelligence and Conflict Resolution," *Human Performance* 17, no. 2 (2004): 195–218.

25. Nicole Bayes-Fleming, "How to Grow Your Emotional Intelligence," *Mindful*, April 6, 2018, https://www.mindful.org/grow-emotional-intelligence/.

26. Peerayuth Charoensukmongkol, "Benefits of Mindfulness Meditation on Emotional Intelligence, General Self-Efficacy, and Perceived Stress: Evidence from Thailand," *Journal of Spirituality in Mental Health* 16, no. 3 (2014): 171–92.

27. Lippincott, "A Study of the Perception," 57–58.

28. Bonnie Rochman, "Samurai Mind Training for Modern American Warriors," *Time*, September 5, 2009.

29. Rachel Salaman, "How Mindfulness Leads to Emotional Intelligence," *Mind-Tools*, August 16, 2018, https://www.mindtools.com/blog/mindfulness-emotional-intel ligence/.

30. Alison Beard, "Mindfulness in the Age of Complexity: An Interview with Ellen Langer," *Mindfulness: Emotional Intelligence Series* (Brighton, MA: Harvard Business Review Press, 2017).

31. Yi-Yuan Tang, Britta Hölzel, and Michael Posner, "The Neuroscience of Mindfulness Meditation," *Nature Reviews Neuroscience* 16 (2015): 214.

32. Lippincott, "A Study of the Perception," 48.

33. Michael D. Mrazek, et al., "Mindfulness Training Improves Working Memory Capacity and GRE Performance While Reducing Mind Wandering," *Psychological Science* 24, no. 5 (2013): 776-81.

34. There is nothing wrong or silly with this choice, if this is your path.

35. Dan Harris, *10% Happier: How I Tamed the Voice in My Head, Reduced Stress Without Losing My Edge, and Found Self-Help That Actually Works—A True Story* (New York: Dey Street Books, 2014).

36. Evan Thompson, "What Is Mindfulness? An Embodied Cognitive Science Perspective," Mind & Life Institute, ISCS 2016, accessed August 2, 2018, https://www.youtube.com/watch?v=Q17_A0CYa8s.

37. Lippincott, "A Study of the Perception," 46.

38. Daniel Goleman and Richard Davidson, *Altered Traits: Science Reveals How Meditation Changes Your Mind, Brain, and Body* (New York: Penguin, 2017), 14.

39. Heleen A. Slagter, et al., "Mental Training Affects Distribution of Limited Brain Resources," *PLOS Biology*, May 8, 2007, http://journals.plos.org/plosbiology/article?id=10.1371/journal.pbio.0050138.

40. Christina Congleton, Britta Hölzel, and Sara Lazar, "Mindfulness Can Literally Change Your Brain," *Mindfulness: Emotional Intelligence Series* (Brighton, MA: Harvard Business Review Press, 2017).

41. Hattie Garlick, "The Madness of Mindfulness," *Financial Times*, February 3, 2017, https://www.ft.com/topics/authors/Hattie_Garlick.

42. "Building the Case for Mindfulness in the Workplace," The Mindfulness Initiative, October 2016, http://themindfulnessinitiative.org.uk/images/reports/MI_Building-the-Case_v1.1_Oct16.pdf.

43. "Burnt! Stress at the Workplace and How It's Reshaping America," Eastern Kentucky University Online, accessed August 23, 2018, https://safetymanagement.eku.edu/blog/work-related-stress-on-employees-health/.

44. Bertie Scott, "Why Meditation and Mindfulness Training Is One of the Best Industries for Starting a Business in 2017," Inc., March 1, 2017, https://www.inc.com/bartie-scott/best-industries-2017-meditation-and-mindfulness-training.html.

45. Shawn Achor and Michelle Gielan, "The Busier You Are, the More You Need Mindfulness," *Harvard Business Review*, December 18, 2015.

46. David Gelles, "The Mind Business," *Financial Times*, August 2012.

47. Mindful Schools, accessed May 2, 2019, https://www.mindfulschools.org/.

48. Charlotte Zenner, Solveig Herrnleben-Kurz, and Harald Walach, "Mindfulness-Based Interventions in Schools—A Systematic Review and Meta-Analysis," *Frontiers in Psychology* 5, no. 603 (2014).

49. Morey, "How Self-Compassion Can Help."

50. Mark Williamson and Renata Salecl, "Autopilot Britain" (white paper prepared for Marks & Spencer, UK, 2017), https://corporate.marksandspencer.com/documents/reports-results-and-publications/autopilot-britain-whitepaper.pdf.

51. Williamson and Salecl, "Autopilot Britain."

52. Matthew A. Killingsworth and Daniel T. Gilbert, "A Wandering Mind Is an Unhappy Mind," *Science* 330, no. 6006 (November 12, 2010).

53. Judson A. Brewer, et al., "Meditation Experience is Associated with Differences in Default Mode Network Activity and Connectivity," *PNAS* 108, no. 50 (2011).

54. Goleman and Davidson, *Altered Traits*, 157.

55. Tang, Hölzel, and Posner, "Neuroscience of Mindfulness Meditation," 213.

56. Theo Winter, "Evidence for Mindfulness: A Research Summary for the Corporate Sceptic," Association for Talent Development, March 25, 2016, https://www.td.org/insights/evidence-for-mindfulness-a-research-summary-for-the-corporate-sceptic.

57. Lippincott, "A Study of the Perception," 40.

58. Lippincott, "A Study of the Perception," 40–41.

59. Goleman and Davidson, *Altered Traits*, 37.
60. Goleman and Davidson, *Altered Traits*, 78.

2. THE BRAIN BEHIND THE BRAIN

1. Lisa Feldman Barrett, "The Secret History of Emotions," *Chronicle of Higher Education*, March 5, 2017, retrieved from: https://www.chronicle.com/article/The-Se cret-History-of-Emotions/239357. See also, Lisa Feldman Barrett, "How to Become a 'Superager,'" *New York Times*, December 31, 2016, retrieved from: https://www .nytimes.com/2016/12/31/opinion/sunday/how-to-become-a-superager.html.

2. Understanding of the brain continues to evolve—daily. If this piques your interest, continue to research and learn—and question what you read and see. In a few years, some of this information may be outdated—perhaps you'll be one of those making new discoveries about the mysteries of our brains.

3. For a few decades, scientists have written about the limbic system as the center for emotional processing. There is now greater understanding that there is no clear boundary between the limbic and non-limbic areas of the brain, nor is the limbic system itself one complete unit.

4. Lisa Feldman Barrett, "Seeing Fear: It's All in the Eyes?" *Science & Society Series: Seminal Neuroscience Papers 1978–2017* 41, no. 9 (September 1, 2018): 559–63.

5. Bob Nease, "Your Brain Is on Autopilot More Than You Think—Here's How to Wake It Up," *Fast Company*, June 29, 2016, https://www.fastcompany.com/3061366/ your-brain-is-on-autopilot-more-than-you-think-heres-how-to-wake-i.

6. Nease, "Your Brain is on Autopilot."

7. John Meiklejohn, et al., "Integrating Mindfulness Training into K–12 Education: Fostering the Resilience of Teachers and Students," *Mindfulness* 1, no. 1 (March 2010).

8. O. Singleton, et al., "Change in Brainstem Gray Matter Concentration Following a Mindfulness-Based Intervention is Correlated with Improvement in Psychological Well-Being," *Frontiers in Human Neuroscience* 8, no. 33 (2014).

9. Tang, Hölzel, and Posner, "Neuroscience of Mindfulness Meditation," 215.

10. Congleton, Hölzel, and Lazar, "Mindfulness Can Literally Change Your Brain."

11. Darren Good, et al., "Contemplating Mindfulness at Work: An Integrative Review," *Journal of Management* 42, no. 1 (2016): 114–42.

12. Ryan, *A Mindful Nation*, 49.

13. Ryan, *A Mindful Nation*, 55.

14. Goleman and Davidson, *Altered Traits*, 6.

15. Goleman and Davidson, *Altered Traits*, 92.

16. Goleman, *Emotional Intelligence*, 79.

17. Goleman and Davidson, *Altered Traits*, 96–97.

18. Goleman and Davidson, *Altered Traits*, 134.

19. Goleman and Davidson, *Altered Traits*, 138.

20. Goleman and Davidson, *Altered Traits*, 160–61.

21. Goleman and Davidson, *Altered Traits*, 274.

22. Goleman and Davidson, *Altered Traits*, 274.

23. Donald L. Gleason, *At What Cost? Defending Adolescent Development in Fiercely Competitive Schools* (Concord, MA: Development Empathy, LLC, 2017), 65.

24. Gleason, *At What Cost?*, 95–96.

25. Goleman, *Emotional Intelligence*, 251.

26. Gleason, *At What Cost?*, 99.

3. EDUCATING MY EMOTIONS

1. Gleason, *At What Cost?*, 92.
2. B. J. Casey, Rebecca M. Jones, and Todd A. Hare, "The Adolescent Brain," *Annals of the New York Academy of Science* 1124, no. 1, April 3, 2008.
3. Gleason, *At What Cost?*, 91.
4. Lawrence E. Williams and John Bargh, "Experiencing Physical Warmth Promotes Interpersonal Warmth," *Science* 322 (2008): 606–7.
5. Lisa Feldman Barrett, *How Emotions Are Made: The Secret Life of the Brain* (Boston: Houghton Mifflin Harcourt, 2017).
6. Lisa Feldman Barrett, "The Theory of Constructed Emotion: An Active Inference Account of Interoception and Categorization," *Social Cognitive and Affective Neuroscience* 12, no. 1 (2017): 1–23.
7. Pendergast, "Role of Resilience," 16–17.
8. J. J. Gross, "Emotion Regulation: Taking Stock and Moving Forward," *Emotion* 13, no. 3 (2013): 356–65.
9. A. Bechara, *Iowa Gambling Task Professional Manual* (Lutz, FL: Psychological Assessment Resources, 2007).
10. William D. S. Killgore, et al., "Sleep Deprivation Reduces Perceived Emotional Intelligence and Constructive Thinking Skills," *Sleep Medicine* 9, no. 5 (July 2008): 517–26.
11. "Technology Addiction: Concern, Controversy, and Finding Balance," Common Sense Media, 2016, https://www.commonsensemedia.org/research/technology-addiction-concern-controversy-and-finding-balance.
12. Chaelin K. Ra, Junhan Cho, and Matthew Stone, "Association of Digital Media Use with Subsequent Symptoms of Attention-Deficit/Hyperactivity Disorder Among Adolescents," *JAMA* 320, no. 3 (2018): 255–63.
13. Erik Peper and Richard Harvey, "Digital Addiction: Increased Loneliness, Anxiety, and Depression," *NeuroRegulation* 5, no. 1 (2018): 3–8.
14. Nellie Bowles, "A Dark Consensus About Screens and Kids Begins to Emerge in Silicon Valley," *New York Times*, October 26, 2018.
15. So Young Kim, et al., "The Associations Between Internet Use Time and School Performance Among Korean Adolescents Differ According to the Purpose of Internet Use," *PLOS*, April 3, 2017.

4. IT'S NOT JUST ABOUT YOU

1. Bill Burnett and Dave Evans, *Designing Your Life: How to Build a Well-Lived, Joyful Life* (New York: Knopf, 2016), x.
2. Carl Benedikt Frey and Michael A. Osborne, "The Future of Employment: How Susceptible Are Jobs to Computerisation?," Oxford Martin Programme on Technology and Employment, September 17, 2013, https://www.oxfordmartin.ox.ac.uk/publications/view/1314.
3. Gallup, "Why Higher Ed? Top Reasons U.S. Consumers Choose Their Educational Pathways," Strada Education Network, January 2018, https://futureu.education/wp-content/uploads/2018/03/Strada-Gallup-January-2018-Why-Choose-Higher-Ed.pdf.
4. Bureau of Labor Statistics, "Employment Projections," accessed 2017, https://www.bls.gov/emp/chart-unemployment-earnings-education.htm.

5. "Lifetime Earnings by Degree Type," The Hamilton Project, April 26, 2017, http://www.hamiltonproject.org/charts/lifetime_earnings_by_degree_type.

6. Philip Trostel, "It's Not Just the Money: The Benefits of College Education to Individuals and to Society," Lumina Foundation, October 14, 2015, https://agb.org/wp-content/uploads/2019/01/report_2017_guardians_roi.pdf.

7. Trostel, "It's Not Just the Money."

8. Anthony Carnevale, Tamara Jayasundera, and Artem Gulish, "America's Divided Recovery: College Haves and Have-Nots, 2016," Center on Education and the Workforce, Georgetown University, https://cew.georgetown.edu/wp-content/uploads/Americas-Divided-Recovery-web.pdf.

9. Trostel, "It's Not Just the Money."

10. "What Are the Social Benefits of Education?," Education Indicators in Focus, OECD, January 2013, https://www.oecd-ilibrary.org/education/what-are-the-social-benefits-of-education_5k4ddxnl39vk-en.

11. Sandy Baum, Jennifer Ma, and Kathleen Payea, "Education Pays 2013: The Benefits of Higher Education for Individuals and Society," College Board, 2013, https://trends.collegeboard.org/sites/default/files/education-pays-2013-full-report.pdf.

12. Trostel, "It's Not Just the Money."

13. Trostel, "It's Not Just the Money."

14. Gallup, "Why Higher Ed?"

15. John Dewey, *How We Think*, revised and expanded edition (Belmont, CA: Wadsworth, 1997).

16. UNESCO, "Role of Education," Social and Human Sciences, accessed July 28, 2018, http://www.unesco.org/new/en/social-and-human-sciences/themes/fight-against-discrimination/role-of-education/.

17. Lorelle Espinosa, "Higher Education Can Lead the Way Toward a More Tolerant Society," Higher Education Today (blog), American Council on Education, January 18, 2017, https://www.higheredtoday.org/2017/01/18/higher-education-can-lead-way-toward-tolerant-society/.

18. Quoted in Jack Allen Yehuda, "The Benefits of Higher Education," HASTAC (Humanities, Arts, Science, and Technology Alliance and Collaboratory), December 8, 2016, https://www.hastac.org/blogs/jackkunis/2016/12/08/benefits-higher-education.

19. Espinosa, "Higher Education Can Lead the Way."

20. Eli Saslow, "The White Flight of Derek Black," *Washington Post,* October 15, 2016.

21. "What Are the Social Benefits?," Education Indicators in Focus, OECD.

22. Baum, Ma, and Payea, "Education Pays."

23. Trostel, "It's Not Just the Money."

24. Baum, Ma, and Payea, "Education Pays."

25. Trostel, "It's Not Just the Money."

26. Adam Grant, *Give and Take: A Revolutionary Approach to Success* (New York: Penguin, 2013).

27. Jennifer L. Trew and Lynn E. Alden, "Kindness Reduces Avoidance Goals in Socially Anxious Individuals," *Motivation and Emotion* 39, no. 6 (2015): 892–907.

28. Tenelle Porter, "The Benefits of Admitting When You Don't Know," *Behavioural Scientist* (April 30, 2018).

29. Fred Rogers, Dartmouth College Commencement Address, June 6, 2002, Hanover, NH.

5. A NEW EDUCATION

1. Ayodeji Awosika, "School Sucks: The Problem with Our Education System," *Thought Catalog*, July 13, 2015, https://thoughtcatalog.com/ayodeji-awosika/2015/07/school-sucks-the-problem-with-the-our-education-system/.

2. Ted Dintersmith, *What School Could Be: Insights and Inspiration from Teachers Across America* (Princeton, NJ: Princeton University Press, 2018), xiv.

3. Dintersmith, *What School Could Be*, xvi.

4. Yuval Noah Harari, "Yuval Noah Harari on What the Year 2050 has in Store for Humankind," *Wired*, August 12, 2018, https://www.wired.co.uk/article/yuval-noah-harari-extract-21-lessons-for-the-21st-century.

5. Leonard Baird, "Do Grades and Tests Predict Adult Accomplishment?," *Research in Higher Education* 23, no. 1 (March 1985): 3–85.

6. Adam Grant, "What Straight-A Students Get Wrong," *New York Times*, December 8, 2018.

7. Sir John Jones, "Fifty Years and Counting—Into the Future on the Road Less Travelled," Annual EARCOS Leadership Conference, Kuala Lumpur, Malaysia, October 25, 2018.

8. Daniel Pink, *A Whole New Mind: Why Right-Brainers Will Rule the Future* (New York: Riverhead Books, 2006).

9. Goleman, *Emotional Intelligence*, 36.

10. Richard Arum and Josipa Roksa, *Academically Adrift: Limited Learning on College Campuses* (Chicago: University of Chicago Press, 2011).

11. Dr. Frank M. Bruno, National Association of Pupil Services Administrators, President's Message, accessed May 5, 2019, http://napsa.com/?page_id=42.

12. Randye Semple, Vita Droutman, and Brittany Ann Reid, "Mindfulness Goes to School: Things Learned (So Far) From Research and Real-World Experiences," *Psychology in Society* 54, no. 1 (January 2017): 29–52.

13. Aspen Institute, "How Learning Happens: Supporting Students' Social, Emotional, and Academic Development," National Commission on Social, Emotional, and Academic Development, January 2018, https://www.aspeninstitute.org/publications/learning-happens-supporting-students-social-emotional-academic-development/.

14. Semple, Droutman, and Reid, "Mindfulness Goes to School."

15. Turnaround for Children, "Building Blocks for Learning: A Framework for Comprehensive Student Development," accessed May 16, 2018, https://www.turnaroundusa.org/what-we-do/tools/building-blocks/.

16. Carol Ryff, "Psychological Well-Being Revisited: Advances in Science and Practice," *Psychotherapy and Psychosomatics* 83, no. 1 (2014): 10–28.

17. Dintersmith, *What School Could Be*, xvi.

18. Nicholas Yoder, "Teaching the Whole Child: Instructional Practices That Support Social-Emotional Learning in Three Teacher Evaluation Frameworks," American Institutes for Research, January 2014.

19. "2016 Children's Mental Health Report," Child Mind Institute, accessed May 9, 2018, https://childmind.org/report/2016-childrens-mental-health-report/.

20. Katherine Weare, "Developing Mindfulness with Children and Young People: Evidence and Policy Context," *Journal of Children's Services* 8, no. 2 (June 2013).

21. Yoder, "Teaching the Whole Child."

22. Kimberly Schonert-Reichl, et al., "Enhancing Cognitive and Social-Emotional Development Through a Simple-to-Administer Mindfulness-Based School Program for Elementary School Children: A Randomized Controlled Trial," *Development Psychology* 51, no. 1 (January 2015): 52–66.

23. Brian Galla, "'Safe in My Own Mind': Supporting Healthy Adolescent Development Through Meditation Retreats," *Journal of Applied Developmental Psychology* 53 (2017): 96–107.

24. Lan Anh Pham, "Northeast Independent Schools Mindfulness Conference Report," Middlesex School, Independent School Health Association, June 10, 2016, accessed June 10, 2016, https://www.mxschool.edu/wp-content/uploads/2017/04/North eastIndependentSchoolMindfulnessConference.2016.pdf.

25. Emily Deruy, "Does Mindfulness Actually Work in Schools?," *Atlantic* (May 20, 2016).

26. Amanda Machado, "Should Schools Teach Kids to Meditate?," *Atlantic* (January 27, 2014).

27. Machado, "Should Schools Teach Kids to Meditate?"

28. Maryanna Klatt, et al., "Feasibility and Preliminary Outcomes for Move-Into-Learning: An Arts-Based Mindfulness Classroom Intervention," *Journal of Positive Psychology* 8, no. 3 (April 2, 2013): 233–41.

29. David S. Black and Randima Fernando, "Mindfulness Training and Classroom Behavior Among Lower-Income and Ethnic Minority Elementary School Children," *Journal of Child and Family Studies* 23, no. 7 (October 2013): 1242–46.

30. Brian Galla, "Within-Person Changes in Mindfulness and Self-Compassion Predict Enhanced Emotional Well-Being in Healthy, but Stressed Adolescents," *Journal of Adolescence* 49 (2016): 204–17.

31. Semple, Droutman, and Reid, "Mindfulness Goes to School."

32. Semple, Droutman, and Reid, "Mindfulness Goes to School."

33. Semple, Droutman, and Reid, "Mindfulness Goes to School."

34. "Wellness Works in Schools Research, 2001–2017," Wellness Works in Schools, accessed September 13, 2018, http://www.wellnessworksinschools.com/uploads/1/3/9/2/13927398/ww_research_infographic.jpg.

35. Eric Hoover, "What Colleges Want in an Applicant (Everything)," *New York Times*, November 1, 2017.

36. Jones, "Fifty Years and Counting."

6. IT'S ONLY GETTING WORSE

1. Jean M. Twenge, "Have Smartphones Destroyed a Generation?," *Atlantic*, September 2017.

2. Twenge, "Have Smartphones Destroyed a Generation?"

3. Twenge, "Have Smartphones Destroyed a Generation?"

4. Lloyd Johnston, et al., "Monitoring the Future: National Survey Results on Drug Use, 1975–2013: Volume 1, Secondary School Students" (Ann Arbor, MI: Institute for Social Research, University of Michigan, 2014), 32–36.

5. Johns Hopkins, "Adderall Misuse Rising Among Young Adults," February 16, 2016, retrieved at https://www.jhsph.edu/news/news-releases/2016/adderall-misuse-rising-among-young-adults.html.

6. FDA, "Youth Tobacco Use: Results from the National Youth Tobacco Survey," 2018, retrieved at https://www.fda.gov/tobacco-products/youth-and-tobacco/youth-tobacco-use-results-national-youth-tobacco-survey.

7. Anuradha Gorukanti, et al., "Adolescents' Attitudes Towards E-Cigarette Ingredients, Safety, Addictive Properties, Social Norms, and Regulation," *Preventive Medicine* 94 (2017): 65–71.

8. Mark Rubinstein, et al., "Adolescent Exposure to Toxic Volatile Organic Chemicals from E-Cigarettes," *Pediatrics* 141, no. 4 (2018).

9. Aaron Scott, et al., "Pro-Inflammatory Effects of E-Cigarette Vapour Condensate on Human Alveolar Macrophages," *Thorax* 73, no. 12 (2018): 1161–69.

10. Janet Raloff, "Vaping May Threaten Brain, Immunity and More," *Toxicology*, February 14, 2016.

11. Hillary Gordon, "Vaping: What You Need to Know," TeensHealth, retrieved at https://kidshealth.org/en/teens/e-cigarettes.html. See also, Rajiv Bahl, "From E-Cigs to Tobacco: Here's How Nicotine Affects the Body," *HealthLine*, August 23, 2018.

12. Alexandra Ossola, "High-Stress High School," *Atlantic*, October 9, 2015.

13. Shawn Achor and Michelle Gielan, "Resilience Is About How You Recharge, Not How You Endure," in *Resilience: HBR Emotional Intelligence Series* (Boston: Harvard Business Review Press, 2017).

14. J. M. Guyon, "New Sleep Guidelines for Kids Stress Need for More Zzzs," NBC News, June 13, 2016, https://www.nbcnews.com/health/kids-health/new-sleep-guidelines-kids-stress-need-more-zzzs-n591596.

15. "Teens and Sleep," National Sleep Foundation, accessed August 2, 2018, https://sleepfoundation.org/sleep-topics/teens-and-sleep.

16. Twenge, "Have Smartphones Destroyed a Generation?"

17. Kyla Wahlstrom, et al., "Examining the Impact of Later High School Start Times on the Health and Academic Performance of High School Students: A Multi-Site Study," Center for Applied Research and Educational Improvement, 2014, https://www.academia.edu/27707568/Examining_the_Impact_of_Later_High_School_Start_Times_on_the_Health_and_Academic_Performance_of_High_School_Students_A_Multi-Site_Study.

18. Harvey M. Hysing, S. J. Linton, K. G. Askeland, and B. Sivertsen, "Sleep and Academic Performance in Later Adolescence: Results from a Large Population-Based Study," *Journal of Sleep Research* 25, no. 3 (2016): 318–24.

19. Yu Jin Lee, et al., "Academic Performance among Adolescents with Behaviorally Induced Insufficient Sleep Syndrome," *Journal of Clinical Sleep Medicine* 11, no. 1 (2015).

20. Arianna Huffington, *The Sleep Revolution* (New York: Random House, 2016), 115.

21. Baylor University, "Bonus for Superior Snoozing: Students Who Meet 8-Hour Sleep Challenge Do Better on Finals," *ScienceDaily*, December 3, 2018.

22. K. L. Wahlstrom, "Later Start Time for Teens Improves Grades, Mood, and Safety," *Phi Delta Kappan* 98, no. 4 (December 2016/January 2017): 8–14.

23. Wahlstrom, "Later Start Time."

24. Susan David, *Emotional Agility: Get Unstuck, Embrace Change, and Thrive in Work and Life* (New York: Penguin, 2016).

25. Bruce Feiler, *The Secrets of Happy Families* (New York: HarperCollins, 2013).

26. Caitlin Gibson, "When Parents Are So Desperate to Get Their Kids into College That They Sabotage Other Students," *Washington Post*, April 3, 2019.

27. Richard Weissbourd, et al., "Turning the Tide II: How Parents and High Schools Can Cultivate Ethical Character and Reduce Distress in the College Admissions Process," Making Caring Common Project, March 2019, 11, retrieved at https://static1.squarespace.com/static/5b7c56e255b02c683659fe43/t/5cacc9ecee6eb05919b9c1f5/1554827826670/Turning+the+Tide+II+FINAL.

28. Kelly McGonigal, *The Upside of Stress: Why Stress Is Good for You, and How to Get Good at It* (New York: Avery, 2015).

29. Alia Crum, Peter Salovey, and Shawn Achor, "Rethinking Stress: The Role of Mindsets in Determining the Stress Response," *Journal of Personality and Social Psychology* 104, no. 4 (2013): 716–33.

30. Clifton B. Parker, "Embracing Stress Is More Important than Reducing Stress, Stanford Psychologist Says," News Release, Stanford University, May 7, 2015.

31. Gleason, *At What Cost? Defending Adolescent Development in Fiercely Competitive Schools*, 11–12.

32. Gleason, *At What Cost?*, 17.

33. Rebecca Schuman, "Confessions of a Grade Inflator," *Slate*, May 14, 2014.

34. Nancy DeGennaro, "One School, 48 Valedictorians: How Many Is Too Many?," *Daily News Journal*, May 13, 2017.

35. Gleason, *At What Cost?*, 47–48.

36. Gleason, *At What Cost?*, 67.

37. Yishai Schwartz, "The T&C Guide to College: Admissions Anxiety," *Town & Country* (August 2017): 89–91.

38. Laura Krantz, "Admissions Consultant Sentenced to Five Years in Scam," *Boston Globe*, September 17, 2015.

39. Peter Jacobs, "A Former Hedge-Funder Guarantees He Can Get Your Kid Into an Ivy League School," *Business Insider*, September 4, 2014.

40. Chris Fuchs, "This Company Will Guarantee to Get Your Student into Their Dream College—For a Price," NBC News, November 20, 2017, accessed October 28, 2018, https://www.nbcnews.com/news/asian-america/company-will-guarantee-get-your-student-their-dream-college-price-n821791.

41. Frank Bruni, "The Real Campus Scourge," *New York Times*, September 2, 2017.

42. Claudia Hammond, "Who Feels Lonely? The Results of the World's Largest Loneliness Study," *The Anatomy of Loneliness*, accessed September 10, 2018, https://www.bbc.co.uk/programmes/articles/2yzhfv4DvqVp5nZyxBD8G23/who-feels-lonely-the-results-of-the-world-s-largest-loneliness-study.

43. Rebecca Muller, "Should We Blame Our Devices for the Rise in Teens with ADHD?," *Thrive Global*, July 27, 2018.

44. Vimita Mohandas, "More Kids in Singapore Seeking Help for Mental Health Issues," Channel News Asia, September 25, 2017.

45. Chao Deng, "China's Cutthroat School System Leads to Teen Suicides," *Wall Street Journal*, May 15, 2014.

46. Scott Jaschik, "Suicide Note Calls Out Pressure on Students," *Inside Higher Ed*, February 12, 2018.

47. Erin Anderssen, "Number of Ontario Teens with Psychological Distress Rising at Alarming Rates: Study," *Globe and Mail*, May 16, 2018.

48. Denis Campbell, "One in Four Girls Have Depression by the Time They Hit 14, Study Reveals," *Guardian*, September 19, 2017.

49. Sophie Bethune, "Teen Stress Rivals That of Adults," *Monitor on Psychology* 45, no. 4 (2014): 20.

50. Alexandra Ossola, "High-Stress High School," *Atlantic*, October 9, 2015.

51. Samantha Olson, "High School Students Are Stressed Out about College Admissions; The Reality of Burning Out Before College," *Medical Daily*, August 12, 2015.

52. Dintersmith, *What School Could Be*, 17.

53. Lea Winerman, "By the Numbers: Stress on Campus," *Monitor on Psychology* 48, no. 8 (2017): 88.

54. Alina Tugend, "Colleges Get Proactive in Addressing Depression on Campus," *New York Times*, June 7, 2017.

55. Amy Novotney, "Students Under Pressure," *Monitor on Psychology* 45, no. 8 (2014): 36.

56. Carolyn Walworth, "Paly Student Tells of School Stress: 'Students are Gasping for Air,'" *Almanac*, March 26, 2015.

57. Gleason, *At What Cost?*, 86.

58. Goleman and Davidson, *Altered Traits*, 54.

7. THE RUMOR MILL AND THE GOSSIP

1. Suzy Lee Weiss, "To (All) the Colleges That Rejected Me," *Wall Street Journal*, March 29, 2013.

2. Annie Monjar, "Penn Only Bothers to Consider 1 of 7 College Essays Submitted by Applicants," *Philadelphia*, February 7, 2013.

3. Gregor Aisch, Larry Buchanan, Amanda Cox, and Kevin Quealy, "Some Colleges Have More Students From the Top 1 Percent Than the Bottom 60. Find Yours," *New York Times*, January 18, 2017.

4. "Nudges, Norms, and New Solutions: Evidence-Based Strategies to Get Students to & Through College," Ideas42, accessed October 11, 2018, https://nudge4.ideas42 .org/wp-content/themes/nudge4/resources/downloads/NudgesNormsNewSolutions.pdf/.

5. Jason England, "Admissions Confidential: The Process Can Make a Fool or Liar Out of Anyone," *Chronicle of Higher Education*, December 3, 2017.

6. England, "Admissions Confidential."

7. Stacy Berg Dale and Alan B. Krueger, "Estimating the Payoff to Attending a More Selective College: An Application of Selection on Observables and Unobservables," National Bureau of Economic Research Working Paper No. 7322, August 1999.

8. Suqin Ge, Elliott Isaac, and Amalia Miller, "Elite Schools and Opting-In: Effects of College Selectivity on Career and Family Outcomes," National Bureau of Economic Research Working Paper 25315, November 2018.

9. Derek Thompson, "Does It Matter Where You Go to College?," *Atlantic*, December 11, 2018.

10. Dintersmith, *What School Could Be*, 31.

11. Ernst & Young, "EY Transforms Its Recruitment Selection Process for Graduates, Undergraduates and School Leavers," August 3, 2015, retrieved at https:// www.ey.com/uk/en/newsroom/news-releases/15-08-03---ey-transforms-its-recruitment-selection-process-for-graduates-undergraduates-and-school-leavers.

12. Goleman, *Emotional Intelligence*, 34.

13. Goleman, *Emotional Intelligence*, 35–36.

8. ROLLING THE DICE AND BETTING ON THE HOUSE

1. Hoover, "What Colleges Want in an Applicant (Everything)."

2. Jeffrey Selingo, "Why Universities Are Phasing Out Luxury Dorms," *Atlantic*, August 21, 2017.

3. "Enrollment Management and Big Data in an Era of Change," Maguire Associates, *Chronicle of Higher Education* (2017): 5, accessed August 17, 2018, https:// www.ellucian.com/assets/en/white-paper/whitepaper-enrollment-management-and-big-data-chronicle.pdf.

4. Sean Hill, *The History of Enrollment Management* (Louisville, KY: Capture Higher Ed, 2016), retrieved from: https://innovate.capturehighered.com/history-of-enrollment.

5. "Enrollment Management and Big Data," 18.

6. Jim Hundrieser, ed., *Strategic Enrollment Planning: A Dynamic Collaboration* (Cedar Rapids, IA: Noel-Levitz, 2012).

7. Julie Bourbon, "The Rules of Attraction: Enrolling Students in (and for) the 21st Century," *Trusteeship*, September/October, 2013.

8. Bourbon, "Rules of Attraction."

9. Bourbon, "Rules of Attraction."

10. "Enrollment Management and Big Data," 6.

11. Suhauna Hussain, "UC-Irvine Withdraws 500 Admissions Offers 2 Months Before Fall Term," *Chronicle of Higher Education*, July 28, 2017.

12. "Enrollment Management and Big Data," 5.

13. Gary Saul Morson and Morton Schapiro, "Commentary: Oh What a Tangled Web Schools Weave: The College Rankings Game," *Chicago Tribune*, August 27, 2017.

14. Harold O. Levy, "Colleges Should Abandon Early Admissions," *Inside Higher Education*, January 12, 2017.

15. Levy, "Colleges Should Abandon Early Admissions."

16. Jonathan Zimmerman, "One Group that Definitely Faces Prejudice in College Admissions," *Washington Post*, August 5, 2018.

17. Susan Cain, *Quiet: The Power of Introverts in a World That Can't Stop Talking* (New York: Random House, 2012).

18. Mlodinow, *Subliminal*.

19. Mlodinow, *Subliminal*.

9. WORRYWARTS AND WORRY-NOTS

1. Maria Konnikova, "How People Learn to Be Resilient," *New Yorker*, February 11, 2016.

2. Leonie Kronberg, et al., "Control and Resilience: The Importance of an Internal Focus to Maintain Resilience in Academically Able Students," *Gifted and Talented International* 32, no. 1 (2017): 59–74.

3. Richard Pérez-Peña, "Best, Brightest and Rejected: Elite Colleges Turn Away Up to 95%," *New York Times*, April 8, 2014.

4. Melissa Clinedinst and Pooja Patel, "2018 State of College Admissions," NACAC, 2018.

5. Anemona Hartocollis, Amy Harmon, and Mitch Smith, "'Lopping,' 'Tips,' and the 'Z-List': Bias Lawsuit Explores Harvard's Admissions Secrets," *New York Times*, July 29, 2018.

6. "Behind the Curtain of College Admissions, Fairness May Not Be Priority No. 1," *All Things Considered*, NPR, May 23, 2015.

10. WE'RE ONLY HUMAN

1. Doug Cook, "Bowdoin's Dean Soule: The Humanity of College Admissions," *Bowdoin Daily Sun*, December 20, 2016, accessed May 9, 2018, https://daily-sun.bowdoin.edu/2016/12/bowdoins-dean-soule-the-humanity-of-college-admissions/.

2. Shai Danziger, et al., "Extraneous Factors in Judicial Decisions," *PNAS* (April 26, 2011): 108.

3. Emily Pronin, Daniel Lin, and Lee Ross, "The Bias Blind Spot: Perceptions of Bias in Self Versus Others," *Personality and Social Psychology* 28, no. 3 (2002): 369–81.

4. Daniel Kahneman, *Thinking, Fast and Slow* (New York: Farrar, Straus and Giroux, 2011).

5. Try a few: https://implicit.harvard.edu/implicit/.

11. ACADEMICS

1. Note that there are some exceptions. For example, some veterans or transfer students may have struggled a bit academically during high school but, after serving in the military and/or going to community college, have demonstrated complete readiness at the time of application.

2. "Children & Nature Network 2017 Annual Report," Children & Nature Network, 2018, accessed September 20, 2018, https://www.childrenandnature.org/annual-reports/2017-annual-report/.

3. William Hiss, "Defining Promise: Optional Standardized Testing Policies in American College and University Admissions" (presentation, International Association for College Admission Counseling, Itasca, IL, May 2, 2014).

4. Emma Garcia and Elaine Weiss, "Education Inequalities at the School Starting Gate," Economic Policy Institute, September 27, 2017.

5. Ozan Jaquette and Karina Salazar, "Colleges Recruit at Richer, Whiter High Schools," *New York Times*, April 13, 2018, accessed April 21, 2018, https://www.nytimes.com/interactive/2018/04/13/opinion/college-recruitment-rich-white.html.

6. Rebecca Zwick, *Who Gets In? Strategies for Fair and Effective College Admissions* (Cambridge, MA: Harvard University Press, 2017).

12. TESTING

1. Clara Ritger, "How Important Is the SAT? Admissions Officers Weigh In," *USA Today*, March 28, 2013.

2. Jennifer Giancola and Richard Kahlenberg, "True Merit: Ensuring Our Brightest Students Have Access to Our Best Colleges and Universities" (report prepared for Jack Kent Cooke Foundation, January 2016), 21.

3. Giancola and Kahlenberg, "True Merit," 22.

4. Giancola and Kahlenberg, "True Merit," 22.

5. Center for Studies in Higher Education, "The Growing Correlation Between Race and SAT Scores: New Findings from California," UC Berkeley, October 27, 2015, accessed March 5, 2018, https://cshe.berkeley.edu/news/growing-correlation-between-race-and-sat-scores-new-findings-california.

6. "Total Group Profile Report," College Board, 2013, accessed April 22, 2018, http://media.collegeboard.com/digitalServices/pdf/research/2013/TotalGroup-2013.pdf.

7. Zachary Goldfarb, "These Four Charts Show How the SAT Favors Rich, Educated Families," *Washington Post*, March 5, 2014.

8. Maria Perez, "Former Texas Official Asks Biracial Student if Harvard Admission Is Based on 'Merit or Quota,'" *Newsweek*, April 21, 2018.

9. Giancola and Kahlenberg, "True Merit," 21.

10. James Murphy, "The SAT-Prep Industry Isn't Going Anywhere," *Atlantic*, March 15, 2014.

11. Murphy, "SAT-Prep Industry."

12. Ben Domingue and Derek C. Briggs, "Using Linear Regression and Propensity Score Matching to Estimate the Effect of Coaching on the SAT" (paper presented at the University of Colorado, May 20, 2009), accessed September 21, 2018, http://www.colorado.edu/education/sites/default/files/attached-files/Domingue_Briggs_Using%20Propensity%20Score%20Matching.pdf.

13. Valerie Strauss, "Can Coaching Truly Boost SAT Scores? For Years, the College Board Said No. Now It Says Yes," *Washington Post*, May 9, 2017.

14. Cory Turner, "Why Are Colleges Really Going Test-Optional?," *Morning Edition*, NPR, September 3, 2015, accessed October 11, 2018, https://www.npr.org/sections/ed/2015/09/03/436584244/why-are-colleges-really-going-test-optional.

15. Steven Syverson, Valerie Franks, and William Hiss, "Defining Access: How Test-Optional Works," National Association for College Admissions Counseling, Spring 2018.

16. Jose Rios, "What Does the Research Say on Test Optional?," College Board, March 28, 2016.

17. "20-Year Bates College Study of Optional SATs Finds No Difference," Bates College, October 1, 2005, accessed May 3, 2018, http://www.bates.edu/news/2005/10/01/sat-study/.

18. Ritger, "How Important Is the SAT?"

19. Caroline J. Edmonds, Rosanna Crombie, and Mark R. Gardner, "Subjective Thirst Moderates Changes in Speed of Responding Associated with Water Consumption," *Frontiers in Human Neuroscience* 7, no. 363 (July 16, 2013).

13. LEADERSHIP

1. Kenji Yoshino and Christie Smith, "Uncovering Talent: A New Model of Inclusion," Deloitte University Leadership Center, December 6, 2013.

2. Angela L. Duckworth, *Grit: The Power of Passion and Perseverance* (New York: Scribner, 2016).

3. Susan Cain, "Not Leadership Material? Good. The World Needs Followers," *New York Times*, March 24, 2017.

4. Cain, "Not Leadership Material? Good."

5. Priyanka B. Carr and Gregory M. Walton, "Cues of Working Together Fuel Intrinsic Motivation," *Journal of Experimental Social Psychology* 53 (2014): 169–84.

6. "How Important Are Extracurricular Activities in Admissions Decisions?," Harvard University, accessed June 25, 2018, https://college.harvard.edu/how-important-are-extracurricular-activities-admissions-decisions.

7. "Teens and Sleep," National Sleep Foundation.

8. Adam Winsler, et al., "Sleepless in Fairfax: The Difference One More Hour of Sleep Can Make for Teen Hopelessness, Suicidal Ideation, and Substance Use," *Journal of Youth and Adolescence* 44, no. 2 (2015): 362–78.

9. Perri Klass, "The Science of Adolescent Sleep," *New York Times*, May 22, 2017.

10. "More Sleep = Better Performance: The Hidden Advantages of a Well-Rested Workforce," Virgin Pulse, Virgin Group, accessed October 5, 2018, https://community.virginpulse.com/moresleep_betterperformance.

11. "Teens and Sleep," National Sleep Foundation.

12. Lee, et al., "Academic Performance among Adolescents."

13. Yu Jin Lee, et al., "Insufficient Sleep and Suicidality in Adolescents," *Sleep* 35, no. 4 (2012): 455–60.

14. "Health and Academic Achievement," National Center for Chronic Disease Prevention and Health Promotion, CDC (Centers for Disease Control and Prevention), accessed September 8, 2018, https://www.cdc.gov/healthyyouth/health_and_academics/pdf/health-academic-achievement.pdf.

14. ACCOLADES

1. "How to Write Good Letters of Recommendation," MIT Admissions, Massachusetts Institute of Technology, http://mitadmissions.org/apply/prepare/writingrecs.

15. SPIRIT

1. Scott Jaschik, "The Freshman Who Lied Her Way In," *Inside Higher Ed*, August 28, 2017.

2. Ed Pilkington, "Student Who Conned His Way into Harvard Says Sorry," *Guardian*, December 17, 2010.

3. Tom Vanderbilt, "The Psychology of Genre," *New York Times*, May 28, 2016.

4. Scott Jaschik, "How They Really Get In," *Inside Higher Ed*, April 9, 2012.

5. Giancola and Kahlenberg, "True Merit."

6. Giancola and Kahlenberg, "True Merit."

CHARTING A NEW COURSE: WHOLE-BEING WELL-BEING

1. David Holmes, "Bringing Educators Together to Embed Character in Admission Practice," *National Association of Independent Schools*, June 26, 2017.

16. AWARENESS

1. CASEL, the Collaborative for Academic, Social, and Emotional Learning, defines social and emotional learning (SEL) as having five components: 1) self-awareness = ability to understand one's own emotions; 2) self-management = ability to manage one's emotions; 3) social awareness = ability to feel and show empathy for others; 4) relationship skills = ability to establish and maintain positive relationships; 5) responsible decision-making = ability to set and achieve positive goals.

2. "The Leader's Mind with Daniel J. Siegel and Daniel Goleman," Leadership: A Master Class (streaming video), Key Step Media, accessed April 20, 2018, https://www.keystepmedia.com/shop/leadership-a-master-class-the-leaders-mind-with-daniel-j-siegel-and-daniel-goleman/.

3. Siegel and Goleman, "The Leader's Mind."

4. Daniel Goleman, "Focusing on Ourselves," in *The Triple Focus: A New Approach to Education*, edited by Daniel Goleman and Peter Senge (Florence, MA: More Than Sound, 2014), 17.

5. Goleman, "Focusing on Ourselves," 18.

6. Drake Baer, "This Psychologist Is Figuring Out How Your Brain Makes Emotions," *The Cut*, March 6, 2017, https://www.thecut.com/2017/03/what-emotions-really-are-according-to-science.html.

7. Baer, "This Psychologist Is Figuring Out."

8. Barbara Holzapfel, "Class of 2030: What Do Today's Kindergartners Need To Be Life-Ready?," Microsoft Education, January 20, 2018, accessed August 20, 2018, https://educationblog.microsoft.com/2018/01/class-of-2030-predicting-student-skills/.

9. Lauri Nummenmaa, Enrico Glerean, Riitta Hari, and Jari K. Hietanen, "Bodily Maps of Emotions," *PNAS* 111, no. 2 (January 14, 2014): 646–51.

10. Baer, "This Psychologist Is Figuring Out."

11. Goleman, "Focusing on Ourselves," 20.

12. Goleman, "Focusing on Ourselves," 22.

13. Angela Lee Duckworth and Martin Seligman, "Self-Discipline Outdoes IQ in Predicting Academic Performance of Adolescents," *Psychological Science* 16, no. 12 (2005): 939–44.

14. Mark Linkins, et al., "Through the Lens of Strength: A Framework for Educating the Heart," *Journal of Positive Psychology* 10, no. 1 (2015): 64–68.

17. THINKING

1. Killingsworth and Gilbert, "A Wandering Mind."

2. Matthew Killingsworth, "The Future of Happiness Research," *Harvard Business Review* 90, nos. 1–2 (January 2012): 88–89.

3. Beard, "Mindfulness in the Age of Complexity."

4. Beard, "Mindfulness in the Age of Complexity."

5. Congleton, Hölzel, and Lazar, "Mindfulness Can Literally Change Your Brain."

6. Jason Snipes and Loan Tran, "Growth Mindset, Performance Avoidance, and Academic Behaviors in Clark County School District," WestEd, National Center for Education Evaluation and Regional Assistance, April 2017.

7. Carol Dweck, "The Power of Believing That You Can Improve," TED video filmed November 2014 in Norrköping, Sweden, accessed April 2, 2018, https://www.ted.com/talks/carol_dweck_the_power_of_believing_that_you_can_improve/transcript?language=en.

8. Hae Yeon Lee, et al., "An Entity Theory of Intelligence Predicts Higher Cortisol Levels When High School Grades Are Declining," *Child Development* (July 10, 2018).

9. Snipes and Tran, "Growth Mindset."

10. Snipes and Tran, "Growth Mindset."

11. Guang Zeng, Hanchao Hou, and Kaiping Peng, "Effect of Growth Mindset on School Engagement and Psychological Well-Being of Chinese Primary and Middle School Students: The Mediating Role of Resilience," *Frontiers in Psychology* 7 (2016).

12. Zeng, Hou, and Peng, "Effect of Growth Mindset."

13. Zeng, Hou, and Peng, "Effect of Growth Mindset."

14. Zeng, Hou, and Peng, "Effect of Growth Mindset."

15. Sonja Lyubomirsky, *The How of Happiness: A Scientific Approach to Getting the Life You Want* (New York: Penguin, 2007).

16. Daniel Gilbert, *Stumbling on Happiness* (New York: Vintage, 2005).

17. Karen Arnold, *Lives of Promise: What Becomes of High School Valedictorians: A Fourteen-Year Study of Achievement and Life Choices* (San Francisco: Jossey-Bass, 1995).

18. Eric Barker, *Barking Up the Wrong Tree: The Surprising Science Behind Why Everything You Know About Success Is (Mostly) Wrong* (New York: HarperCollins, 2017).

19. Shana Lebowitz, "Why Valedictorians Rarely Become Rich and Famous—and the Average Millionaire's College GPA was 2.9," *Business Insider*, May 29, 2017.

20. Malcolm Gladwell, *David and Goliath: Underdogs, Misfits, and the Art of Battling Giants* (New York: Back Bay Books, 2015).

21. Goleman, *Emotional Intelligence*, 86.

22. Goleman, *Emotional Intelligence*, 83.

23. Goleman, *Emotional Intelligence*, 84.

24. Goleman, *Emotional Intelligence*, 88.

25. Goleman, *Emotional Intelligence*, 88.

26. Daniel Goleman and Richard Boyatzis, *Positive Outlook: A Primer* (Florence, MA: Key Step Media).

27. Slagter, et al., "Mental Training Affects Distribution."

28. Walter Mischel, Ebbe Ebbeson, and Antonette Raskoff Zeiss, "Cognitive and Attentional Mechanisms in Delay of Gratification," *Journal of Personality and Social Psychology* 21, no. 2 (1972): 204–18. See also, Walter Mischel, Yuichi Shoda, and M. L. Rodriguez, "Delay of Gratification in Children," *Science* 244, no. 4907 (1989): 933–38. Yuichi Shoda, Walter Mischel, and Philip Peake, "Predicting Adolescent Cognitive and Self-Regulatory Competencies from Preschool Delay of Gratification: Identifying Diagnostic Conditions," *Developmental Psychology* 26, no. 6 (1990): 976–86. Tanya Schlam, et al., "Preschoolers' Delay of Gratification Predicts Their Body Mass 30 Years Later," *Journal of Pediatrics* 162, no. 1 (2013): 90–93. B. J. Casey, et al., "Behavioral and Neural Correlates of Delay of Gratification 40 Years Later," *Proceedings of the National Academy of Sciences* 108, no. 36 (2011): 14998–15003.

29. The Dunedin Study, retrieved at https://dunedinstudy.otago.ac.nz/.

30. Jack Scanlan, "The Exceptional Scientific Study That's Been Going on for Over 40 Years," *Science: SBS Australia*, May 24, 2016, retrieved at https://www.sbs.com.au/topics/science/humans/article/2016/05/24/exceptional-scientific-study-thats-been-going-over-40-years.

31. Goleman, "Focusing on Ourselves," 24–25.

32. Angela Lee Duckworth and James J. Gross, "Self-Control and Grit: Related but Separable Determinants of Success," *Current Directions in Psychological Science* 23, no. 5 (2014): 319–25.

33. K. Anders Ericsson, Ralf Th. Krampe, and Clemens Tesch-Romer, "The Role of Deliberate Practice in the Acquisition of Expert Performance," *Psychological Review* 100, no. 3 (1993): 363–406.

34. Leah Shafer, "Resilience for Anxious Students," *Usable Knowledge*, Harvard Graduate School of Education, November 20, 2017, accessed September 14, 2018, https://www.gse.harvard.edu/news/uk/17/11/resilience-anxious-students.

35. Diane Coutu, "How Resilience Works," *Harvard Business Review*, May 2002.

36. Gleason, *At What Cost?*, 135.

37. Daniel Goleman, "Resilience for the Rest of Us," *Harvard Business Review,* April 25, 2011.

38. Ephrat Livni, "Forget Happiness, You Should Be Aiming for Resilience," contributor, World Economic Forum, May 30, 2018, https://www.weforum.org/agenda/authors/ephrat-livni/.

39. Scott Barry Kaufman, "Schools Are Missing What Matters About Learning," *Atlantic*, July 24, 2017.

40. Kaufman, "Schools Are Missing What Matters."

41. Kaufman, "Schools Are Missing What Matters."

42. Rasmus Hougaard, Jacqueline Carter, and Gillian Coutts, *One Second Ahead: Enhance Your Performance at Work with Mindfulness* (New York: Palgrave Macmillan, 2015), 184.

18. LISTENING

1. Amos Tversky and Daniel Kahneman, "Availability: A Heuristic for Judging Frequency and Probability," *Cognitive Psychology* 5, no. 2 (1973): 207–32.

2. Mlodinow, *Subliminal*.

3. Jesse Chandler, Tiffany M. Griffin, and Nicholas Sorensen, "In the 'I' of the Storm: Shared Initials Increase Disaster Donations," *Judgment and Decision Making* 3, no. 5 (June 2008): 404–10.

4. Jonathan Passmore and Lindsey Oades, "Positive Psychology Coaching Techniques: Active Constructive Responding," *Coaching Psychologist* 10, no. 2 (2014): 71–73.

5. Mlodinow, *Subliminal*.

6. Jack Zenger and Joseph Folkman, "What Great Listeners Actually Do," *Harvard Business Review*, July 14, 2016.

7. Daniel Goleman, "What is Empathy? And Why It's Important," in *Empathy: HBR Emotional Intelligence Series* (Boston: Harvard Business Review Press, 2017).

8. Lippincott, "A Study of the Perception," 37.

9. Paul D. Cherulnik, Kristina A. Donley, Tay Sha R. Wiewel, and Susan R. Miller, "Charisma Is Contagious: The Effect of Leaders' Charisma on Observers' Affect," *Journal of Applied Social Psychology* 31, no. 10 (July 31, 2006).

10. Olga Khazan, "Ending Extracurricular Privilege: One Man's Mission to Make College Admissions Sane (and Fair) Again," *Atlantic*, December 21, 2016.

11. Sung Soo Kim, Stan Kaplowitz, and Mark V. Johnston, "The Effects of Physician Empathy on Patient Satisfaction and Compliance," *Evaluation & the Health Professions* 27, no. 3 (September 1, 2004): 237–51.

12. William A. Gentry, Todd J. Weber, and Golnaz Sadri, "Empathy in the Workplace: A Tool for Effective Leadership," Center for Creative Leadership, New York, April 2007.

13. Goleman, *Emotional Intelligence*, 179.

14. Christina N. Armenta, Megan M. Fritz, and Sonja Lyubomirsky, "Functions of Positive Emotions: Gratitude as a Motivator of Self-Improvement and Positive Change," *Emotion Review* 9, no. 3 (July 7, 2017).

15. Robert Emmons and Michael McCullough, "Counting Blessings versus Burdens: An Experimental Investigation of Gratitude and Subjective Well-Being in Daily Life," *Journal of Personality and Social Psychology* 84, no. 2 (2003): 377–89.

16. Jeffrey J. Froh, et al., "Gratitude and the Reduced Costs of Materialism in Adolescents," *Journal of Happiness Studies* 12, no. 2 (April 2011): 289–302.

17. Christina Armenta, Megan Fritz, Lisa Walsh, and Sonja Lyubomirsky, "Gratitude and Self-Improvement in Adolescents," poster at University of California, Riverside.

18. Elliott Kruse, Joseph Chancellor, Peter M. Ruberton, and Sonja Lyubomirsky, "An Upward Spiral Between Gratitude and Humility," *Social Psychology and Personality Science* 5 (May 30, 2014).

19. Weissbourd, et al., "Turning the Tide II," 15.
20. Emmons and McCullough, "Counting Blessings versus Burdens," 377–89.
21. Roland Zahn, et al., "The Neural Basis of Human Social Values: Evidence from Functional MRI," *Cerebral Cortex* 19, no. 2 (February 2009): 276–83.

19. ALIGNMENT

1. Burnett and Evans, *Designing Your Life*, xxix.
2. Goleman, "Focusing on Ourselves," 18.
3. Daniel Pink, *Drive: The Surprising Truth About What Motivates Us* (New York: Riverhead Books, 2011).
4. Burnett and Evans, *Designing Your Life*, 32.
5. Mihaly Csikszentmihalyi, "Flow, the Secret to Happiness," TED video filmed February 2004 in Monterey, California, accessed May 6, 2018, https://www.ted.com/talks/mihaly_csikszentmihalyi_on_flow?language=en.
6. Ryan, *A Mindful Nation*, 48.
7. Gardiner Morse, "The Science Behind the Smile," *Harvard Business Review*, January–February 2012.
8. Goleman, *Emotional Intelligence*, 95.
9. Jennifer Moss, "Happiness Isn't the Absence of Negative Feelings," *Harvard Business Review*, August 20, 2015.
10. Siegel and Goleman, "The Leader's Mind."
11. Elizabeth Svoboda, "What Happens When We Seek Status Instead of Goodness?," *Greater Good Magazine* (April 3, 2019).

20. SELF-COMPASSION

1. Robb Willer, "Groups Reward Individual Sacrifice: The Status Solution to the Collective Action Problem," *American Sociological Review* 74 (2009): 23–43.
2. Amy Harmon, "College Admissions Is Not a Personality Contest. Or Is It?," *New York Times*, June 15, 2018.
3. Daniel Goleman, "Tuning in to Other People," in *The Triple Focus: A New Approach to Education*, edited by Daniel Goleman and Peter Senge (Florence, MA: More Than Sound, 2014), 31–32.
4. Frank Bruni, *Where You Go Is Not Who You'll Be: An Antidote to the College Admissions Mania* (New York: Grand Central/Hachette, 2015).
5. Brian M. Galla, "Within-Person Changes in Mindfulness and Self-Compassion Predict Enhanced Emotional Well-Being in Healthy, but Stressed Adolescents," *Journal of Adolescence* 49 (2016): 204–17.
6. Imogen C. Marsh, Stella W. Y. Chan, and Angus MacBeth, "Self-Compassion and Psychological Distress in Adolescents—A Meta-Analysis," *Mindfulness* 9, no. 4 (November 25, 2017): 1011–27, accessed August 6, 2018, https://doi.org/10.1007/s12671-017-0850-7.
7. Kristin Neff, "The Space Between Self-Esteem and Self-Compassion," TEDx Talk, February 6, 2013.
8. Neff, "The Space Between."
9. Neff, "The Space Between."

10. Kristin Neff, "Self-Compassion: The Proven Power of Being Kind to Yourself," live talk, January 10, 2018, for Search Inside Yourself Leadership Institute.

11. "Stanford Mindfulness Lecture," YouTube, February 10, 2015, accessed August 6, 2018, at https://www.youtube.com/watch?v=FIUvbXkywWs.

12. Antoine Lutz, "The Neuroscience of Compassion—Empathy and Compassion in Society 2013," YouTube, December 2013, accessed June 6, 2018, https://www.youtube.com/watch?v=8fleI6sfX6E.

13. Tenzin Gyatso, *The Compassionate Life* (Somerville, MA: Wisdom, 2003), 17.

14. Gyatso, *Compassionate Life*, 40.

15. Rebecca Klein, "New Study Finds Students Who Want to Get Better Grades Should Start Volunteering More," (blog) HuffPost, October 29, 2015.

16. Klein, "New Study."

17. Christine I. Celio, Joseph Durlak, and Allison Dymnicki, "A Meta-Analysis of the Impact of Service-Learning on Students," *Journal of Experiential Education* 34, no. 2 (2011).

18. Goleman and Davidson, *Altered Traits*, 106.

19. Juliana Breines and Serena Chen, "Self-Compassion Increases Self-Improvement Motivation," *Personality and Social Psychology* 38, no. 9 (2012): 1133–43.

20. Breines and Chen, "Self-Compassion Increases Self-Improvement."

21. Marsh, Chan, and MacBeth, "Self-Compassion and Psychological Distress."

22. Livni, "Forget Happiness, You Should Be Aiming for Resilience."

23. His Holiness the Dalai Lama, *Beyond Religion: Ethics for a Whole World* (New York: Houghton Mifflin Harcourt, 2011), 45.

24. Dalai Lama, *Beyond Religion*, 153.

25. "10% Happier Podcast with Dr. Amish Jha & Major General Walter Piatt," accessed July 13, 2018, https://www.youtube.com/watch?v=JF09RhhVEME.

26. "10% Happier Podcast."

21. COLLEGE 101

1. Kathryn Schulz, *Being Wrong: Adventures in the Margin of Error* (New York: Ecco, 2010).

2. Frank Bruni, "How to Get the Most Out of College," *New York Times*, August 17, 2018.

3. Susan Sargeant and Myriam Mongrain, "An Online Optimism Intervention Reduces Depression in Pessimistic Individuals," *Journal of Consulting and Clinical Psychology* 82, no. 2 (January 2013).

4. Goleman, *Emotional Intelligence*, xv.

5. Bloomberg Next, "Building Tomorrow's Talent: Collaboration Can Close Emerging Skills Gap," Bureau of National Affairs, 2018.

6. Gallup, "21st Century Skills and the Workplace," Microsoft Partners in Learning and Pearson Foundation Study, May 30, 2013, https://www.gallup.com/services/176699/21st-century-skills-workplace.aspx.

7. Tomas Chamorro-Premuzic and Becky Franciewicz, "Does Higher Education Still Prepare People for Jobs?," *Harvard Business Review*, January 16, 2019.

22. A PREFERENCE FOR MANUAL DRIVING

1. John F. Helliwell, Richard Layard, and Jeffrey D. Sachs, "World Happiness Report 2018," March 14, 2018, UN Sustainable Development Solutions Network, https://worldhappiness.report/ed/2018/.

2. Vijay Govindarajan, "Strategy for Leading Innovation," Tuck School of Business Global Leadership Program, Hanover, NH, September 22, 2018.

3. Marshall Goldsmith, "What Got You Here Won't Get You There," Tuck School of Business Global Leadership Program, Hanover, NH, September 25, 2018.

4. Goldsmith, "What Got You Here."

Index

About the Author

Belinda H. Y. Chiu, EdD, believes in the power of play to bring authenticity and compassion for a happier planet. A former senior associate director of admissions at Dartmouth College, she has worked in university admissions for institutions such as Barnard College, the Kenan-Flagler Business School (UNC–Chapel Hill), and the Fletcher School of Law and Diplomacy, and as an evaluator with organizations such as the Jack Kent Cooke Foundation, the Mandela Washington Fellowship for Young African Leaders, and the National Honor Society Scholarship Program. She is on the forefront of the movement to democratize emotional intelligence through Goleman EI as a faculty member and certified coach with the Daniel Goleman Emotional Intelligence Coaching Certification Program. She also works to cultivate resilient leaders with Ignition Coaching LLC and as founder of Hummingbird research coaching consulting. A certified teacher with the Google-born Search Inside Yourself Leadership Institute, a RYT© yoga instructor, and a Myers-Briggs® certified facilitator, Chiu writes on emotional intelligence, mindfulness, and leadership. She has written a book of yoga meditations for children and on the Camino de Santiago for women. A member of Valley Improv, she currently lives in New Hampshire with Bandit, the pink-nosed pup.